# ACCA

## FINANCIAL REPORTING
## (FR)

P
R
A
C
T
I
C
E

&

R
E
V
I
S
I
O
N

K
I
T

BPP Learning Media is an **ACCA Approved Content Provider** for the ACCA qualification. This means we work closely with ACCA to ensure our products fully prepare you for your ACCA exams.

In this Practice & Revision Kit, which has been reviewed by the **ACCA examining team,** we:

- Discuss the **best strategies** for revising and taking your ACCA exams

- Ensure you are well **prepared** for your exam

- Provide you with **lots of great guidance** on tackling questions

- Provide you with **three** mock exams

Our **Passcards** also support the Financial Reporting syllabus

**FOR EXAMS IN SEPTEMBER 2018, DECEMBER 2018, MARCH 2019 AND JUNE 2019**

**BPP**
LEARNING MEDIA

First edition 2008

Twelth edition February 2018
ISBN 9781 5097 1668 5
(previous ISBN 9781 5097 0858 1)
e-ISBN 9781 5097 1698 2

British Library Cataloguing-in-Publication Data

A catalogue record for this book
is available from the British Library

**Published by**

BPP Learning Media Ltd
BPP House, Aldine Place
London W12 8AA

www.bpp.com/learningmedia

Printed in the United Kingdom

Your learning materials, published by BPP Learning Media Ltd, are
printed on paper obtained from traceable sustainable sources.

# About this Practice & Revision Kit

ACCA have commenced the transition of this paper to computer-based examination (CBE), beginning with a pilot in limited markets in September 2016. Students will initially have the choice of CBE or paper exams and as a result, changes will be made to BPP's learning materials to ensure that we fully support students through this transition.

This Practice & Revision Kit is valid for exams from the September 2018 sitting through to the June 2019 sitting and in this Practice & Revision Kit you will find questions in both multiple choice question (MCQ) and objective testing question (OTQ) format. OTQs include a wider variety of questions types including MCQ as well as number entry, multiple response and drag and drop. More information on these question types will be available on the ACCA website.

OTQs will only appear in computer-based exams but these questions will still provide valuable practice for all students whichever version of the exam is taken. These are clearly marked on the contents page as either CBE style, OTQ bank or CBE style OTQ case.

More information on the exam formats can be found on page xv.

All timings given throughout this Practice & Revision Kit are based on the computer-based exam which is 3 hours and 20 minutes long. Within session CBEs there will be additional questions used for quality assurance purposes, to ensure that all students now and in the future receive fair and equal exams. These extra questions are referred to by the technical term 'seeded questions' and do not contribute to a student's result. As a result, session CBEs will contain 110 marks of exam content, 100 marks contributing to the student result. Exam timings are allocated on the basis of 110 marks across the 3 hours and 20 minutes. Time management is a key skill for success in this exam and so we recommend you use these indicative timings when attempting questions to time on paper.

ACCA are recommending that all students consult the ACCA website on a regular basis for updates on the launch of the new CBEs.

These materials are reviewed by the ACCA examining team. The objective of the review is to ensure that the material properly covers the syllabus and study guide outcomes, used by the examining team in setting the exams, in the appropriate breadth and depth. The review does not ensure that every eventuality, combination or application of examinable topics is addressed by the ACCA Approved Content. Nor does the review comprise a detailed technical check of the content as the Approved Content Provider has its own quality assurance processes in place in this respect.

# Contents

BPP
LEARNING MEDIA

# Question index

The headings in this checklist/index indicate the main topics of questions, but many questions cover several different topics.

Each topic area begins with Section A questions on the topic. Your exam will have 15 section A questions.

BPP
LEARNING MEDIA

## Part D: Preparation of financial statements

**Mock exam 1 (Specimen exam CBE)**

**Mock exam 2 (September 2016 CBE)**

**Mock exam 3 (December 2016 PBE)**

BPP
LEARNING MEDIA

# Revising Financial Reporting (FR)

From September 2017 the FR exam has a Section A with 15 2-mark OTQs and a Section B with a further 15 2-mark OTQs based on three scenarios. This gives the examining team greater scope to examine the whole of the syllabus and bring in topics that do not feature in the longer questions. Section C will have two 20-mark questions. Sections A and B account for 60% of the marks on the exam. So it is really not possible to pass this exam by only revising certain topics.

A consolidation question could feature in Section C and can be a statement of financial position or statement of profit or loss or both, and it may include an associate, so be prepared for all of this. Therefore you must revise all the consolidation workings, and you must know how to account for an associate. All questions are compulsory.

A single company accounts preparation question allows the examining team to bring in more complex issues that they would not test in the consolidation question. Make sure you can deal with leases, deferred tax, calculating finance costs using the effective interest rate, prior period adjustments and discontinued operations.

Other possibilities for Section C are statements of cash flow or interpretation of accounts. You have studied both of these at Financial Accounting, so make sure you can do them well. A question on interpretation of group financial statements is also a possibility in Section C. For these questions you also have to consider group-related/consolidation issues.

Issues that could appear anywhere are non-current assets and impairment, intangible assets, EPS, provisions and regulatory issues.

## Question practice

This is the most important thing to do if you want to get through. Many of the most up-to-date exam questions are in this Kit, amended to reflect the new exam format. Practise doing them under timed conditions, then go through the answers and go back to the Study Text for any topic you are really having trouble with. Come back to a question a week later and try it again – you will be surprised at how much better you are getting. Be very ruthless with yourself at this stage – you have to do the question in the time, without looking at the answer. This will really sharpen your wits and make the exam experience less worrying. Just keep doing this and you will get better at doing questions and you will really find out what you know and what you don't know.

# Passing the FR exam

If you have honestly done your revision then you can pass this exam. What you must do is remain calm and tackle it in a professional manner. There are a number of points which you should bear in mind. These apply particularly to the long questions.

- You must read the question properly. Students often fail to read the question properly and miss some of the information. Time spent reading the question a second time would be time well spent. Make yourself do this, don't just rush into it in a panic.

- Workings must be clear and cross-referenced. If the marker can read and understand your workings they can give you credit for using the right method, even if your answer is wrong. If your answer is wrong and there are no workings, or they are illegible and incomprehensible, you will get no marks for that part of the question.

- Stick to the timings and answer all questions. Do not spend too long on one question at the expense of others. The number of extra marks you will gain on that question will be minimal, and you could have at least obtained the easy marks on the next question.

- Do not neglect the short parts of the question. If you get a consolidation with a five-mark discussion topic at the end, leave time for that last part. You can't afford to throw away five marks.

- Make sure you get the easy marks. If an accounts preparation question contains something that you are unable to do, just ignore it and do the rest. You will probably only lose a few marks and if you start trying to puzzle it out you might waste a lot of minutes.

- Answer the question. In a discussion-type question, such as an interpretation question, you may be tempted to just write down everything you know about the topic. This will do you no good. The marking parameters for these questions are quite precise. You will only get marks for making points that answer the question exactly as it has been set. So don't waste your time waffling – you could be scoring marks somewhere else.

## Avoiding weaknesses

- There is no choice in this exam all questions have to be answered. You must therefore study the entire syllabus, there are no short-cuts.

- Ability to answer multiple choice questions and cases improves with practice. Try to get as much practice with these questions as you can.

- The longer questions will be based on simple scenarios and answers must be focused and specific to the organisation.

# Gaining the easy marks

Easy marks in this exam tend to fall into three categories.

## Objective test questions (OTQs)

Some OTQs are easier than others. Answer those that you feel fairly confident about as quickly as you can. Come back later to those you find more difficult. This could be a way of making use of the time in the examination most efficiently and effectively. Some OTQs will not involve calculations. Make sure that you understand the wording of 'written' OTQs before selecting your answer.

## Calculations in Section C questions

There will be some relatively straightforward calculations at the start of the question and they will then probably get progressively more difficult. If you get stuck, make an assumption, state it and move on. Do not miss out on easy marks by not learning your proformas properly.

## Discussions in Section C questions

A Section C question may separate discussion requirements from calculations, so that you do not need to do the calculations first in order to answer the discussion part. This means that you should be able to gain marks from making sensible, practical comments without having to complete the calculations.

Discussions that are focused on the specific organisation in the question will gain more marks than regurgitation of knowledge. Read the question carefully and more than once, to ensure you are actually answering the specific requirements.

Pick out key words such as 'describe', 'evaluate' and 'discuss'. These all mean something specific.

- 'Describe' means to communicate the key features of
- 'Evaluate' means to assess the value of
- 'Discuss' means to examine in detail by argument

Clearly label the points you make in discussions so that the marker can identify them all rather than getting lost in the detail.

Provide answers in the form requested. Use a report format if asked for and give recommendations if required.

# Tackling Objective Test Questions

First, read the whole case scenario. Make a note of any specific instructions or assumptions, such as 'Ignore the calculation of depreciation' for a non-current asset question. Then skim through the requirements of the five questions. The questions are independent of each other and can be answered in any order.

Some of the OTQs will be easier than others. Answer these OTQs quickly.

Other OTQs will be more difficult and/or complex. There are two types of OTQ that may take you longer to answer.

The first more time-consuming OTQ will involve doing a computation. You will probably need to jot down a quick proforma to answer a computational question. If the OTQ is a multiple choice question, remember that the wrong answers will usually involve common errors so don't assume that because you have the same answer as one of the options that your answer is necessarily correct! Double check to make sure you haven't made any silly mistakes, If you haven't got the same answer as any of the options, rework your computation, thinking carefully about what errors you could have made. If you still haven't got one of the options, choose the one which is nearest to your answer.

The second more time-consuming OTQ is one where you are asked to consider a number of statements and identify which one (or more) of them is correct. Make sure that you read each statement at least twice before making your selection. Be careful to follow the requirements of the OTQ exactly, for example if you are asked to identify **two** correct statements.

# Exam information

## Computer-based exams

ACCA have commenced the launch of computer-based exams (CBEs) for this exam. They have been piloting computer-based exams in limited markets since September 2016 with the aim of rolling out into all markets internationally over a five-year period. Paper-based examinations will be run in parallel while the CBEs are phased in and BPP materials have been designed to support you, whichever exam option you choose.

## Format of the exam

The exam format is the same irrespective of the mode of delivery and will comprise three exam sections:

| Section | Style of question type | Description | Proportion of exam, % |
|---------|------------------------|-------------|----------------------|
| A | Objective test (OTQ) | 15 questions × 2 marks | 30 |
| B | Objective test (OTQ) case | 3 questions × 10 marks<br><br>Each question will contain 5 subparts each worth 2 marks | 30 |
| C | Constructed Response (Long questions) | 2 questions × 20 marks | 40 |
| Total | | | 100 |

Section A and B questions will be selected from the entire syllabus. The paper version of these objective test questions contain multiple choice only and the computer based versions will contain a variety. The responses to each question or subpart in the case of OT cases are marked automatically as either correct or incorrect by computer.

Section C questions will mainly focus on the following syllabus areas but a minority of marks can be drawn from any other area of the syllabus

* Interpretation of financial statements of a single entity or groups (syllabus area C)
* Preparation of financial statements of a single entity or groups (syllabus area D)

The responses to these questions are human marked.

The ACCA website has specimen exams for both the paper-based and CBE exams and a constructed response workspace to give you practice answering questions using word processing and spreadsheet tools. There are no questions set up in the workspace, so you can use it to answer the questions in this kit.

www.accaglobal.com/uk/en/student/exam-support-resources/fundamentals-exams-study-resources/f7/specimen-exams.html

## Additional information

The Study Guide provides more detailed guidance on the syllabus and can be found by visiting the exam resource finder on the ACCA website: www.accaglobal.com/uk/en/student/exam-support-resources.html

# Useful websites

The websites below provide additional sources of information of relevance to your studies for *Financial Reporting*.

- www.accaglobal.com

  ACCA's website. The students' section of the website is invaluable for detailed information about the qualification, past issues of Student Accountant (including technical articles) and a free downloadable Student Planner App.

- www.bpp.com

  Our website provides information about BPP products and services, with a link to the ACCA website.

# Helping you with your revision

## Tackling revision and the exam

Using feedback obtained from ACCA examining team review:

- We look at the dos and don'ts of revising for, and taking, ACCA exams

- We focus on Financial Reporting (FR); we discuss revising the syllabus, what to do (and what not to do) in the exam, how to approach different types of question and ways of obtaining easy marks

## Selecting questions

We provide a full **question index** to help you plan your revision.

## Making the most of question practice

At BPP Learning Media we realise that you need more than just questions and model answers to get the most from your question practice.

- Our **top tips** included for certain questions provide essential advice on tackling questions, presenting answers and the key points that answers need to include.

- We show you how you can pick up **easy marks** on some questions, as we know that picking up all readily available marks often can make the difference between passing and failing.

- We include **marking guides** to show you what the examining team rewards.

- We include **comments from the examining team** to show you where students struggled or performed well in the actual exam.

- We refer to the **2017 BPP Study Text** (for exams in September 2018, December 2018, March 2019 and June 2019) for detailed coverage of the topics covered in questions.

## Attempting mock exams

There are three mock exams that provide practice at coping with the pressures of the exam day. We strongly recommend that you attempt them under exam conditions. **Mock exam 1** is the Specimen exam paper. **Mock exam 2** is the September 2016 computer-based exam. **Mock exam 3** is the December 2016 exam paper.

# Questions

PART A THE CONCEPTUAL AND REGULATORY FRAMEWORK FOR FINANCIAL REPORTING

Questions 1 to 11 cover the Conceptual Framework and the regulatory framework for financial reporting.

Inflation is an important concept and questions 12-17 review the impact of historical and current costs of assets on the financial performance of the company. It is worth leaving those questions until after you have covered Chapter 22 in your studies.

The Section B questions 18-22 cover the Conceptual Framework and the regulatory framework.

# Conceptual framework

1   How does the *Conceptual Framework* define an asset?

    A    A resource owned by an entity as a result of past events and from which future economic benefits are expected to flow to the entity

    B    A resource over which an entity has legal rights as a result of past events and from which economic benefits are expected to flow to the entity

    C    A resource controlled by an entity as a result of past events and from which future economic benefits are expected to flow to the entity

    D    A resource to which an entity has a future commitment as a result of past events and from which future economic benefits are expected to flow from the entity     **(2 marks)**

2   Which of the following would be classified as a liability?

    A    Dexter's business manufactures a product under licence. In 12 months' time the licence expires and Dexter will have to pay $50,000 for it to be renewed.

    B    Reckless purchased an investment 9 months ago for $120,000. The market for these investments has now fallen and Reckless's investment is valued at $90,000.

    C    Carter has estimated the tax charge on its profits for the year just ended as $165,000.

    D    Expansion is planning to invest in new machinery and has been quoted a price of $570,000.

    **(2 marks)**

3   Which of the following would correctly describe the net realisable value of a two year old asset?

    A    The original cost of the asset less two years' depreciation
    B    The amount that could be obtained from selling the asset, less any costs of disposal
    C    The cost of an equivalent new asset less two years' depreciation
    D    The present value of the future cash flows obtainable from continuing to use the asset     **(2 marks)**

4   The *Conceptual Framework* identifies an **UNDERLYING ASSUMPTION** in preparing financial statements. This is:

    A    Going concern
    B    Materiality
    C    Substance over form
    D    Accruals     **(2 marks)**

5   The *Conceptual Framework* identifies four enhancing qualitative characteristics of financial information. For which of these characteristics is **DISCLOSURE OF ACCOUNTING POLICIES** particularly important?

    A    Verifiability
    B    Timeliness
    C    Comparability
    D    Understandability     **(2 marks)**

6       Which of the following are purposes of the IASB's *Conceptual Framework*?

☐       To assist the IASB in the preparation and review of IFRS
☐       To assist auditors in forming an opinion on whether financial statements comply with IFRS
☐       To assist in determining the treatment of items not covered by an existing IFRS
☐       To be authoritative where a specific IFRS conflicts with the *Conceptual Framework*          **(2 marks)**

7       Recognition is the process of including within the financial statements items which meet the definition of an element according to the IASB's *Conceptual Framework for Financial Reporting*.

Which of the following items should be recognised as an asset in the statement of financial position of a company?

A       A skilled and efficient workforce which has been very expensive to train. Some of these staff are still in the employment of the company.

B       A highly lucrative contract signed during the year which is due to commence shortly after the year end

C       A government grant relating to the purchase of an item of plant several years ago, which has a remaining life of four years

D       A receivable from a customer which has been sold (factored) to a finance company. The finance company has full recourse to the company for any losses.          **(2 marks)**

8       Comparability is identified as an enhancing qualitative characteristic in the IASB's *Conceptual Framework for Financial Reporting*.

Which of the following does **NOT** improve comparability?

A       Restating the financial statements of previous years when there has been a change of accounting policy

B       Prohibiting changes of accounting policy unless required by an IFRS or to give more relevant and reliable information

C       Disclosing discontinued operations in financial statements

D       Applying an entity's current accounting policy to a transaction which an entity has not engaged in before          **(2 marks)**

# Regulatory Framework

9       The process for developing an International Financial Reporting Standard involves a number of stages. Following receipt and review of comments on a Discussion Paper, what will be the next step undertaken by the IASB?

A       Publication of an Exposure Draft
B       Establishment of an Advisory Committee
C       Consultation with the Advisory Committee
D       Issue of a final IFRS          **(2 marks)**

10      Which of the following would **NOT** be an advantage of adopting IFRS?

A       It would be easier for investors to compare the financial statements of companies with those of foreign competitors.

B       Cross-border listing would be facilitated.

C       Accountants and auditors would have more defence in case of litigation.

D       Multinational companies could more easily transfer accounting staff across national borders.

          **(2 marks)**

11    Which **TWO** of the following statements regarding systems of regulation of accounting are true?

☐    A principles-based system will require more detailed regulations than a rules-based system.

☐    A rules-based system will tend to give rise to a larger number of accounting standards than a principles-based system.

☐    A principles-based system seeks to cover every eventuality.

☐    A principles-based system requires the exercise of more judgement in application than a rules-based system.                                                                  **(2 marks)**

# Accounting for inflation

12    Historical cost accounting remains in use because of its practical advantages.

Which of the following is **NOT** an advantage of historical cost accounting?

A    Amounts of transactions are reliable and can be verified

B    Amounts in the statement of financial position can be matched to amounts in the statement of cash flows

C    It avoids the overstatement of profit which can arise during periods of inflation

D    It provides fewer opportunities for creative accounting than systems of current value accounting                                                                                    **(2 marks)**

13    Overstatement of profits can arise during periods of inflation. This then leads to a number of other consequences. Which of the following is **NOT** a likely consequence of overstatement of profits?

A    Higher wage demands from employees
B    Higher tax bills
C    Reduced dividends to shareholders
D    Overstated EPS                                                                                     **(2 marks)**

14    Drexler acquired an item of plant on 1 October 20X2 at a cost of $500,000. It has an expected life of five years (straight-line depreciation) and an estimated residual value of 10% of its historical cost or current cost as appropriate. As at 30 September 20X4, the manufacturer of the plant still makes the same item of plant and its current price is $600,000.

What is the correct carrying amount to be shown in the statement of financial position of Drexler as at 30 September 20X4 under historical cost and current cost?

|   | Historical cost | Current cost |
|---|---|---|
|   | $ | $ |
| A | 320,000 | 600,000 |
| B | 320,000 | 384,000 |
| C | 300,000 | 600,000 |
| D | 300,000 | 384,000 |

**(2 marks)**

15    The 'physical capital maintenance' concept states that profit is the increase in the physical productive capacity of the business over the period. This concept is applied in:

A    Current cost accounting
B    Historical cost accounting
C    Current value accounting
D    Current purchasing power accounting                                                                **(2 marks)**

16    Which method of accounting adjusts income and capital values to allow for the effects of general price inflation?

    A     Historical cost accounting
    B     Current purchasing power accounting
    C     Current cost accounting
    D     Current value accounting          **(2 marks)**

17    Under current cost accounting, goods sold are charged to profit or loss at:

    A     Historical cost
    B     Replacement cost
    C     Net realisable value
    D     Economic value          **(2 marks)**

**(Total = 6 marks)**

# Section B

## Lisbon – case question

**Information relevant to questions 18–22**

The accountant of Lisbon is considering a number of transactions and events and how they should be treated in accordance with the concepts and qualitative characteristics of financial information as set out in the *Conceptual Framework*.

During the year ended 31 March 20X6, Lisbon experienced the following transactions or events:

(i) Lisbon sold an asset to a finance company and leased it back for the remainder of its useful life. The accountant has decided that this should be treated as a secured loan.

(ii) The company's statement of profit or loss prepared using historical costs showed a loss from operating its shops, but Lisbon is aware that the increase in the value of its properties during the period far outweigh the operating loss.

(iii) Inventory has up to this year been valued using FIFO but the accountant is considering changing to the weighted average method for the year to 31 March 20X6.

18  The accountant is aware that some members of the board of Lisbon have little understanding of accounting and he is worried about his presentation of the financial statements at the board meeting.

   How should he deal with this situation?

   A   In doing his presentation he should omit any complex issues, so that everybody can understand what he is saying.

   B   He should open his presentation with the advice that some of them may not understand all of it.

   C   He should classify, characterise and present the information clearly and precisely.

   D   He should deliver his presentation just to those who are financially qualified.

19  Which concept or qualitative characteristic has influenced the decision in (i) above?

   A   Faithful representation
   B   Verifiability
   C   Accruals
   D   Comparability

20  In looking at issue (ii) above, the accountant decides that the properties should be revalued.

   Which concept or qualitative characteristic has been applied in making this decision?

   A   Materiality
   B   Going concern
   C   Relevance
   D   Timeliness

21 Because of the loss arising from operating the shops, the accountant is considering the issue of going concern. If it were decided that Lisbon was no longer a going concern at 31 March 20X6, which of the following would apply in accordance with the *Conceptual Framework*?

    A    Financial statements do not need to be prepared.

    B    All the assets should be liquidated.

    C    The financial statements should be prepared on a different basis.

    D    The financial statements should be prepared as normal and the going concern status disclosed in the notes.

22 In applying the principle of comparability, how should the change of inventory valuation basis be accounted for?

    A    The change should just be disclosed.

    B    The financial statements for 31 March 20X6 should show both methods.

    C    The notes should show what the profit would have been if the change had not taken place.

    D    The financial statements for the prior period as shown at 31 March 20X6 should be restated using the weighted average basis.

# Section A
# Tangible non-current assets

23   Foster Co has built a new factory incurring the following costs:

|  | $'000 |
|---|---|
| Land | 1,200 |
| Materials | 2,400 |
| Labour | 3,000 |
| Architect's fees | 25 |
| Surveyor's fees | 15 |
| Site overheads | 300 |
| Apportioned administrative overheads | 150 |
| Testing of fire alarms | 10 |
| Business rates for first year | 12 |
|  | 7,112 |

What will be the total amount capitalised in respect of the factory?

A    $6,112,000
B    $6,950,000
C    $7,112,000
D    $7,100,000                                                                      (2 marks)

24   Carriageways Co had the following bank loans outstanding during the whole of 20X8:

|  | $m |
|---|---|
| 9% loan repayable 20X9 | 15 |
| 11% loan repayable 20Y2 | 24 |

Carriageways Co began construction of a qualifying asset on 1 April 20X8 and withdrew funds of $6 million on that date to fund construction. On 1 August 20X8 an additional $2 million was withdrawn for the same purpose.

Calculate the borrowing costs which can be capitalised in respect of this project for the year ended 31 December 20X8.

A    $549,333
B    $411,999
C    $750,000
D    $350,000                                                                        (2 marks)

25    Leclerc Co has borrowed $2.4 million to finance the building of a factory. Construction is expected to take two years. The loan was drawn down and incurred on 1 January 20X9 and work began on 1 March 20X9. $1 million of the loan was not utilised until 1 July 20X9 so Leclerc was able to invest it until needed.

Leclerc Co is paying 8% on the loan and can invest surplus funds at 6%.

Calculate the borrowing costs to be capitalised for the year ended 31 December 20X9 in respect of this project.

     A      $140,000
     B      $192,000
     C      $100,000
     D      $162,000              **(2 marks)**

---

26    Which of the following would be recognised as an investment property under IAS 40 in the consolidated financial statements of Build Co?

     A      A property intended for sale in the ordinary course of business
     B      A property being constructed for a customer
     C      A property held by Build Co as a right-of-use asset and leased out under a six-month lease
     D      A property owned by Build Co and leased out to a subsidiary        **(2 marks)**

---

27    Match the statement to whether the treatment of investment properties is allowed under IAS 40?

| Statement | |
| --- | --- |
| Following initial recognition, investment property can be held at either cost or fair value. | |
| If an investment property is held at fair value, this must be applied to all of the entity's investment property. | True |
| An investment property is initially measured at cost, including transaction costs. | False |
| A gain or loss arising from a change in the fair value of an investment property should be recognised in other comprehensive income. | |

             **(2 marks)**

---

28    Fido Feed Ltd has the following loans in place throughout the year ended 31 December 20X8.

|  | $m |
| --- | --- |
| 10% bank loan | 140 |
| 8% bank loan | 200 |

On 1 July 20X8 $50 million was drawn down for construction of a qualifying asset which was completed during 20X9.

What amount should be capitalised as borrowing costs at 31 December 20X8 in respect of this asset?

     A      $5.6 million
     B      $2.8 million
     C      $4.4 million
     D      $2.2 million              **(2 marks)**

---

29    Wetherby Co purchased a machine on 1 July 20X7 for $500,000. It is being depreciated on a straight-line basis over its expected life of ten years. Residual value is estimated at $20,000. On 1 January 20X8, following a change in legislation, Wetherby Co fitted a safety guard to the machine. The safety guard cost $25,000 and has a useful life of five years with no residual value.

What amount will be charged to profit or loss for the year ended 31 March 20X8 in respect of depreciation on this machine?

     $ [＿＿＿＿＿＿]                    **(2 marks)**

30    An aircraft requires a planned overhaul each year at a cost of $5,000 every three years. This is a condition of being allowed to fly.

How should the cost of the overhaul be treated in the financial statements? Select the correct option from those stated here:

A    Accrued for over the year and charged to maintenance expenses
B    Provided for in advance and charged to maintenance expenses
C    Capitalised and depreciated over the period to the next overhaul
D    Charged to profit or loss when the expenditure takes place                    **(2 marks)**

---

31    Auckland Co purchased a machine for $60,000 on 1 January 20X7 and assigned it a useful life of 15 years. On 31 March 20X9 it was revalued to $64,000 with no change in useful life.

What will be depreciation charge in relation to this machine in the financial statements of Auckland Co for the year ending 31 December 20X9?

$ [          ]                                                                    **(2 marks)**

---

32    Carter Co vacated an office building and let it out to a third party on 30 June 20X8. The building had an original cost of $900,000 on 1 January 20X0 and was being depreciated over 50 years. It was judged to have a fair value on 30 June 20X8 of $950,000. At the year-end date of 31 December 20X8 the fair value of the building was estimated at $1.2 million.

Carter Co uses the fair value model for investment property.

What amount will be shown in revaluation surplus at 31 December 20X8 in respect of this building?

$ [          ]                                                                    **(2 marks)**

# Intangible non-current assets

33    Geek Co is developing a new product and expects to be able to capitalise the costs. Which of the following would preclude capitalisation of the costs?

A    Development of the product is not yet complete.
B    No patent has yet been registered in respect of the product.
C    No sales contracts have yet been signed in relation to the product.
D    It has not been possible to reliably allocate costs to development of the product.    **(2 marks)**

---

34    Assoria Co had $20 million of capitalised development expenditure at cost brought forward at 1 October 20X7 in respect of products currently in production and a new project began on the same date.

The research stage of the new project lasted until 31 December 20X7 and incurred $1.4 million of costs. From that date the project incurred development costs of $800,000 per month. On 1 April 20X8 the directors of Assoria Co became confident that the project would be successful and yield a profit well in excess of costs. The project was still in development at 30 September 20X8. Capitalised development expenditure is amortised at 20% per annum using the straight-line method.

What amount will be charged to profit or loss for the year ended 30 September 20X8 in respect of research and development costs?

A    $8,280,000
B    $6,880,000
C    $7,800,000
D    $3,800,000                                                                    **(2 marks)**

35    Which of the following internally generated items may be eligible for capitalisation as intangible assets in accordance with IAS 38 *Intangible Assets?* (Ignore business combinations.)

    A     A customer list
    B     A pre-production prototype
    C     Goodwill
    D     The cost of researching new material           **(2 marks)**

36    At 30 September 20X9 Sandown Co's trial balance showed a brand at cost of $30 million, less accumulated amortisation brought forward at 1 October 20X8 of $9 million. Amortisation is based on a ten year useful life. An impairment review on 1 April 20X9 concluded that the brand had a value in use of $12 million and a remaining useful life of three years. However, on the same date Sandown Co received an offer to purchase the brand for $15 million.

    What should be the carrying amount of the brand in the statement of financial position of Sandown Co as at 30 September 20X9? (Answer to the nearest $'000)

    $ ☐                                                 **(2 marks)**

37    Dempsey Co's year end is 30 September 20X4. Dempsey Co commenced the development stage of a project to produce a new pharmaceutical drug on 1 January 20X4. Expenditure of $40,000 per month was incurred until the project was completed on 30 June 20X4 when the drug went into immediate production. The directors became confident of the project's success on 1 March 20X4. The drug has an estimated lifespan of five years; time apportionment is used by Dempsey Co where applicable.

    What amount will Dempsey Co charge to profit or loss for development costs, including any amortisation, for the year ended 30 September 20X4?

    $ ☐                                                 **(2 marks)**

# Impairment of assets

38    A cash-generating unit comprises the following assets:

|  | $'000 |
| --- | --- |
| Building | 700 |
| Plant and equipment | 200 |
| Goodwill | 90 |
| Current assets | 20 |
|  | 1,010 |

One of the machines, carried at $40,000, is damaged and will have to be scrapped. The recoverable amount of the cash-generating unit is estimated at $750,000.

What will be the carrying amount of the building when the impairment loss has been recognised? (to the nearest $'000)

    A     $597,000
    B     $577,000
    C     $594,000
    D     $548,000                          **(2 marks)**

39    What is the **RECOVERABLE AMOUNT** of an asset?

    A    Its current market value less costs of disposal
    B    The lower of carrying amount and value in use
    C    The higher of fair value less costs of disposal and value in use
    D    The higher of carrying amount and market value        **(2 marks)**

---

40    Lichen Ltd owns a machine that has a carrying amount of $85,000 at the year end of 31 March 20X9. Its market value is $78,000 and costs of disposal are estimated at $2,500. A new machine would cost $150,000. Lichen Ltd expects it to produce net cash flows of $30,000 per annum for the next three years. The cost of capital of Lichen Ltd is 8%.

What is the impairment loss on the machine to be recognised in the financial statements at 31 March 20X9?

$ [        ]        **(2 marks)**

---

41    IAS 36 *Impairment of Assets* suggests how indications of impairment might be recognised.

Which **TWO** of the following would be **EXTERNAL INDICATORS** that one or more of an entity's assets may be impaired?

☐    An unusually significant fall in the market value of one or more assets

☐    Evidence of obsolescence of one or more assets

☐    A decline in the economic performance of one or more assets

☐    An increase in market interest rates used to calculate value in use of the assets    **(2 marks)**

---

42    The following information relates to an item of plant owned by Bazaar Co:

(i)    Its carrying amount in the statement of the financial position is $3 million.

(ii)    Bazaar Co has received an offer of $2.7 million from a company in Japan interested in buying the plant.

(iii)    The present value of the estimated cash flows from continued use of the plant is $2.6 million.

(iv)    The estimated cost of shipping the plant to Japan is $50,000.

What is the amount of the impairment loss that should be recognised on the plant?

$ [        ]        **(2 marks)**

43    A business which comprises a single cash-generating unit has the following assets:

|  | $m |
|---|---|
| Goodwill | 3 |
| Patent | 5 |
| Property | 10 |
| Plant and equipment | 15 |
| Net current assets | 2 |
|  | 35 |

Following an impairment review it is estimated that the value of the patent is $2 million and the recoverable amount of the business is $24 million.

At what amount should the property be measured following the impairment review?

A    $8 million
B    $10 million
C    $7 million
D    $5 million                                                                (2 marks)

---

44    Riley Co acquired a non-current asset on 1 October 20W9 (ten years before 20X9) at a cost of $100,000 which had a useful life of ten years and a nil residual value. The asset had been correctly depreciated up to 30 September 20X4. At that date the asset was damaged and an impairment review was performed. On 30 September 20X4, the fair value of the asset less costs of disposal was $30,000 and the expected future cash flows were $8,500 per annum for the next five years. The current cost of capital is 10% and a five-year annuity of $1 per annum at 10% would have a present value of $3.79.

What amount would be charged to profit or loss for the impairment of this asset for the year ended 30 September 20X4?

A    $17,785
B    $20,000
C    $30,000
D    $32,215                                                                (2 marks)

---

45    The net assets of Fyngle Co, a cash-generating unit (CGU), are:

|  | $ |
|---|---|
| Property, plant and equipment | 200,000 |
| Allocated goodwill | 50,000 |
| Product patent | 20,000 |
| Net current assets (at net realisable value) | 30,000 |
|  | 300,000 |

As a result of adverse publicity, Fyngle Co has a recoverable amount of only $200,000.

What would be the value of Fyngle Co's property, plant and equipment after the allocation of the impairment loss?

A    $154,545
B    $170,000
C    $160,000
D    $133,333                                                                (2 marks)

---

46    Which of the following is **NOT** an indicator of impairment under IAS 36 *Impairment of Assets*?

A    Advances in the technological environment in which an asset is employed have an adverse impact on its future use

B    An increase in interest rates which increases the discount rate an entity uses

C    The carrying amount of an entity's net assets is lower than the entity's number of shares in issue multiplied by its share price

D    The estimated net realisable value of inventory has been reduced due to fire damage although this value is greater than its carrying amount                                                                (2 marks)

# Section B

# Plethora plc – case

### Information relevant to questions 47–51

The draft financial statements of Plethora plc for the year to 31 December 20X9 are being prepared and the accountant has requested your advice on dealing with the following issues.

(i)     Plethora plc has an administration building which it no longer needs. On 1 July 20X9 Plethora plc entered into an agreement to lease the building out to another company. The building cost $600,000 on 1 January 20X0 and is being depreciated over 50 years, based on the IAS 16 cost model. Plethora plc applies the fair value model under IAS 40 *Investment Property* and the fair value of the building was judged to be $800,000 on 1 July 20X9. This valuation had not changed at 31 December 20X9.

(ii)    Plethora plc owns another building which has been leased out for a number of years. It had a fair value of $550,000 at 31 December 20X8 and $740,000 at 31 December 20X9.

(iii)   Plethora plc owns a retail business which has suffered badly during the recession. Plethora plc treats this business as a separate cash-generating unit.

The carrying amounts of the assets comprising the retail business are:

|                       | $'000 |
|-----------------------|-------|
| Building              | 900   |
| Plant and equipment   | 300   |
| Inventory             | 70    |
| Other current assets  | 130   |
| Goodwill              | 40    |

An impairment review has been carried out as at 31 December 20X9 and the recoverable amount of the cash-generating unit is estimated at $1.3m.

47     What is the amount of the revaluation surplus that will be recognised in respect of the building in (i)?

$

48     In respect of the building in (ii), how will the increase in value from $550,000 to $740,000 be accounted for?

   A     Credited to profit or loss
   B     Credited to the revaluation surplus
   C     Credited to retained earnings
   D     Credited to an investment property reserve

49     Using the picklist provided, select the amount at which a potentially impaired asset is measured, following an impairment review?

**Picklist**

Fair value
Value in use
Recoverable amount
Carrying amount

50    What will be the carrying amount of the inventory after the impairment loss in (iii) has been accounted for?

    A    $64,000
    B    $70,000
    C    Nil
    D    $65,000

51    What will be the carrying amount of the building after the impairment loss has been accounted for?

    A    $900,000
    B    $836,000
    C    $795,000
    D    $825,000

(10 marks)

# Dearing Co OTQ case

18 mins

**Information relevant to questions 52–56**

(a)    On 1 October 20X5 Dearing Co acquired a machine under the following terms.

|  | $ |
| --- | --- |
| Manufacturer's base price | 1,050,000 |
| Trade discount (applying to base price only) | 20% |
| Early settlement discount taken (on the payable amount of the base cost only) | 5% |
| Freight charges | 30,000 |
| Electrical installation cost | 28,000 |
| Staff training in use of machine | 40,000 |
| Pre-production testing | 22,000 |
| Purchase of a three-year maintenance contract | 60,000 |

On 1 October 20X7 Dearing Co decided to upgrade the machine by adding new components at a cost of $200,000. This upgrade led to a reduction in the production time per unit of the goods being manufactured using the machine.

52    What amount should be recognised under non-current assets as the cost of the machine?

    A    $840,000
    B    $920,000
    C    $898,000
    D    $870,000

53    How should the $200,000 worth of new components be accounted for?

    A    Added to the carrying amount of the machine
    B    Charged to profit or loss
    C    Capitalised as a separate asset
    D    Debited to accumulated depreciation

54    Every five years the machine will need a major overhaul in order to keep running. How should this be accounted for?

    A    Set up a provision at year 1
    B    Build up the provision over years 1–5
    C    Capitalise the cost when it arises and amortise over five years
    D    Write the overhaul off to maintenance costs

55  By 27 September 20X7 internal evidence had emerged suggesting that Dearing Co's machine was impaired. Which of the following would be internal evidence of impairment?

A    The economic performance of the machine had declined.
B    There were legal and regulatory changes affecting the operating of the machine.
C    There was an unexpected fall in the market value of the machine.
D    New technological innovations were producing better machines.

56  On 30 September 20X7 the impairment review was carried out. The following amounts were established in respect of the machine:

|  | $ |
|---|---|
| Carrying amount | 850,000 |
| Value in use | 760,000 |
| Fair value | 850,000 |
| Costs of disposal | 30,000 |

What should be the carrying amount of the machine following the impairment review?

A    $760,000
B    $820,000
C    $850,000
D    $790,000

(10 marks)

# Elite Leisure Co OTQ case                                   18 mins

**The following scenario relates to questions 57–61.**

Elite Leisure Co is a private limited liability company that operates a single cruise ship. The ship was acquired on 1 October 20W6 (ten years before 20X6). Details of the cost of the ship's components and their estimated useful lives are:

| Component | Original cost $m | Depreciation basis |
|---|---|---|
| Ship's fabric (hull, decks etc) | 300 | 25 years straight-line |
| Cabins and entertainment area fittings | 150 | 12 years straight-line |
| Propulsion system | 100 | Useful life of 40,000 hours |

At 30 September 20X4 no further capital expenditure had been incurred on the ship.

The measured expired life of the propulsion system at 30 September 20X4 was 30,000 hours. Due to the unreliability of the engines, a decision was taken in early October 20X4 to replace the whole of the propulsion system at a cost of $140 million. The expected life of the new propulsion system was 50,000 hours and in the year ended 30 September 20X5 the ship had used its engines for 5,000 hours.

At the same time as the propulsion system replacement, Elite Leisure Co took the opportunity to do a limited upgrade to the facilities at a cost of $60 million and repaint the ship's fabric at a cost of $20 million. After the upgrade of the facilities it was estimated that their remaining life was five years (from the date of the upgrade). For the purpose of calculating depreciation, all the work on the ship can be assumed to have been completed on 1 October 20X4. All residual values can be taken as nil.

57  At 30 September 20X4 the ship is eight years old. What is the carrying amount of the ship at that date?

A    $279m
B    $275m
C    $229m
D    $254m

58 What is the amount of depreciation that should be charged in respect of the propulsion system for the year ended 30 September 20X5?

   A   $14m
   B   $39m
   C   $17.5m
   D   $16.5m

59 Apart from depreciation, what is the total charge to profit or loss for the year ended 30 September 20X5?

   $ [          ]

60 Elite Leisure Co's ship has to have a safety check carried out every five years at a cost of $50,000 in order to be licensed to operate. How should this be accounted for?

   A   Set up a provision for the discounted present value and unwind over five years
   B   Accrue the cost of the check over five years until it takes place
   C   Charge $50,000 to profit or loss when incurred
   D   Capitalise the cost when incurred and amortise over five years

61 Elite Leisure Co is being sued for $250,000 by a passenger who slipped on one of the gangways and twisted an ankle. The company's lawyer estimates that there is a 55% chance that it will lose the case. Legal costs for Elite Leisure Co will be $40,000. What amount should Elite Leisure Co provide in respect of this case?

   $ [          ]

(10 marks)

# Dexterity Co OTQ case

18 mins

### Information relevant to questions 62–66

Dexterity Co is a public listed company. It has been considering the accounting treatment of its intangible assets and how the matters below should be treated in its financial statements for the year to 31 March 20X4.

1   On 1 October 20X3 Dexterity Co acquired Temerity Co, a small company that specialises in pharmaceutical drug research and development. The purchase consideration was by way of a share exchange and valued at $35 million. The fair value of Temerity Co's net assets was $15 million (excluding any items referred to below). Temerity Co owns a patent for an established successful drug that has a remaining life of eight years. A firm of specialist advisors, Leadbrand, has estimated the current value of this patent to be $10 million, however the company is awaiting the outcome of clinical trials where the drug has been tested to treat a different illness. If the trials are successful, the value of the drug is then estimated to be $15 million. Also included in the company's statement of financial position is $2 million for medical research that has been conducted on behalf of a client.

2   Dexterity Co has developed and patented a new drug which has been approved for clinical use. The costs of developing the drug were $12 million. Based on early assessments of its sales success, Leadbrand have estimated its market value at $20 million, which can be taken as a reliable measurement.

3   Dexterity Co's manufacturing facilities have recently received a favourable inspection by government medical scientists. As a result of this the company has been granted an exclusive five-year licence to manufacture and distribute a new vaccine. Although the licence had no direct cost to Dexterity Co, its directors feel its granting is a reflection of the company's standing and have asked Leadbrand to value the licence. Accordingly they have placed a value of $10 million on it.

4   In the current accounting period, Dexterity Co has spent $3 million sending its staff on specialist training courses. While these courses have been expensive, they have led to a marked improvement in production quality and staff now need less supervision. This in turn has led to an increase in revenue and cost reductions. The directors of Dexterity Co believe these benefits will continue for at least three years and wish to treat the training costs as an asset.

62    Which of the following items should be recognised as intangible assets?

(i)    Patent for new drug
(ii)   Licence for new vaccine
(iii)  Specialist training courses

A    (i) and (ii)
B    (ii) and(iii)
C    (i) and (iii)
D    (i) only

63    Which of the following is one of the criteria for the recognition of development costs as an intangible asset?

A    The asset has been completed and is available for sale or use
B    It is possible that the asset can be sold or used
C    The proceeds from sale or use of the asset can be reliably measured
D    The asset will generate probable future economic benefits

64    IAS 38 gives examples of activities that would be regarded as research and therefore not eligible for recognition as an intangible asset.

Which of the following would be an example of research costs?

A    The design and construction of chosen alternative products or processes
B    The design of pre-production prototypes and models
C    The design of possible new or improved product or process alternatives
D    The design, construction and operation of a pilot plant

65    At what amount should the patent acquired from Temerity Co be valued at 31 March 20X4?

A    $10,000,000
B    $9,375,000
C    $15,000,000
D    Nil

66    How should Dexterity Co treat the goodwill arising on its acquisition of Temerity Co?

A    It should be capitalised and amortised over 20 years.
B    It should be capitalised and reviewed for impairment every year.
C    It should be capitalised and reviewed for impairment every five years.
D    It should be written off to retained earnings.

**(10 marks)**

# Advent Co OTQ case

**18 mins**

The following scenario relates to questions 67–71.

Advent Co is a publicly listed company. Details of Advent Co's non-current assets at 1 October 20X8 were:

|  | Land and building $m | Plant $m | Telecommunications licence $m | Total $m |
|---|---|---|---|---|
| Cost/valuation | 280 | 150 | 300 | 730 |
| Accumulated depreciation/amortisation | (40) | (105) | (30) | (175) |
| Carrying amount | 240 | 45 | 270 | 555 |

The following information is relevant:

(i) The land and building were revalued on 1 October 20X3 with $80 million attributable to the land and $200 million to the building. At that date the estimated remaining life of the building was 25 years. A further revaluation was not needed until 1 October 20X8 when the land and building were valued at $85 million and $180 million respectively. The remaining estimated life of the building at this date was 20 years.

(ii) Plant is depreciated at 20% per annum on cost with time apportionment where appropriate. On 1 April 20X9 new plant costing $45 million was acquired. In addition, this plant cost $5 million to install and commission. No plant is more than four years old.

(iii) The telecommunications licence was bought from the government on 1 October 20X7 and has a ten-year life. It is amortised on a straight-line basis. In September 20X9, a review of the sales of the products related to the licence showed them to be very disappointing. As a result of this review the estimated recoverable amount of the licence at 30 September 20X9 was estimated at only $100 million.

There were no disposals of non-current assets during the year to 30 September 20X9.

67 What is the carrying amount of the land and buildings at 30 September 20X9?

A $256m
B $265m
C $240m
D $271m

68 What is the depreciation charge on the plant for the year ended 30 September 20X9?

A $30m
B $25m
C $20m
D $35m

69 Having revalued its property Advent Co is required to make certain disclosures in respect of the revaluation.

Which of the following is **NOT** one of these disclosures?

A Effective date of revaluation
B Professional qualifications of valuer
C Basis used to revalue assets
D Carrying amount of assets if no revaluation had taken place

70 What is the amount of the impairment loss on the licence? Select your answer from the drop down box options below.

$ [          ▼ ]

**Picklist**

$100m
$140m
$170m
$240m

BPP
LEARNING MEDIA

71    Advent Co's licence is now carried at its recoverable amount. How is recoverable amount measured?

    A       Higher of fair value less costs of disposal and value in use
    B       Lower of fair value less costs of disposal and value in use
    C       Higher of carrying amount and fair value less costs of disposal
    D       Lower of carrying amount and fair value less costs of disposal

(10 marks)

# Systria Co OTQ case

**18 mins**

**The following information is relevant to questions 72–76.**

Systria Co is preparing its financial statements for the year ended 31 December 20X7 and has a number of issues to deal with regarding non-current assets.

(i)    Systria Co has suffered an impairment loss of $90,000 to one of its cash-generating units. The carrying amounts of the assets in the cash-generating unit prior to adjusting for impairment are:

|  | $'000 |
|---|---|
| Goodwill | 50 |
| Patent | 10 |
| Land and buildings | 100 |
| Plant and machinery | 50 |
| Net current assets | 10 |

The patent is now estimated to have no value.

(ii)    During the year to 31 December 20X7 Systria Co acquired Dominica for $10 million, its tangible assets being valued at $7 million and goodwill on acquisition being $3 million. Assets with a carrying amount of $2.5 million were subsequently destroyed. Systria Co has carried out an impairment review and has established that Dominica Co could be sold for $6 million, while its value in use is $5.5 million.

(iii)    A freehold property originally costing $100,000 with a 50-year life has accumulated depreciation to date of $20,000. The asset is to be revalued to $130,000 at 31 December 20X7.

72    What is the post-impairment carrying amount of plant and machinery in (i) above?

$ ☐

73    The finance director has been asked to report to the board on the reasons for the impairment review on the cash-generating unit. Which **TWO** of the following would be an internal indicator of impairment of an asset under IAS 36 *Impairment of Assets*?

☐    The market value of the asset has fallen significantly.

☐    There are adverse changes to the use to which the asset is put.

☐    The asset is fully depreciated.

☐    The operating performance of the asset has declined.

74    What is the carrying amount of the goodwill in (ii) following the impairment review?  Select your answer from the drop down box options below.

$ ☐ ▼

**Picklist**

$1.5 million
$2 million
$2.5 million
$3 million

75    Using the drag and drop options below, select the double entries required to record the revaluation in (iii)?

|                           | Debit | Credit |
|---------------------------|-------|--------|
| Accumulated depreciation  |       |        |
| Property at cost          |       |        |
| Revaluation surplus       |       |        |

$20,000

$30,000

$50,000

76    What will be the depreciation charge on the asset in (iii) for the year ended 31 December 20X8?

A    $2,000
B    $2,600
C    $3,250
D    $2,750

**(10 marks)**

# Section A

# Revenue

77 Confidence Co entered into a contract on 1 January 20X5 to build a factory. The total contract revenue was $2.8 million. At 31 December 20X5 the contract was certified as 35% complete. Costs incurred during the year were $740,000 and costs to complete are estimated at $1.4 million. $700,000 has been billed to the customer but not yet paid.

What amount will be recognised as a contract asset or liability in respect of this contract in the statement of financial position of Confidence Co as at 31 December 20X5?

   A    $271,000 contract asset
   B    $509,000 contract asset
   C    $271,000 contract liability
   D    $509,000 contract liability                                                          **(2 marks)**

78 Which of the following are acceptable methods of accounting for a government grant relating to an asset in accordance with IAS 20 *Accounting for Government Grants and Disclosure of Government Assistance*?

   (i)     Set up the grant as deferred income
   (ii)    Credit the amount received to profit or loss
   (iii)   Deduct the grant from the carrying amount of the asset
   (iv)    Add the grant to the carrying amount of the asset

   A    (i) and (ii)
   B    (ii) and (iv)
   C    (i) and (iii)
   D    (iii) and (iv)                                                                        **(2 marks)**

79  On 1 October 20X2 Pricewell Co entered into a contract to construct a bridge over a river. The total contract revenue was $50 million and construction is expected to be completed on 30 September 20X4. Costs to date are:

|  | $m |
|---|---|
| Materials, labour and overheads | 12 |
| Specialist plant acquired 1 October 20X2 | 8 |

The sales value of the work done at 31 March 20X3 has been agreed at $22 million and the estimated cost to complete (excluding plant depreciation) is $10 million. The specialist plant will have no residual value at the end of the contract and should be depreciated on a monthly basis. Pricewell Co recognises satisfaction of performance obligations on the percentage of completion basis as determined by the agreed work to date compared to the total contract price.

What is the profit to date on the contract at 31 March 20X3?

A  $8,800,000
B  $13,200,000
C  $11,440,000
D  $10,000,000                                                              (2 marks)

80  The following details apply to a contract where performance obligations are satisfied over time at 31 December 20X5.

|  | $ |
|---|---|
| Total contract revenue | 120,000 |
| Costs to date | 48,000 |
| Estimated costs to completion | 48,000 |
| Amounts invoiced | 50,400 |

The contract is agreed to be 45% complete at 31 December 20X5.
What amount should appear in the statement of financial position as at 31 December 20X5 as a contract asset?

A  $8,400
B  $48,000
C  $6,000
D  $50,400                                                                  (2 marks)

81  Sale and repurchase arrangements can be used to disguise the substance of loan transactions by taking them 'off balance sheet'. In this case the legal position is that the asset has been sold but the substance is that the seller still retains the benefits of ownership.

Which of the following is **NOT** a feature which suggests that the substance of a transaction differs from its legal form?

A  The seller of an asset retains the ability to use the asset.
B  The seller has no further exposure to the risks of ownership
C  The asset has been transferred at a price substantially above or below its fair value.
D  The 'sold' asset remains on the sellers premises.                       (2 marks)

82    Springthorpe Co entered into a three-year contract on 1 January 20X2 to build a factory. This is a contract where performance obligations are satisfied over time. The percentage of performance obligations satisfied is measured according to certificates issued by a surveyor. The contract price was $12 million. At 31 December 20X2 details of the contract were as follows.

|                             | $m   |
|-----------------------------|------|
| Costs to date               | 6    |
| Estimated costs to complete | 9    |
| Amounts invoiced            | 4    |
| Certified complete          | 40%  |

What amount should appear in the statement of financial position of Springthorpe Co as at 31 December 20X2 as contract assets/liabilities in respect of this contract?

A    $1 million contract liability
B    $2 million contract liability
C    $1 million contract asset
D    $2 million contract asset                                                          **(2 marks)**

83    On 25 June 20X9 Cambridge Co received an order from a new customer, Circus Co, for products with a sales value of $900,000. Circus Co enclosed a deposit with the order of $90,000.

On 30 June Cambridge Co had not completed credit checks on Circus and had not despatched any goods. Cambridge is considering the following possible entries for this transaction in its financial statements for the year ended 30 June 20X9.

(i)     Include $900,000 in revenue for the year
(ii)    Include $90,000 in revenue for the year
(iii)   Do not include anything in revenue for the year
(iv)    Create a trade receivable for $810,000
(v)     Show $90,000 as a current liability

According to IFRS 15 *Revenue from Contracts with Customers*, how should Cambridge Co record this transaction in its financial statements for the year ended 30 June 20X9?

A    (i) and (iv)
B    (ii) and (v)
C    (ii) and (iv)
D    (iii) and (v)                                                                      **(2 marks)**

84    Repro Co, a company which sells photocopying equipment, has prepared its draft financial statements for the year ended 30 September 20X4. It has included the following transactions in revenue at the stated amounts below.

Which of these has been correctly included in revenue according to IFRS 15 *Revenue from Contracts with Customers*?

A    Agency sales of $250,000 on which Repro Co is entitled to a commission.

B    Sale proceeds of $20,000 for motor vehicles which were no longer required by Repro Co.

C    Sales of $150,000 on 30 September 20X4. The amount invoiced to and received from the customer was $180,000, which included $30,000 for ongoing servicing work to be done by Repro Co over the next two years.

D    Sales of $200,000 on 1 October 20X3 to an established customer which, (with the agreement of Repro Co), will be paid in full on 30 September 20X5. Repro Co has a cost of capital of 10%.

                                                                                        **(2 marks)**

85    Yling Co entered into a contract in respect of which performance obligations are satisfied over time on 1 January 20X4. The contract is expected to last 24 months. The price which has been agreed for the contract is $5 million. At 30 September 20X4 the costs incurred on the contract were $1.6 million and the estimated remaining costs to complete were $2.4 million. On 20 September 20X4 Yling Co received a payment from the customer of $1.8 million which was equal to the total of the amounts invoiced. Yling Co calculates the stage of completion of its performance obligations on contracts on the basis of amounts invoiced to the contract price.

What amount would be reported in Yling Co's statement of financial position as at 30 September 20X4 as the contract asset arising from the above contract?

A    Nil
B    $160,000
C    $800,000
D    $200,000

**(2 marks)**

---

86    Consignment inventory is an arrangement whereby inventory is held by one party but owned by another party. It is common in the motor trade.

Which **TWO** of the following indicate that the inventory in question is consignment inventory?

☐    Manufacturer can require dealer to return the inventory
☐    Dealer has no right of return of the inventory
☐    Manufacturer bears obsolescence risk
☐    Dealer bears slow movement risk

**(2 marks)**

---

87    Intellect Intelligence Co receives a government grant of $400,000 on 1 April 20X6 to facilitate purchase on the same day of an asset which costs $600,000. The asset has a five-year useful life and is depreciated on a 25% reducing balance basis. Company policy is to account for all grants received as deferred income.

What amount of income will be recognised in respect of the grant in the year to 31 March 20X8?

$ ☐

**(2 marks)**

---

88    Newmarket Co's revenue as shown in its draft statement of profit or loss for the year ended 31 December 20X9 is $27 million. This includes $8 million for a consignment of goods sold on 31 December 20X9 on which Newmarket Co will incur ongoing service and support costs for two years after the sale.

The supply of the goods and the provision of service and support are separate performance obligations under the terms of IFRS 15 *Revenue from Contracts with Customers*.

The cost of providing service and support is estimated at $800,000 per annum. Newmarket Co applies a 30% mark-up to all service costs.

At what amount should revenue be shown in the statement of profit or loss of Newmarket Co for the year ended 31 December 20X9? (Ignore the time value of money.)

$ ☐

**(2 marks)**

# Introduction to groups

89    On what basis may a subsidiary be excluded from consolidation?

    A    The activities of the subsidiary are dissimilar to the activities of the rest of the group.

    B    The subsidiary was acquired with the intention of reselling it after a short period of time.

    C    The subsidiary is based in a country with strict exchange controls which make it difficult for it to transfer funds to the parent.

    D    There is no basis on which a subsidiary may be excluded from consolidation.            **(2 marks)**

90    When a bargain purchase arises, IFRS 3 *Business Combinations* requires that the amounts involved in computing the bargain purchase should first be reassessed. When the amount of the bargain purchase has been confirmed, how should it be accounted for?

    A    Charged as an expense in profit or loss
    B    Capitalised and presented under non-current assets
    C    Credited to profit or loss
    D    Shown as a deduction from non-current assets            **(2 marks)**

91    Which of the following is the criterion for treatment of an investment as an associate?

    A    Ownership of a majority of the equity shares
    B    Ability to exercise control
    C    Existence of significant influence
    D    Exposure to variable returns from involvement with the investee            **(2 marks)**

92    Which **TWO** of the following statements are correct when preparing consolidated financial statements?

    ☐    A subsidiary cannot be consolidated unless it prepares financial statements to the same reporting date as the parent.

    ☐    A subsidiary with a different reporting date may prepare additional statements up to the group reporting date for consolidation purposes.

    ☐    A subsidiary's financial statements can be included in the consolidation if the gap between the parent and subsidiary reporting dates is five months or less.

    ☐    Where a subsidiary's financial statements are drawn up to a different reporting date from those of the parent, adjustments should be made for significant transactions or events occurring between the two reporting dates.            **(2 marks)**

93    IFRS 3 *Business Combinations* requires an acquirer to measure the assets and liabilities of the acquiree at the date of consolidation at fair value. IFRS 13 *Fair Value Measurement* provides guidance on how fair value should be established.

    Which of the following is **NOT** one of the issues to be considered according to IFRS 13 when arriving at the fair value of a non-financial asset?

    A    The characteristics of the asset
    B    The price paid to acquire the asset
    C    The principal or most advantageous market for the asset
    D    The highest and best use of the asset            **(2 marks)**

94      IFRS 10 *Consolidated Financial Statements* provides a definition of control and identifies three separate elements of control. Which of the following is **NOT** one of these elements of control?

   A    Power over the investee
   B    The power to participate in the financial and operating policies of the investee
   C    Exposure to, or rights to, variable returns from its involvement with the investee
   D    The ability to use its power over the investee to affect the amount of the investor's returns  **(2 marks)**

95      Petre Co owns 100% of the share capital of the following companies. The directors are unsure of whether the investments should be consolidated.

   In which of the following circumstances would the investment **NOT** be consolidated?

   A    Petre Co has decided to sell its investment in Alpha Co as it is loss-making; the directors believe its exclusion from consolidation would assist users in predicting the group's future profits

   B    Beta Co is a bank and its activity is so different from the engineering activities of the rest of the group that it would be meaningless to consolidate it

   C    Delta Co is located in a country where local accounting standards are compulsory and these are not compatible with IFRS used by the rest of the group

   D    Gamma Co is located in a country where a military coup has taken place and Petre Co has lost control of the investment for the foreseeable future              **(2 marks)**

# Financial instruments

96      An 8% $30 million convertible loan note was issued on 1 April 20X5 at par. Interest is payable in arrears on 31 March each year. The loan note is redeemable at par on 31 March 20X8 or convertible into equity shares at the option of the loan note holders on the basis of 30 shares for each $100 of loan. A similar instrument without the conversion option would have an interest rate of 10% per annum.

   The present values of $1 receivable at the end of each year based on discount rates of 8% and 10% are:

|              |            | 8%   | 10%  |
| ------------ | ---------- | ---- | ---- |
| End of year  | 1          | 0.93 | 0.91 |
|              | 2          | 0.86 | 0.83 |
|              | 3          | 0.79 | 0.75 |
|              | Cumulative | 2.58 | 2.49 |

   What amount will be credited to equity on 1 April 20X5 in respect of this financial instrument?

   A    $5,976,000
   B    $1,524,000
   C    $324,000
   D    $9,000,000                                                        **(2 marks)**

97      A 5% loan note was issued on 1 April 20X0 at its face value of $20 million. Direct costs of the issue were $500,000. The loan note will be redeemed on 31 March 20X3 at a substantial premium. The effective interest rate applicable is 10% per annum.

   At what amount will the loan note appear in the statement of financial position as at 31 March 20X2?

   A    $21,000,000
   B    $20,450,000
   C    $22,100,000
   D    $21,495,000                                                       **(2 marks)**

98 Using the drag and drop options below, complete the statement to show how IFRS 9 *Financial Instruments* require investments in equity instruments to be measured and accounted for (in the absence of any election at initial recognition)?

| | | |
|---|---|---|
| [ ] | with changes going through | [ ] |

| Fair value | | profit or loss |
|---|---|---|
| Amortised cost | | other comprehensive income |

(2 marks)

99 On 1 January 20X1 Penfold Co purchased a debt instrument for its fair value of $500,000. It had a principal amount of $550,000 and was due to mature in five years. The debt instrument carries fixed interest of 6% paid annually in arrears and has an effective interest rate of 8%. It is held at amortised cost.

At what amount will the debt instrument be shown in the statement of financial position of Penfold Co as at 31 December 20X2?

A  $514,560
B  $566,000
C  $564,560
D  $520,800

(2 marks)

100 Which of the following are **NOT** classified as financial instruments under IAS 32 *Financial Instruments: Presentation*?

A  Share options
B  Intangible assets
C  Trade receivables
D  Redeemable preference shares

(2 marks)

101 Dexon Co's draft statement of financial position as at 31 March 20X8 shows financial assets at fair value through profit or loss with a carrying amount of $12.5 million as at 1 April 20X7.

These financial assets are held in a fund whose value changes directly in proportion to a specified market index. At 1 April 20X7 the relevant index was 1,200 and at 31 March 20X8 it was 1,296.

What amount of gain or loss should be recognised at 31 March 20X8 in respect of these assets?

$ [ ]

(2 marks)

102 On 1 January 20X8 Zeeper Ltd purchased 40,000 $1 listed equity shares at a price of $3 per share. An irrevocable election was made to recognise the shares at fair value through other comprehensive income. Transaction costs were $3,000. At the year end of 31 December 20X8 the shares were trading at $6 per share.

What amount in respect of these shares will be shown under 'investments in equity instruments' in the statement of financial position of Zeeper Ltd as at 31 December 20X8?

$ [ ]

(2 marks)

# Leasing

103 On 1 January 20X6 Fellini Co hired a machine under a five year lease. A non-refundable deposit of $700,000 was payable on 1 January 20X6. The present value of the future lease payments was $2,426,000. The remaining 4 instalments of $700,000 are payable annually in advance with the first payment made on 1 January 20X6. The interest rate implicit in the lease is 6%.

What amount will appear under non-current liabilities in respect of this lease in the statement of financial position of Fellini Co at 31 December 20X6? [Answers to nearest $'000]

A    $742,000
B    $1,726,000
C    $1,872,000
D    $2,572,000

(2 marks)

104 Which of the following situations does **NOT** suggest that an arrangement constitutes a lease under IFRS 16 *Leases*?

A    The lessee obtains substantially all of the economic benefits from use of the asset.
B    Ownership in the asset is transferred at the end of the lease term.
C    The contract relates to an identified asset.
D    If it suits them to do so, the lessor can substitute an identical asset.

(2 marks)

105 Pebworth Co acquired an item of plant under a lease on 1 April 20X7. The present value of the lease payments was $15.6 million and the rentals are $6 million per annum paid in arrears for three years on 31 March each year.

The interest rate implicit in the lease is 8% per annum.

What amount will appear under current liabilities in respect of this lease in the statement of financial position at 31 March 20X8? (Answers to nearest $'000)

A    $5,132,000
B    $5,716,000
C    $6,000,000
D    $4,752,000

(2 marks)

106 At what amount does IFRS 16 Leases require a lessee to measure a right-of-use asset acquired under a lease?

A    Lease liability + other direct costs + incentives received
B    Lease liability – other direct costs – prepayments
C    Lease liability + other direct costs + prepayments – incentives received
D    Lease liability – other direct costs – prepayments + incentives received

(2 marks)

107 On 1 October 20X3, Fresco Co acquired an item of plant under a five-year lease agreement. The lease required an immediate deposit of $2 million. The present value of the future payments was $25 million. The agreement had an implicit finance cost of 10% per annum and annual rentals of $6 million paid on 30 September each year for five years.

What will be the non-current liability in Fresco Co's statement of financial position as at 30 September 20X5?

A    $2,500,000
B    $2,300,000
C    $2,150,000
D    $3,850,000

(2 marks)

108    The objective of IFRS 16 *Leases* is to prescribe the appropriate accounting treatment and required disclosures in relation to leases.

Which **TWO** of the following are among the criteria set out in IFRS 16 for an arrangement to be classified as a lease?

- [ ] The lessee has the right to substantially all of the economic benefits from use of the asset.
- [ ] The lease term is for substantially all of the estimated useful life of the asset.
- [ ] The agreement concerns an identified asset which cannot be substituted.
- [ ] The lessor has the right to direct the use of the asset.                                     **(2 marks)**

109    Tourmalet Co sold an item of plant for $50 million on 1 April 20X4. The plant had a carrying amount of $40 million at the date of sale, which was charged to cost of sales. On the same date, Tourmalet Co entered into an agreement to lease back the plant for the next five years (being the estimated remaining life of the plant) at a cost of $14 million per annum payable annually in arrears. An arrangement of this type is normally deemed to have a financing cost of 10% per annum. Tourmalet Co retained the rights to direct the use of and retain substantially all the remaining benefits from the plant.

Using the drop down box, select what amount will be shown as income from this transaction in the statement of profit or loss for the year ended 30 September 20X4?

[ ▼ ]

**Picklist**

Nil
$10 million
$40 million
$50 million                                                                                  **(2 marks)**

110    A sale and leaseback transaction involves the sale of an asset and the leasing back of the same asset. If the arrangement meets the IFRS 15 criteria to be recognised as a sale, how should any 'profit' on the sale be treated?

A    Recognise whole amount of profit immediately in profit or loss
B    Defer profit and amortise over the lease term
C    Recognise proportion relating to right-of-use retained
D    Recognise proportion relating to right-of-use transferred                                   **(2 marks)**

111    During the year ended 30 September 20X4 Hyper Co entered into two lease transactions:

On 1 October 20X3 a payment of $90,000, being the first of five equal annual payments of a lease for an item of plant which has a five-year useful life. The lease has an implicit interest rate of 10% and the initial measurement of the right-of-use asset and the lease liability on 1 October 20X3 was $340,000.

On 1 August 20X4 a payment of $18,000 for a nine-month lease of an item of excavation equipment.

What amount in total would be charged to Hyper Co's statement of profit or loss for the year ended 30 September 20X4 in respect of the above transactions?

$[          ]                                                                                 **(2 marks)**

112    On 1 January 20X6 Platinum Co entered into a lease agreement. The initial lease liability was $360,000 and the terms of the lease were a deposit of $120,000 payable on 1 January 20X6 and three further instalments of $100,000 payable on 31 December 20X6, 31 December 20X7 and 31 December 20X8. The rate of interest implicit in the lease is 12%.

What will be the amount of the finance charge arising from this lease which will be charged to profit or loss for the year ended 31 December 20X7?

$[          ]                                                                                 **(2 marks)**

# Provisions and events after the reporting period

113 Candel Co is being sued by a customer for $2 million for breach of contract over a cancelled order. Candel Co has obtained legal opinion that there is a 20% chance that Candel Co will lose the case. Accordingly Candel Co has provided $400,000 ($2 million × 20%) in respect of the claim. The unrecoverable legal costs of defending the action are estimated at $100,000. These have not been provided for as the case will not go to court until next year.

What is the amount of the provision that should be made by Candel Co in accordance with IAS 37 *Provisions, Contingent Liabilities and Contingent Assets*?

A    $2,000,000
B    $2,100,000
C    $500,000
D    $100,000                                                                                (2 marks)

114 During the year Peterlee Co acquired an iron ore mine at a cost of $6 million. In addition, when all the ore has been extracted (estimated ten years' time) the company will face estimated costs for landscaping the area affected by the mining that have a present value of $2 million. These costs would still have to be incurred even if no further ore was extracted.

How should this $2 million future cost be recognised in the financial statements?

A    Provision $2 million and $2 million capitalised as part of cost of mine
B    Provision $2 million and $2 million charged to operating costs
C    Accrual $200,000 per annum for next ten years
D    Should not be recognised as no cost has yet arisen                                       (2 marks)

115 Which of the following would **NOT** be valid grounds for a provision?

A    Aston Ltd has a policy has a policy of cleaning up any environmental contamination caused by its operations, but is not legally obliged to do so.

B    Brum Ltd  is leasing an office building for which it has no further use. However, it is tied into the lease for another year.

C    Coleshill Co  is closing down a division. The board has prepared detailed closure plans which have been communicated to customers and employees.

D    Dudley Co has acquired a machine which requires a major overhaul every three years. The cost of the first overhaul is reliably estimated at $120,000.                                 (2 marks)

116 Which of the following events taking place after the year end but before the financial statements were authorised for issue would require adjustment in accordance with IAS 10 *Events After the Reporting Period*?

A    Three lines of inventory held at the year end were destroyed by flooding in the warehouse.
B    The directors announced a major restructuring.
C    Two lines of inventory held at the year end were discovered to have faults rendering them unsaleable.
D    The value of the company's investments fell sharply.                                    (2 marks)

117 Which of the following statements are correct in accordance with IAS 37 *Provisions, Contingent Liabilities and Contingent Assets*?

(i)    Provisions should be made for both constructive and legal obligations.

(ii)   Discounting may be used when estimating the amount of a provision.

(iii)  A restructuring provision must include the estimated costs of retraining or relocating continuing staff.

(iv)   A restructuring provision may only be made when a company has a detailed plan for the restructuring and has communicated to interested parties a firm intention to carry it out.

A    All four statements are correct
B    (i), (ii) and (iv) only
C    (i), (iii) and (iv) only
D    (ii) and (iii) only                                                                      (2 marks)

118 Tynan's year end is 30 September 20X4 and the following potential liabilities have been identified:

Which **TWO** of the above should Tynan recognise as liabilities as at 30 September 20X4?

☐ The signing of a non-cancellable contract in September 20X4 to supply goods in the following year on which, due to a pricing error, a loss will be made

☐ The cost of a reorganisation which was approved by the board in August 20X4 but has not yet been implemented, communicated to interested parties or announced publicly

☐ An amount of deferred tax relating to the gain on the revaluation of a property during the current year. Tynan has no intention of selling the property in the foreseeable future.

☐ The balance on the warranty provision which related to products for which there are no outstanding claims and whose warranties had expired by 30 September 20X4 **(2 marks)**

119 On 1 October 20X3 Xplorer Co commenced drilling for oil from an undersea oilfield. The extraction of oil causes damage to the seabed which has a restorative cost (ignore discounting) of $10,000 per million barrels of oil extracted. Xplorer Co extracted 250 million barrels in the year ended 30 September 20X4.

Xplorer Co is also required to dismantle the drilling equipment at the end of its five-year licence. This has an estimated cost of $30 million on 30 September 20X8. Xplorer Co's cost of capital is 8% per annum and $1 has a present value of 68 cents in five years' time.

What is the total provision (extraction plus dismantling) which Xplorer Cowould report in its statement of financial position as at 30 September 20X4 in respect of its oil operations?

$ ☐ **(2 marks)**

120 Hopewell Co sells a line of goods under a six-month warranty. Any defect arising during that period is repaired free of charge. Hopewell Co has calculated that if all the goods sold in the last six months of the year required repairs the cost would be $2 million. If all of these goods had more serious faults and had to be replaced the cost would be $6 million.

The normal pattern is that 80% of goods sold will be fault-free, 15% will require repairs and 5% will have to be replaced.

Using the drop down box options, select what is the amount of the provision required?

☐ ▼

**Picklist**

$0.6 million
$0.8 million
$1.6 million
$2 million **(2 marks)**

121 Which **TWO** of the following events which occur after the reporting date of a company but before the financial statements are authorised for issue are classified as **ADJUSTING** events in accordance with IAS 10 *Events After the Reporting Period*?

☐ A change in tax rate announced after the reporting date, but affecting the current tax liability

☐ The discovery of a fraud which had occurred during the year

☐ The determination of the sale proceeds of an item of plant sold before the year end

☐ The destruction of a factory by fire **(2 marks)**

# Inventories and biological assets

122 Caminas Co has the following products in inventory at the year end.

| Product | Quantity | Cost | Selling price | Selling cost |
|---------|----------|------|---------------|--------------|
| A | 1,000 | $40 | $55 | $8 |
| B | 2,500 | $15 | $25 | $4 |
| C | 800 | $23 | $27 | $5 |

At what amount should total inventory be stated in the statement of financial position?

A    $95,900
B    $103,100
C    $95,100
D    $105,100

(2 marks)

123 In which of the following situations is the net realisable value of an item of inventory likely to be lower than cost?

A    The production cost of the item has been falling.
B    The selling price of the item has been rising.
C    The item is becoming obsolete.
D    Demand for the item is increasing.

(2 marks)

124 At what amount is a biological asset measured on initial recognition in accordance with IAS 41 *Agriculture*?

A    Production cost
B    Fair value
C    Cost less estimated costs to sell
D    Fair value less estimated costs to sell

(2 marks)

125 Which of the following is **NOT** the outcome of a biological transformation according to IAS 41?

A    Growth
B    Harvest
C    Procreation
D    Degeneration

(2 marks)

126 How is a gain or loss arising on a biological asset recognised in accordance with IAS 41?

A    Included in profit or loss for the year
B    Adjusted in retained earnings
C    Shown under 'other comprehensive income'
D    Deferred and recognised over the life of the biological asset

(2 marks)

127 Which of the following statements about IAS 2 *Inventories* are correct?

1    Production overheads should be included in cost on the basis of a company's actual level of activity in the period.

2    In arriving at the net realisable value of inventories, settlement discounts must be deducted from the expected selling price.

3    In arriving at the cost of inventories, FIFO, LIFO and weighted average cost formulas are acceptable.

4    It is permitted to value finished goods inventories at materials plus labour cost only, without adding production overheads.

A    1 only
B    1 and 2
C    3 and 4
D    None of them

(2 marks)

128 Isaac Ltd is a company which buys agricultural produce from wholesale suppliers for retail to the general public. It is preparing its financial statements for the year ending 30 September 20X4 and is considering its closing inventory.

In addition to IAS 2 *Inventories*, which of the following IFRSs may be relevant to determining the figure to be included in its financial statements for closing inventories?

    A    IAS 10 *Events After the Reporting Period*
    B    IAS 38 *Intangible Assets*
    C    IAS 16 *Property, Plant and Equipment*
    D    IAS 41 *Agriculture*             **(2 marks)**

129 In preparing financial statements for the year ended 31 March 20X6, the inventory count was carried out on 4 April 20X6. The value of inventory counted was $36 million. Between 31 March and 4 April goods with a cost of $2.7 million were received into inventory and sales of $7.8 million were made at a mark-up on cost of 30%.

Using the drop down box. select at what amount inventory should be stated in the statement of financial position as at 31 March 20X6?

**Picklist**

$39.3 million
$36.0 million
$33.3 million
$41.1 million             **(2 marks)**

130 At 31 March 20X7 Tentacle Ltd had 12,000 units of product W32 in inventory, included at cost of $6 per unit. During April and May 20X7 units of W32 were being sold at a price of $5.40 each, with sales staff receiving a 15% commission on the sales price of the product.

At what amount should inventory of product W32 be recognised in the financial statements of Tentacle Ltd as at 31 March 20X7?

$ ☐             **(2 marks)**

# Accounting for taxation

131 Ullington Co's trial balance shows a debit balance of $2.1 million brought forward on current tax and a credit balance of $5.4 million on deferred tax. The tax charge for the current year is estimated at $16.2 million and the carrying amounts of net assets are $13 million in excess of their tax base. The income tax rate is 30%

What amount will be shown as income tax in the statement of profit or loss of Ullington Co for the year?

    A    $15.6 million
    B    $12.6 million
    C    $16.8 million
    D    $18.3 million             **(2 marks)**

132 Jasper Orange Co's trial balance at 31 December 20X3 shows a debit balance of $700,000 on current tax and a credit balance of $8,400,000 on deferred tax. The directors have estimated the provision for income tax for the year at $4.5 million and the required deferred tax provision is $5.6 million, $1.2 million of which relates to a property revaluation..

What is the profit or loss income tax liability for the year ended 31 December 20X3?

    A    $1 million
    B    $2.4 million
    C    $1.2 million
    D    $3.6 million             **(2 marks)**

133 The following information relates to an entity:

(i) At 1 January 20X8 the carrying amount of non-current assets exceeded their tax written down value by $850,000.

(ii) For the year to 31 December 20X8 the entity claimed depreciation for tax purposes of $500,000 and charged depreciation of $450,000 in the financial statements.

(iii) During the year ended 31 December 20X8 the entity revalued a property. The revaluation surplus was $250,000. There are no current plans to sell the property.

(iv) The tax rate was 30% throughout the year.

What is the provision for deferred tax required by IAS 12 *Income Taxes* at 31 December 20X8?

A    $240,000
B    $270,000
C    $315,000
D    $345,000                                                                    (2 marks)

134 The statements of financial position of Nedburg Co include the following extracts:

Statements of financial position as at 30 September

|                          | 20X2 $m | 20X1 $m |
|--------------------------|---------|---------|
| Non-current liabilities  |         |         |
| Deferred tax             | 310     | 140     |
| Current liabilities      |         |         |
| Taxation                 | 130     | 160     |

The tax charge in the statement of profit or loss for the year ended 30 September 20X2 is $270 million.

What amount of tax was paid during the year to 30 September 20X2?

$ _____ million                                                                 (2 marks)

135 The trial balance of Highwood Co at 31 March 20X6 showed credit balances of $800,000 on current tax and $2.6 million on deferred tax. A property was revalued during the year giving rise to deferred tax of $3.75 million. This has been included in the deferred tax provision of $6.75 million at 31 March 20X6.

The income tax liability for the year ended 31 March 20X6 is estimated at $19.4 million.

What will be shown as the income tax charge in the statement of profit or loss of Highwood at 31 March 20X6?

$ _____ million                                                                 (2 marks)

# Section B

## Derringdo Co OTQ case

**Information relevant to questions136–140**

Derringdo Co is a broadband provider which receives government assistance to provide broadband to remote areas. Derringdo Co invested in a new server at a gross cost of $800,000 on 1 October 20X2. The server has an estimated life of ten years with a residual value equal to 15% of its gross cost. Derringdo Co uses straight-line depreciation on a time apportioned basis.

The company received a government grant of 30% of its cost price of the server at the time of purchase. The terms of the grant are that if the company retains the asset for four years or more, then no repayment liability will be incurred. Derringdo Co has no intention of disposing of the server within the first four years. Derringdo Co's accounting policy for capital-based government grants is to treat them as deferred credits and release them to income over the life of the asset to which they relate.

136  What is the net amount that will be charged to operating expenses in respect of the server for the year ended 31 March 20X3?

    A    $10,000
    B    $28,000
    C    $22,000
    D    $34,000

137  What amount will be presented under non-current liabilities at 31 March 20X3 in respect of the grant?

    A    $228,000
    B    $216,000
    C    $240,000
    D    $204,000

138  Derringdo Co also sells a package which gives customers a free laptop when they sign a two-year contract for provision of broadband services. The laptop has a stand-alone price of $200 and the broadband contract is for $30 per month.

In accordance with IFRS 15 *Revenue from Contracts with Customers*, what amount will be recognised as revenue on each package in the first year?

    A    $439
    B    $281
    C    $461
    D    $158

139  Determining the amount to be recognised in the first year is an example of which step in the IFRS 15 five-step model?

    A    Determining the transaction price
    B    Recognising revenue when a performance obligation is satisfied
    C    Identifying the separate performance obligations
    D    Allocating the transaction price to the performance obligations

140  Derringdo Co is carrying out a transaction on behalf of another entity and the finance director is unsure whether Derringdo Co should be regarded as an agent or a principal in respect of this transaction.

Which of the following would indicate that Derringdo Co is acting as an agent?

    A    Derringdo Co is primarily responsible for fulfilling the contract.
    B    Derringdo Co is not exposed to credit risk for the amount due from the customer.
    C    Derringdo Co is responsible for negotiating the price for the contract.
    D    Derringdo Co will not be paid in the form of commission.

**(10 marks)**

# Bridgenorth Co OTQ case

**Information relevant to questions 141–145**

Bridgenorth Co has undertaken a $5 million contract to repair a railway tunnel. The contract was signed on 1 April 20X8 and the work is expected to take two years. This is a contract where performance obligations are satisfied over time and progress in satisfying performance obligations is to be measured according to % of work completed as certified by a surveyor. Bridgenorth Co has an enforceable right to payment for performance completed to date.

At 31 December 20X9 the details of the contract were as follows:

|  | 20X9 | 20X8 |
| --- | --- | --- |
|  | $ | $ |
| Total contract value | 5,000,000 | 5,000,000 |
| Costs to date | 3,600,000 | 2,300,000 |
| Estimated costs to completion | 700,000 | 2,100,000 |
| Work invoiced to date | 3,000,000 | 2,000,000 |
| Cash received to date | 2,400,000 | 1,500,000 |
| % certified complete | 75% | 40% |

141  What is the profit recognised for the year ended 31 December 20X8?

$ _____

142  Using the drop down box, select what amount would have been included in trade receivables at 31 December 20X8?

▼ _____

**Picklist**

$200,000
$500,000
$2,000,000
$3,000,000

143  What is the contract asset to be recognised at 31 December 20X9?

$ _____

144  Bridgenorth Co measures performance obligations completed by reference to percentage of completion.

Identify which **TWO** of the following would be an acceptable method of measuring the performance obligations completed?

☐ Work invoiced to date as a percentage of total contract price

☐ Cash received to date as a percentage of total contract price

☐ Costs incurred as a percentage of total expected costs

☐ Time spent as a percentage of total expected contract time

145  If at 31 December 20X8 Bridgenorth Co had completed only 10% of the contract for costs of $400,000 and felt that it was too early to predict whether or not the contract would be profitable, what amount, if any, could Bridgenorth Co have recognised as revenue?

$ _____

**(10 marks)**

# Apex Co OTQ case

**The following scenario relates to questions 146–150**

Apex Co is a publicly listed supermarket chain. During the current year it started the building of a new store. The directors are aware that in accordance with IAS 23 *Borrowing Costs* certain borrowing costs have to be capitalised.

Details relating to construction of Apex Co's new store:

Apex Co issued a $10 million unsecured loan with a coupon (nominal) interest rate of 6% on 1 April 20X8. The loan is redeemable at a premium which means the loan has an effective finance cost of 7.5% per annum. The loan was specifically issued to finance the building of the new store which meets the definition of a qualifying asset in IAS 23. Construction of the store commenced on 1 May 20X8 and it was completed and ready for use on 28 February 20X9, but did not open for trading until 1 April 20X9.

146 Apex Co's new store meets the definition of a qualifying asset. Which of the following describes a qualifying asset?

    A      An asset that is ready for use or sale when purchased
    B      An asset that takes over 12 months to get ready for use or sale
    C      An asset that is intended for use rather than sale
    D      An asset that takes a substantial period of time to get ready for use or sale

147 Apex Co issued the loan stock on 1 April 20X8. Three events or transactions must be taking place for capitalisation of borrowing costs to commence in accordance with IAS 23. Which of the following is **NOT** one of these?

    A      Expenditure on the asset is being incurred.
    B      Borrowing costs are being incurred.
    C      Physical construction of the asset is nearing completion.
    D      Necessary activities are in progress to prepare the asset for use or sale.

148 What is the total of the finance costs which can be capitalised in respect of Apex Co's new store?

    $ ☐

149 Rather than take out a loan specifically for the new store Apex Co could have funded the store from existing borrowings which are:

    (i)     10% bank loan  $50 million
    (ii)    8% bank loan   $30 million

In this case it would have applied a 'capitalisation rate' to the expenditure on the asset. What would that rate have been?

    A      10%
    B      8.75%
    C      9%
    D      9.25%

150 If Apex Co had been able to temporarily invest the proceeds of the loan from 1 April to 1 May when construction began, how would the proceeds be accounted for?

    A      Deducted from finance costs
    B      Deducted from the cost of the asset
    C      Recognised as investment income in the statement of profit or loss
    D      Deducted from administrative expenses in the statement of profit or loss

**(10 marks)**

# Bertrand Co OTQ case

**Information relevant to questions 151–155**

Bertrand Co issued $10 million convertible loan notes on 1 October 20X0 that carry a nominal interest (coupon) rate of 5% per annum. They are redeemable on 30 September 20X3 at par for cash or can be exchanged for equity shares in Bertrand Co on the basis of 20 shares for each $100 of loan. A similar loan note, without the conversion option, would have required Bertrand Co to pay an interest rate of 8%.

The present value of $1 receivable at the end of each year, based on discount rates of 5% and 8%, can be taken as:

|  |  | 5% | 8% |
|---|---|---|---|
| End of year | 1 | 0.95 | 0.93 |
|  | 2 | 0.91 | 0.86 |
|  | 3 | 0.86 | 0.79 |
|  | cumulative | 2.72 | 2.58 |

151 How should the convertible loan notes be accounted for?

    A    As debt

    B    As debt and equity

    C    As equity

    D    As debt until conversion, then as equity

---

152 What is the amount that will be recognised as finance costs for the year ended 30 September 20X1?

    $ ☐

---

153 What is the amount that should be shown under liabilities at 30 September 20X1?

    A    $9,425,000

    B    $9,925,000

    C    $9,690,000

    D    Nil

---

154 If Bertrand Co had incurred transaction costs in issuing these loan notes, how should these have been accounted for?

    A    Added to the proceeds of the loan notes

    B    Deducted from the proceeds of the loan notes

    C    Amortised over the life of the loan notes

    D    Charged to finance costs

---

155 Later that year Bertrand Co purchased a debt instrument which will mature in five years' time. Bertrand Co intends to hold the debt instrument to maturity to collect interest payments. How should this debt instrument be measured in the financial statements of Bertrand Co?

    A    As a financial liability at fair value through profit or loss

    B    As a financial liability at amortised cost

    C    As a financial asset at fair value through profit or loss

    D    As a financial asset at amortised cost

---

**(10 marks)**

# Fino Co OTQ case

**Information relevant to questions 156–160**

On 1 April 20X7, Fino Co increased the operating capacity of its plant. On the recommendation of the finance director, Fino Co entered into an agreement to lease the plant from the manufacturer. The present value of the future payments is $350,000. The lease requires three annual payments in advance of $100,000 each, commencing on 1 April 20X8. The rate of interest implicit in the lease is 10%. The lease does not transfer ownership of the plant to Fino Co by the end of the lease term and there is no purchase option available. A non-refundable deposit of $100,000 is payable on 1 April 20X7.

156 Over what period should Fino Co depreciate the right-of-use asset?

A   From the commencement of the lease to the end of the lease term

B   From the commencement of the lease to the end of the useful life of the plant

C   From the commencement of the lease to the longer of the end of the lease term and the end of the useful life of the plant

D   From the commencement of the lease to the shorter of the end of the lease term and the end of the useful life of the plant

---

157 Fino Co incurred initial direct costs of $20,000 and received lease incentives from the manufacturer totalling $7,000. After four years it will have to dismantle the plant at an estimated (discounted) cost of $15,000.

What is the measurement of the right-of-use asset as at 1 April 20X7?

A   $350,000
B   $378,000
C   $385,000
D   $478,000

---

158 The finance director questions why the lease payments cannot be simply charged to profit or loss. Which **TWO** of the following, if true, would indicate that this was the correct treatment?

(i)     Ownership is transferred at the end of the lease term.
(ii)    The lease is for less than 12 months.
(iii)   The asset has a low underlying value.
(iv)    The asset has been specially adapted for the use of the lessee.

A   (i) and (ii)
B   (ii) and (iii)
C   (iii) and (iv)
D   (i) and (iv)

---

159 What is the amount that should be shown under non-current liabilities at 31 March 20X9 in respect of this plant?

A   $247,380
B   $262,500
C   $250,000
D   $100,000

160    On 1 April 20X7 Fino Co also took out a lease on another piece of equipment. The lease runs for ten months and payments of $1,000 per month are payable in arrears. As an incentive to enter into the lease, Fino received the first month rent free.

What amount should be recognised as payments under short-term leases for the period up to 30 September 20X7?

A    $5,000
B    $6,000
C    $4,500
D    $5,400

**(10 marks)**

# Rainbird Co OTQ case      18 mins

### Information relevant to questions 161–165

Rainbird Co decided to reorganise a manufacturing facility during November 20X1 and commissioned a consulting engineer to carry out a feasibility study. A provision for the reorganisation was created at 31 December 20X1.

Staff functions will change following the reorganisation, so in December 20X1 Rainbird Co contracted with a training company to provide retraining to take place in January 20X2. A provision for this expenditure was created at 31 December 20X1.

Rainbird Co hopes that reorganising its manufacturing facility will improve quality control. It gives a one-year warranty with all products and the rate of returns under warranty is 12%. 5% of the returned items can be repaired at a cost of $5 (free of charge to the customer). The other 95% are scrapped and a full refund of $30 is given. Rainbird Co sold 525,000 units during the year to 31 December 20X1.

In five years' time Rainbird Co will have to dismantle its factory and return the site to the local authority. A provision was set up for the present value of the dismantling costs when the factory was first acquired. The opening balance on the provision at 1 January 20X1 was $2.63 million. Rainbird Cohas a cost of capital of 8%.

161    Rainbird Co's accountant is preparing the financial statements for the year to 31 December 20X1 and is not too sure about the provisions set up for the reorganisation of the facility and the staff training.

Which of these is a correct provision under IAS 37?

A    The reorganisation
B    The staff training
C    The reorganisation and the staff training
D    Neither the reorganisation nor the staff training

162    Rainbird Co's finance director is checking some of the financial estimates involved. In accordance with IAS 37 if the reporting entity is presently obliged to transfer economic benefit to another party, the occurrence is probable but the amount cannot be measured with sufficient reliability.

Using the picklist below, select the correct option stating what this should give rise to in the financial statements

**Picklist**

A provision
A contingent liability
A long-term liability
A contingent asset

163 What is the amount of the provision that should be created at 31 December 20X1 for returns under warranty?

    A     $1,890,000
    B     $1,811,250
    C     $1,795,500
    D     $1,575,000

164 What is the amount of the provision that should be carried forward at 31 December 20X1 for the dismantling of the factory?

    A     $2,630,000
    B     $2,419,600
    C     $2,435,185
    D     $2,840,400

165 During January 20X2, before the financial statements of Rainbird Co for the year ended 31 December 20X1 had been finalised, a number of events took place.

Which of these events would require an adjustment to the financial statements as at 31 December 20X1 in accordance with IAS 10 *Events After the Reporting Period*?

    A     Rainbird Co's board announced a plan to discontinue one of its operations and dispose of the plant. The loss on disposal is estimated at $2 million.

    B     The employees of the operation to be discontinued commenced a case against Rainbird Co for constructive dismissal. The total cost could be $3 million.

    C     A legal case for which Rainbird Co had provided $1.7 million at 31 December 20X1 to cover possible damages was unexpectedly settled in its favour.

    D     One of Rainbird Co's warehouses was destroyed by fire and half of the inventory on hand at 31 December 20X1, valued at $2.5 million, was destroyed.

**(10 marks)**

# Julian Co OTQ case      18 mins

**Information relevant to questions 166–170**

The carrying amount of Julian Co's property, plant and equipment at 31 December 20X3 was $310,000 and the tax written down value was $230,000.

The following data relates to the year ended 31 December 20X4:

(i) At the end of the year the carrying amount of property, plant and equipment was $460,000 and the tax written down value was $270,000. During the year some items were revalued by $90,000. No items had previously required revaluation. In the tax jurisdiction in which Julian Co operates revaluations of assets do not affect the tax base of an asset or taxable profit. Gains due to revaluations are taxable on sale.

(ii) Julian Co began development of a new product during the year and capitalised $60,000 in accordance with IAS 38. The expenditure was deducted for tax purposes as it was incurred. None of the expenditure had been amortised by the year end.

The corporate income tax rate is 30%. The current tax charge was calculated for the year as $45,000.

166 Julian Co's accountant is confused by the term 'tax base'. What is meant by 'tax base'?

    A     The amount of tax payable in a future period
    B     The tax regime under which an entity is assessed for tax
    C     The amount attributed to an asset or liability for tax purposes
    D     The amount of tax deductible in a future period

167 Using the drag and drop options below, show the taxable temporary difference to be accounted for at 31 December 20X4 in relation to property, plant and equipment and development expenditure?

Property, plant and equipment          Development expenditure

|                |
|----------------|
| Nil            |

| $60,000        |

| $190,000       |

| $270,000       |

---

168 What amount should be charged to the revaluation surplus at 31 December 20X4 in respect of deferred tax?

A    $60,000
B    $90,000
C    $18,000
D    $27,000

---

169 What amount will be shown as tax payable in the statement of financial position of Julian Co at 31 December 20X4?

A    $45,000
B    $72,000
C    $63,000
D    $75,000

---

170 Deferred tax assets and liabilities arise from taxable and deductible temporary differences. Which of the following is **NOT** a circumstance giving rise to a temporary difference?

A    Depreciation accelerated for tax purposes
B    Development costs amortised in profit or loss but tax was deductible in full when incurred
C    Accrued expenses which have already been deducted for tax purposes
D    Revenue included in accounting profit when invoiced but only liable for tax when the cash is received.

**(10 marks)**

# Section A

# Reporting financial performance

171    Which of the following would be treated under IAS 8 *Accounting Policies, Changes in Accounting Estimates and Errors* as a change of accounting policy?

    A    A change in valuation of inventory from a weighted average to a FIFO basis

    B    A change of depreciation method from straight line to reducing balance

    C    Adoption of the revaluation model for non-current assets previously held at cost

    D    Capitalisation of borrowing costs which have arisen for the first time    **(2 marks)**

172    For an asset to be classified as 'held for sale' under IFRS 5 *Non-current Assets Held for Sale and Discontinued Operations* its sale must be 'highly probable'. Which of the following is **NOT** a requirement if the sale is to be regarded as highly probable?

    A    Management must be committed to a plan to sell the asset.

    B    A buyer must have been located for the asset.

    C    The asset must be marketed at a reasonable price.

    D    The sale should be expected to take place within one year from the date of classification.    **(2 marks)**

173    At what amount should an asset classified as 'held for sale' be measured?

    A    Lower of carrying amount and fair value less costs of disposal

    B    Lower of carrying amount and value in use

    C    Higher of value in use and fair value less costs of disposal

    D    Higher of carrying amount and recoverable amount    **(2 marks)**

174    Which of the following would be a change in accounting policy in accordance with IAS 8 *Accounting Policies, Changes in Accounting Estimates and Errors*?

    A    Adjusting the financial statements of a subsidiary prior to consolidation as its accounting policies differ from those of its parent

    B    A change in reporting depreciation charges as cost of sales rather than as administrative expenses

    C    Depreciation charged on reducing balance method rather than straight line

    D    Reducing the value of inventory from cost to net realisable value due to a valid adjusting event after the reporting period    **(2 marks)**

175 Which of the following items is a change of accounting policy under IAS 8 *Accounting Policies, Changes in Accounting Estimates and Errors*?

    A    Classifying commission earned as revenue in the statement of profit or loss, having previously classified it as other operating income

    B    Switching to purchasing plant using leases from a previous policy of purchasing plant for cash

    C    Changing the value of a subsidiary's inventory in line with the group policy for inventory valuation when preparing the consolidated financial statements

    D    Revising the remaining useful life of a depreciable asset    **(2 marks)**

176 As at 30 September 20X3 Dune Co's property in its statement of financial position was:

Property at cost (useful life 15 years)    $45 million
Accumulated depreciation    $6 million

On 1 April 20X4 Dune Co decided to sell the property. The property is being marketed by a property agent at a price of $42 million, which was considered a reasonably achievable price at that date. The expected costs to sell have been agreed at $1 million. Recent market transactions suggest that actual selling prices achieved for this type of property in the current market conditions are 10% less than the price at which they are marketed.

At 30 September 20X4 the property has not been sold.

At what amount should the property be reported in Dune Co's statement of financial position as at 30 September 20X4?

    A    $36 million
    B    $37.5 million
    C    $36.8 million
    D    $42 million    **(2 marks)**

177 Steeplechase Co sold a machine to a Greek company which it agreed to invoice in €. The sale was made on 1 October 20X6 for €250,000. €125,000 was received on 1 November 20X6 and the balance is due on 1 January 20X7.

The exchange rate moved as follows:

1 October 20X6 – €0.91 to $1
1 November 20X6 – €0.95 to $1
31 December 20X6 – €0.85 to $1

At what amount will the receivable be shown in the financial statements at 31 December 20X6?

$ [        ] (to the nearest $)    **(2 marks)**

178 IAS 21 sets out how entities that carry out transactions in a foreign currency should measure the results of these transactions at the year end.

Using the picklist provided, select which exchange rate should non-monetary items carried at historical cost be measured?

**Picklist**

Closing rate
Average rate
Rate at date of transaction
Rate at beginning of the year    **(2 marks)**

179  Miston Co buys goods priced at €50,000 from a Dutch company on 1 November 20X8. The invoice is due for settlement in two equal instalments on 1 December 20X8 and 1 January 20X9.

The exchange rate moved as follows:

1 November 20X8 - 1.63 to $1
1 December 20X8 – 1.61 to $1
31 December 20X8 – 1.64 to $1

What will be the net exchange gain or loss to be reported in the financial statements of Miston Co at 31 December 20X8?

$ ☐ gain / (loss) (to nearest $)                                            **(2 marks)**

# Earnings per share

180  Barwell Co had 10 million ordinary shares in issue throughout the year ended 30 June 20X3. On 1 July 20X2 it had issued $2 million of 6% convertible loan stock, each $5 of loan stock convertible into 4 ordinary shares on 1 July 20X6 at the option of the holder.

Barwell Co had profit after tax for the year ended 30 June 20X3 of $1,850,000. It pays tax on profits at 30%.

What was diluted earnings per share for the year?

A    $0.167
B    $0.185
C    $0.161
D    $0.17                                                                  **(2 marks)**

181  At 30 September 20X2 the trial balance of Cavern Co includes the following balances:

|                          | $'000  |
|--------------------------|--------|
| Equity shares of 20c each | 50,000 |
| Share premium            | 15,000 |

Cavern Co has accounted for a fully subscribed rights issue of equity shares made on 1 April 20X2 of one new share for every four in issue at 42 cents each. This was the only share issue made during the year.

Using the drag and drop options below, show the balances on the share capital and share premium accounts at 30 September 20X1?

*Share capital*          *Share premium*
*$'000*                  *$'000*

☐                        ☐


4,000


11,250


37,500


40,000
                                                                            **(2 marks)**

182  Aqua Co has correctly calculated its basic earnings per share (EPS) for the current year.

Which of the following items need to be additionally considered when calculating the diluted EPS of Aqua Co for the year?

(i)    A 1 for 5 rights issue of equity shares during the year at $1.20 when the market price of the equity shares was $2.00

(ii)   The issue during the year of a convertible (to equity shares) loan note

(iii)  The granting during the year of directors' share options exercisable in three years' time

(iv)   Equity shares issued during the year as the purchase consideration for the acquisition of a new subsidiary company

A    All four
B    (i) and (ii) only
C    (ii) and (iii) only
D    (iii) and (iv) only                                                              **(2 marks)**

---

183  Many commentators believe that the trend of earnings per share (EPS) is a more reliable indicator of underlying performance than the trend of net profit for the year.

Which of the following statements supports this view?

A    Net profit can be manipulated by the choice of accounting policies but EPS cannot be manipulated in this way

B    EPS takes into account the additional resources made available to earn profit when new shares are issued for cash, whereas net profit does not

C    The disclosure of a diluted EPS figure is a forecast of the future trend of profit

D    The comparative EPS is restated where a change of accounting policy affects the previous year's profits                                                              **(2 marks)**

---

184  At 1 January 20X8 Artichoke Co had 5 million $1 equity shares in issue. On 1 June 20X8 it made a 1 for 5 rights issue at a price of $1.50. The market price of the shares on the last day of quotation with rights was $1.80.

Total earnings for the year ended 31 December 20X8 was $7.6 million.

What was the earnings per share for the year?

A    $1.35
B    $1.36
C    $1.27
D    $1.06                                                                            **(2 marks)**

---

185  Waffle Co had share capital of $7.5 million in 50c equity shares at 1 October 20X6. On 1 January 20X7 it made an issue of 4 million shares at full market price immediately followed by a 1 for 3 bonus issue.

The financial statements at 30 September 20X7 showed profit for the year of $12 million.

What was the earnings per share for the year? State your answer to two decimal places.

$ [        ]                                                                          **(2 marks)**

---

186  Plumstead Co had 4 million equity shares in issue throughout the year ended 31 March 20X7. On 30 September 20X7 it made a 1 for 4 bonus issue. Profit after tax for the year ended 31 March 20X8 was $3.6 million, out of which an equity dividend of 20c per share was paid. The financial statements for the year ended 31 March 20X7 showed earnings per share (EPS) of $0.70.

What is the EPS for the year ended 31 March 20X8 and the restated EPS for the year ended 31 March 20X7?

20X8 $ [        ]

20X7 $ [        ]                                                                      **(2 marks)**

# Section B

## Tunshill Co (Dec10) OTQ case

**18 mins**

**Information relevant to questions 187–191**

The directors of Tunshill Co are disappointed by the draft profit for the year ended 30 September 20X3. The company's assistant accountant has suggested two areas where she believes the reported profit may be improved:

(i)    A major item of plant that cost $20 million to purchase and install on 1 October 20X0 is being depreciated on a straight-line basis over a five-year period (assuming no residual value). The plant is wearing well and at the beginning of the current year (1 October 20X2) the production manager believed that the plant was likely to last eight years in total (ie from the date of its purchase). The assistant accountant has calculated that, based on an eight-year life (and no residual value) the accumulated depreciation of the plant at 30 September 20X3 would be $7.5 million ($20 million / 8 years × 3). In the financial statements for the year ended 30 September 20X2, the accumulated depreciation was $8 million ($20 million / 5 years × 2). Therefore, by adopting an eight-year life, Tunshill Co can avoid a depreciation charge in the current year and instead credit $0.5 million ($8 million − $7.5 million) to profit or loss in the current year to improve the reported profit.

(ii)    Most of Tunshill Co's competitors value their inventory using the average cost (AVCO) basis, whereas Tunshill Co uses the first in first out (FIFO) basis. The value of Tunshill Co's inventory at 30 September 20X3 on the FIFO basis, is $20 million, however on the AVCO basis it would be valued at $18 million. By adopting the same method (AVCO) as its competitors, the assistant accountant says the company would improve its profit for the year ended 30 September 20X3 by $2 million. Tunshill Co's inventory at 30 September 20X2 was reported as $15 million, however on the AVCO basis it would have been reported as $13.4 million.

187    What is the nature of the change being proposed by the assistant accountant in (i) and how should it be applied?

    A    Change of accounting policy: Retrospective application

    B    Change of accounting policy: Prospective application

    C    Change of accounting estimate: Retrospective application

    D    Change of accounting estimate: Prospective application

188    Adjusting for the change of useful life, what will be the carrying amount of the plant at 30 September 20X3?

    $ ☐

189    Which of the following would be treated as a change of accounting policy?

    A    Tunshill Co has received its first government grant and is applying the deferred income method.

    B    Tunshill Co has changed the rate of depreciation used for its office equipment from 25% to 20% straight line basis.

    C    Tunshill Co has reclassified development costs from other operating expenses to cost of sales.

    D    Tunshill Co has increased its irrecoverable debt allowance from 10% to 12%.

190    What will be the effect of the change in (ii) on profits for the year ended 30 September 20X3?

    A    Increased by $400,000

    B    Reduced by $400,000

    C    Increased by $1,600,000

    D    Reduced by $1,600,000

191   Using the drag and drop options below, select the correct account to show the accounting entry for the change in inventory value for the year ended 30 September 20X3?

Account

| Debit | | Cost of sales |
| Credit | | Inventory |
| | | Revenue |

(10 marks)

This covers a large portion of the syllabus at Financial Reporting (FR).

The questions in this section will enable you to practice your application skills as well as being able to understand the mechanics behind accounting. Learn your proformas and apply answers to ratio questions to answer the specific scenario. Understanding the limitations of using these analytical tools.

**Section A questions**

Questions 192-197: Calculation and interpretation of ratios (Chapter 19)
Questions 198-205: Limitations of financial statements (Chapter 20)
Questions 206-212: Specialised, not-for-profit and public sector entities (Chapter 23)
**Section B questions** on these topics are in questions 213-217

**Section C** questions are the longer, written questions worth 20 marks. Where the Examining Team's feedback is available (the question coming from a former exam paper), this feedback is given, together with top tips and easy marks.

Question 218 Bengal Co
Question 219 Woodbank Co
Question 220 Greenwood Co
Question 221 Funject Co
Question 222 Harbin Co
Question 223 Quartile Co

# Section A

# Calculation and interpretation of accounting ratios and trends

192 Charlton Co has an average operating profit margin of 23% and an average asset turnover of 0.8, which is similar to the averages for the industry.

The entity is likely to be:

A    An architectural practice
B    A supermarket
C    An estate agent
D    A manufacturer                                                                                    **(2 marks)**

193 Using the drop down options provided, select the correct option to complete this statement.

Reducing the [          ▼ ] will increase the length of a company's operating cycle?

**Picklist**

receivables collection period
inventory holding period
payables payment period
time taken to produce goods                                                                            **(2 marks)**

194　In the year to 31 December 20X9 Weston Co pays an interim equity dividend of 3.4c per share and declares a final equity dividend of 11.1c. It has 5 million $1 shares in issue and the ex div share price is $3.50.

What is the dividend yield?

A　4%
B　24%
C　3.2%
D　4.1%　　　　　　　　　　　　　　　　　　　　　　　　　　　　　　　　　**(2 marks)**

195　Analysis of the financial statements of Capricorn Co at 31 December 20X8 yields the following information:

| | |
|---|---|
| Gross profit margin | 30% |
| Current ratio | 2.14 |
| ROCE | 16.3% |
| Asset turnover | 4.19 |
| Inventory turnover | 13.9 |

What is the profit margin?

A　3.9%
B　7.6%
C　16.1%
D　7.1%　　　　　　　　　　　　　　　　　　　　　　　　　　　　　　　　　**(2 marks)**

196　Camargue Co is a listed company with four million 50c ordinary shares in issue. The following extract is from its financial statements for the year ended 30 September 20X4.

STATEMENT OF PROFIT OR LOSS

| | $'000 |
|---|---|
| Profit before tax | 900 |
| Income tax expense | (100) |
| Profit for the year | 800 |

At 30 September 20X4 the market price of Camargue Co 's shares was $1.50. What was the P/E ratio on that date?

☐☐☐☐　　　　　　　　　　　　　　　　　　　　　　　　　　　　　　　　　　**(2 marks)**

197　Extracts from the financial statements of Perseus Co are as follows:

STATEMENT OF PROFIT OR LOSS

| | $'000 |
|---|---|
| Operating profit | 230 |
| Finance costs | (15) |
| Profit before tax | 215 |
| Income tax | (15) |
| Profit for the year | 200 |

STATEMENT OF FINANCIAL POSITION

| | $'000 |
|---|---|
| Ordinary shares | 2,000 |
| Revaluation surplus | 300 |
| Retained earnings | 1,200 |
| | 3,500 |
| 10% loan notes | 1,000 |
| Current liabilities | 100 |
| Total equity and liabilities | 4,600 |

What is the return on capital employed?

☐☐☐☐　　　　　　　　　　　　　　　　　　　　　　　　　　　　　　　　　　**(2 marks)**

# Limitations of financial statements and interpretation techniques

198 Cyan Co carries its property at revalued amount. Property values have fallen during the current period and an impairment loss has been recognised on the property, however its carrying amount is still higher than its depreciated historical cost.

Complete the statement using the picklist below, showing the effect of the impairment on the ROCE and gearing ratios of Cyan Co.

The effect of this impairment will [ ▼ ] the ROCE ratio of Cyan Co, and [ ▼ ] its gearing ratio.

**Picklist**

Decrease

Increase                                                                                    **(2 marks)**

199 Magenta Ltd has a current ratio of 1.5, a quick ratio of 0.4 and a positive cash balance. If it purchases inventory on credit, what is the effect on these ratios?

|   | *Current ratio* | *Quick ratio* |
|---|---|---|
| A | Decrease | Decrease |
| B | Decrease | Increase |
| C | Increase | Decrease |
| D | Increase | Increase |

**(2 marks)**

200 Fritwel Co has an asset turnover of 2.0 and an operating profit margin of 10%. It is launching a new product which is expected to generate additional sales of $1.6 million and additional profit of $120,000. It will require additional assets of $500,000.

Assuming there are no other changes to current operations, how will the new product affect these ratios?

Select the impact on the ratios below using the drag and drop options

*Operating profit margin*            *ROCE*

[                    ]            [                    ]

[ Decrease ]

[ Increase ]                                                                     **(2 marks)**

201 Which of the following is a possible reason why a company's inventory holding period increases from one year to the next?

A    An increase in demand for its products
B    A reduction in selling prices
C    Obsolete inventory lines
D    Seasonal fluctuations in orders                                              **(2 marks)**

202 Use of historical cost accounting means asset values can be reliably verified but it has a number of shortcomings which need to be considered when analysing financial statements.

Which of these is a possible result of the use of historical cost accounting during a period of inflation?

A    Overstatement of non-current asset values
B    Overstatement of profits
C    Understatement of interest costs
D    Understatement of ROCE                                                       **(2 marks)**

203 Creative accounting measures are often aimed at reducing gearing.

Which of these is **NOT** a measure which can be used to reduce (or not increase) gearing?

A  Renegotiating a loan to secure a lower interest rate
B  Treating a lease as a short-term rental agreement
C  Repaying a loan just before the year end and taking it out again at the beginning of the next year.
D  'Selling' an asset under a sale and leaseback agreement **(2 marks)**

204 If a company wished to maintain the carrying amount in the financial statements of its non-current assets, which of the following would it be unlikely to do?

A  Enter into a sale and short-term leaseback

B  Account for asset-based government grants using the deferral method

C  Revalue its properties

D  Change the depreciation method for new asset acquisitions from 25% reducing balance to ten years straight line **(2 marks)**

205 Trent uses the formula: (trade receivables at year end/revenue for the year) × 365 to calculate how long on average (in days) its customers take to pay.

Which of the following would **NOT** affect the correctness of the above calculation of the average number of days a customer takes to pay?

A  Trent experiences considerable seasonal trading
B  Trent makes a number of cash sales through retail outlets
C  Reported revenue does not include a 15% sales tax whereas the receivables do include the tax
D  Trent factors with recourse the receivable of its largest customer **(2 marks)**

# Specialised, not-for-profit and public sector entities

206 Which of the following are unlikely to be stakeholders in a charity?

A  Taxpayers
B  Financial supporters
C  Shareholders
D  Government **(2 marks)**

207 The International Public Sector Accounting Standards Board regulates public sector entities and is developing a set of accounting standards which closely mirror IFRS.

Which of these is the main concept which needs to be introduced into public sector accounting?

A  Materiality
B  Accruals
C  Relevance
D  Faithful representation **(2 marks)**

208 Public sector entities have performance measures laid down by government, based on Key Performance Indicators. Which of the following are likely to be financial KPIs for a local council?

    (i)     Rent receipts outstanding
    (ii)    Interest paid
    (iii)   Interest received
    (iv)   Interest cover
    (v)    Dividend cover
    (vi)   Financial actuals against budget
    (vii)  Return on capital employed

    A     (i),(ii),(iii),(iv),(vi)
    B     (i),(ii),(vi),(vii)
    C     (ii),(iii),(iv),(v)
    D     All of them                                                  **(2 marks)**

209 Which of the following is **NOT** true of entities in the charity sector?

    A     Their objective is to provide services to recipients and not to make a profit.
    B     They have to be registered.
    C     Their revenues arise mainly from contributions rather than sales.
    D     They have only a narrow group of stakeholders to consider.      **(2 marks)**

210 Which of the following is the main aspect in which public sector bodies differ from charities?

    A     Importance of budgeting
    B     Funded by government
    C     Performance measured by KPIs
    D     No requirement to earn a return on assets                  **(2 marks)**

211 Although the objectives and purposes of not-for-profit entities are different from those of commercial entities, the accounting requirements of not-for-profit entities are moving closer to those entities to which IFRSs apply.

Which of the following IFRS requirements would **NOT** be relevant to a not-for-profit entity?

    A     Preparation of a statement of cash flows
    B     Requirement to capitalise a leased asset
    C     Disclosure of dividends per share
    D     Disclosure of non-adjusting events after the reporting date     **(2 marks)**

212 Which **TWO** of the following statements about a not-for-profit entity are valid?

    ☐    There is no requirement to calculate an earnings per share figure as it is not likely to have shareholders who need to assess its earnings performance.

    ☐    The revaluation of its property, plant and equipment is not relevant as it is not a commercial entity.

    ☐    It prioritising non-financial KPIs over financial targets.

    ☐    Its financial statements will not be closely scrutinised as it does not have any investors.   **(2 marks)**

# Section B

## Sandbag plc– OTQ case

**The following scenario relates to questions 213–217.**

Sandbag plc is a listed manufacturing company. Its summarised statement of financial position is given below.

STATEMENT OF FINANCIAL POSITION AS AT 31 DECEMBER 20X4

|  | $m |
|---|---|
| Non-current assets | 610 |
| | |
| Inventories | 96 |
| Trade receivables | 29 |
| Current asset investments | 5 |
| Cash and cash equivalents | 3 |
| | 133 |
| | 743 |
| | |
| *Equity and liabilities* | |
| $1 ordinary shares | 400 |
| Retained earnings | 190 |
| | 590 |
| Non-current liabilities – loans | 50 |
| Trade and other payables | 103 |
| | 743 |

213 What is Sandbag plc's current ratio at 31 December 20X4?

    A    0.37
    B    1.29
    C    0.87
    D    1.26

214 The finance director of Sandbag plc is worried about its current ratio. He is considering a number of actions that he hopes will improve Sandbag plc's current ratio.

Which of the following would increase Sandbag plc's current ratio?

    A    Offer a settlement discount to customers
    B    Make a bonus issue of ordinary shares
    C    Make a rights issue of ordinary shares
    D    Sell current asset investments at the carrying amount

215 What is Sandbag plc's acid test (quick) ratio at 31 December 20X4?

216 The finance director of Sandbag plc knows that the acid test ratio is below 1. He is planning two changes:

Proposal 1: Offering a 2% early settlement discount to credit customers
Proposal 2: Delaying payment to all trade payables by one extra month

What effect would each of these proposals have on the acid test ratio?

    A    Proposal 1 – increase ratio / Proposal 2 – decrease ratio
    B    Proposal 1 – increase ratio / Proposal 2 – increase ratio
    C    Proposal 1 – decrease ratio / Proposal 2 – decrease ratio
    D    Proposal 1 – decrease ratio / Proposal 2 – increase ratio

BPP
LEARNING MEDIA

217 Sandbag plc is a manufacturing company. Which of the following ratios would best assess the efficiency of Sandbag plc?

A   Price/earnings ratio
B   Gearing ratio
C   Non-current asset turnover
D   Current ratio

**(10 marks)**

# 218 Bengal Co (Jun11 amended)

**36 mins**

Bengal Co is a public company. Its most recent financial statements are shown below:

STATEMENTS OF PROFIT OR LOSS FOR THE YEAR ENDED 31 MARCH

|  | 20X1 | 20X0 |
|---|---|---|
|  | $'000 | $'000 |
| Revenue | 25,500 | 17,250 |
| Cost of sales | (14,800) | (10,350) |
| Gross profit | 10,700 | 6,900 |
| Distribution costs | (2,700) | (1,850) |
| Administrative expenses | (2,100) | (1,450) |
| Finance costs | (650) | (100) |
| Profit before taxation | 5,250 | 3,500 |
| Income tax expense | (2,250) | (1,000) |
| Profit for the year | 3,000 | 2,500 |

STATEMENTS OF FINANCIAL POSITION AS AT 31 MARCH

|  | 20X1 | | 20X0 | |
|---|---|---|---|---|
|  | $'000 | $'000 | $'000 | $'000 |
| *Non-current assets* |  |  |  |  |
| Property, plant and equipment |  | 9,500 |  | 5,400 |
| Intangibles |  | 6,200 |  | nil |
|  |  | 15,700 |  | 5,400 |
| *Current assets* |  |  |  |  |
| Inventories | 3,600 |  | 1,800 |  |
| Trade receivables | 2,400 |  | 1,400 |  |
| Cash and cash equivalents | nil |  | 4,000 |  |
| Non-current assets held for sale | 2,000 | 8,000 | nil | 7,200 |
| Total assets |  | 23,700 |  | 12,600 |
| *Equity and liabilities* |  |  |  |  |
| *Equity* |  |  |  |  |
| Equity shares of $1 each |  | 5,000 |  | 5,000 |
| Retained earnings |  | 4,500 |  | 2,250 |
|  |  | 9,500 |  | 7,250 |
| *Non-current liabilities* |  |  |  |  |
| 5% loan notes |  | 2,000 |  | 2,000 |
| 8% loan notes |  | 7,000 |  | nil |
| *Current liabilities* |  |  |  |  |
| Bank overdraft | 200 |  | nil |  |
| Trade payables | 2,800 |  | 2,150 |  |
| Current tax payable | 2,200 | 5,200 | 1,200 | 3,350 |
| Total equity and liabilities |  | 23,700 |  | 12,600 |

Additional information:

(i) There were no disposals of non-current assets during the period; however Bengal Co does have some non-current assets classified as 'held for sale' at 31 March 20X1.

(ii) Depreciation of property, plant and equipment for the year ended 31 March 20X1 was $640,000.

A disappointed shareholder has observed that although revenue during the year has increased by 48% (8,250 / 17,250 × 100), profit for the year has only increased by 20% (500 / 2,500 × 100).

*Required*

(a) Comment on the performance (including addressing the shareholder's observation) and financial position of Bengal Co for the year ended 31 March 20X1. Up to five marks are available for the calculation of appropriate ratios. **(15 marks)**

(b) Explain the limitations of ratio analysis. **(5 marks)**

**(Total = 20 marks)**

# 219 Woodbank Co (Jun14 amended)                    36 mins

Shown below are the financial statements of Woodbank Co for its most recent two years:

STATEMENTS OF PROFIT OR LOSS FOR THE YEAR ENDED 31 MARCH:

|  | 20X4 | 20X3 |
|---|---|---|
|  | $'000 | $'000 |
| Revenue | 150,000 | 110,000 |
| Cost of sales | 117,000 | (85,800) |
| Gross profit | 33,000 | 24,200 |
| Distribution costs | (6,000) | (5,000) |
| Administrative expenses | (9,000) | (9,200) |
| Finance costs – loan note interest | (1,750) | (500) |
| Profit before tax | 16,250 | 9,500 |
| Income tax expense | (5,750) | (3,000) |
| Profit for the year | 10,500 | 6,500 |

STATEMENTS OF FINANCIAL POSITION AS AT 31 MARCH

|  | 20X4 | 20X3 |
|---|---|---|
|  | $'000 | $'000 |
| ASSETS |  |  |
| *Non-current assets* |  |  |
| Property, plant and equipment | 118,000 | 85,000 |
| Goodwill | 30,000 | – |
|  | 148,000 | 85,000 |
| *Current assets* |  |  |
| Inventories | 15,500 | 12,000 |
| Trade receivables | 11,000 | 8,000 |
| Cash and cash equivalents | 500 | 5,000 |
|  | 27,000 | 25,000 |
| Total assets | 175,000 | 110,000 |

EQUITY AND LIABILITIES
*Equity*

| | | |
|---|---|---|
| Equity shares of $1 each | 80,000 | 80,000 |
| Retained earnings | 15,000 | 10,000 |
| | 95,000 | 90,000 |
| *Non-current liabilities* | | |
| 10% loan notes | 55,000 | 5,000 |
| *Current liabilities* | | |
| Trade payables | 21,000 | 13,000 |
| Current tax payable | 4,000 | 2,000 |
| | 25,000 | 15,000 |
| Total equity and liabilities | 175,000 | 110,000 |

The following information is available:

(i)     On 1 January 20X4, Woodbank Co purchased the trading assets and operations of Shaw Co for $50 million and, on the same date, issued additional 10% loan notes to finance the purchase. Shaw Co was an unincorporated entity and its results (for three months from 1 January 20X4 to 31 March 20X4) and net assets (including goodwill not subject to any impairment) are included in Woodbank Co's financial statements for the year ended 31 March 20X4. There were no other purchases or sales of non-current assets during the year ended 31 March 20X4.

(ii)    Extracts of the results (for three months) of the previously separate business of Shaw Co, which are included in Woodbank Co's statement of profit or loss for the year ended 31 March 20X4, are:

| | $'000 |
|---|---|
| Revenue | 30,000 |
| Cost of sales | (21,000) |
| Gross profit | 9,000 |
| Distribution costs | (2,000) |
| Administrative expenses | (2,000) |

(iii)   The following six ratios have been correctly calculated for Woodbank Co for the years ended 31 March:

| | 20X3 |
|---|---|
| Return on capital employed (ROCE) | 10.5% |
| (profit before interest and tax/year-end total assets less current liabilities) | |
| Net asset (equal to capital employed) turnover | 1.16 times |
| Gross profit margin | 22% |
| Profit before interest and tax margin | 9.1% |
| Current ratio | 1.7:1 |
| Gearing (debt/(debt + equity)) | 5.3% |

*Required*

(a)     Calculate the ratios in (iii) above for Woodbank Co for the year ended 31 March 20X4.        **(5 marks)**

(b)     Calculate for the year ended 31 March 20X4 equivalent ratios to the first **FOUR** only for Woodbank Co excluding the effects of the purchase of Shaw Co.        **(4 marks)**

(c)     Assess the comparative financial performance and position of Woodbank Co for the year ended 31 March 20X4. Your answer should refer to the effects of the purchase of Shaw Co.        **(11 marks)**

**(Total = 20 marks)**

# 220 Greenwood Co

**36 mins**

Greenwood Co is a public listed company. On 31 March 20X7 Greenwood Co sold its 80%-owned subsidiary – Deadwood Co – for $6 million. The directors have been advised that the disposal qualifies as a discontinued operation and it has been accounted for accordingly. The disposal proceeds were not collected until after the year end.

Extracts from Greenwood Co's financial statements are set out below.

CONSOLIDATED STATEMENTS OF PROFIT OR LOSS FOR THE YEAR ENDED 31 MARCH

|  | 20X7 | 20X6 |
|---|---|---|
|  | $'000 | $'000 |
| Revenue | 27,500 | 21,200 |
| Cost of sales | (19,500) | (15,000) |
| Gross profit | 8,000 | 6,200 |
| Operating expenses | (2,900) | (2,450) |
|  | 5,100 | 3,750 |
| Finance costs | (600) | (250) |
| Profit before taxation | 4,500 | 3,500 |
| Income tax expense | (1,000) | (800) |
| Profit for the year from continuing operations | 3,500 | 2,700 |
| Profit/(loss) from discontinued operations | (1,500) | 320 |
| Profit for the year | 2,000 | 3,020 |
| Profit attributable to: |  |  |
| Owners of Greenwood | 2,300 | 2,956 |
| Non-controlling interest | (300) | 64 |
|  | 2,000 | 3,020 |

| Analysis of discontinued operation: | 20X7 | 20X6 |
|---|---|---|
| Revenue | 7,500 | 9,000 |
| Cost of sales | (8,500) | (8,000) |
| Gross profit/(loss) | (1,000) | 1,000 |
| Operating expenses | (400) | (550) |
| Profit/(loss) before tax | (1,400) | 450 |
| Tax (expense)/relief | 300 | (130) |
|  | (1,100) | 320 |
| Loss on measurement to fair value of disposal group | (500) | – |
| Tax relief on disposal group | 100 | – |
| Profit/(loss) from discontinued operations | (1,500) | 320 |

STATEMENTS OF FINANCIAL POSITION AS AT 31 MARCH

|  | 20X7 | | 20X6 | |
|---|---|---|---|---|
|  | $'000 | $'000 | $'000 | $'000 |
| *Non-current assets* |  |  |  |  |
| Property, plant and equipment |  | 17,500 |  | 17,600 |
| Goodwill |  |  |  | 1,500 |
| *Current assets* |  |  |  |  |
| Inventories | 1,500 |  | 1,350 |  |
| Trade receivables | 2,000 |  | 2,300 |  |
| Due on sale of subsidiary | 6,000 |  | nil |  |
| Cash and cash equivalents | nil | 9,500 | 50 | 3,700 |
| Total assets |  | 27,000 |  | 22,800 |

| | 20X7 | | 20X6 | |
|---|---|---|---|---|
| | $'000 | $'000 | $'000 | $'000 |
| *Equity and liabilities* | | | | |
| Equity shares of $1 each | | 10,000 | | 10,000 |
| Retained earnings | | 4,500 | | 2,750 |
| | | 14,500 | | 12,750 |
| Non-controlling interest | | | | 1,250 |
| | | | | 14,000 |
| *Non-current liabilities* | | | | |
| 5% loan notes | | 8,000 | | 5,000 |
| *Current liabilities* | | | | |
| Bank overdraft | 1,150 | | nil | |
| Trade payables | 2,400 | | 2,800 | |
| Current tax payable | 950 | 4,500 | 1,000 | 3,800 |
| Total equity and liabilities | | 27,000 | | 22,800 |

**Note.** The carrying amount of the assets of Deadwood Co at 31 March 20X6 was $6.25 million. Greenwood Comeasures non-controlling interest at share of net assets.

*Required*

Analyse the financial performance and position of Greenwood Co for the two years ended 31 March 20X7. (Ignore working capital and gearing.)

**Note.** Your analysis should be supported by appropriate ratios (up to 6 marks available) and refer to the effects of the disposal.

**(20 marks)**

# 221 Funject Co (Mar/Jun 2017)

## 36 mins

Funject Co has identified Aspect Co as a possible acquisition within the same industry. Aspect Co is currently owned by the Gamilton Group and the following are extracts from the financial statements of Aspect Co:

EXTRACT FROM THE STATEMENT OF PROFIT OR LOSS FOR THE YEAR ENDED 31 DECEMBER 20X4

| | $'000 |
|---|---|
| Revenue | 54,200 |
| Cost of sales | 21,500 |
| Gross profit | 32,700 |
| Operating expenses | 11,700 |
| Operating profit | 21,000 |

STATEMENT OF FINANCIAL POSITION AS AT 31 DECEMBER 20X4

| | $'000 | $'000 |
|---|---|---|
| Assets | | |
| Non-current assets | | 24,400 |
| *Current assets* | | |
| Inventory | 4,900 | |
| Receivables | 5,700 | |
| Cash at bank | 2,300 | 12,900 |
| Total assets | | 37,300 |
| Equity and liabilities | | |
| *Equity* | | |
| Equity shares | | 1,000 |
| Retained earnings | | 8,000 |
| | | 9,000 |

|  | $'000 | $'000 |
|---|---|---|
| Liabilities | | |
| *Non-current liabilities* | | |
| Loan | | 16,700 |
| *Current liabilities* | | |
| Trade payables | 5,400 | |
| Current tax payable | 6,200 | 11,600 |
| Total equity and liabilities | | 37,300 |

Additional information:

(i)  On 1 April 20X4, Aspect Co decided to focus on its core business and so disposed of a non-core division. The disposal generated a loss of $1·5m which is included within operating expenses. The following extracts show the results of the non-core division for the period prior to disposal which were included in Aspect Co's results for 20X4:

|  | $'000 |
|---|---|
| Revenue | 2,100 |
| Cost of sales | (1,200) |
| Gross profit | 900 |
| Operating expenses | (700) |
| Operating profit | 200 |

(ii)  At present Aspect Co pays a management charge of 1% of revenue to the Gamilton Group which is included in operating expenses. Funject Co imposes a management charge of 10% of gross profit on all of its subsidiaries.

(iii)  Aspect Co's administration offices are currently located within a building owned by the Gamilton Group. If Aspect Co were acquired, the company would need to seek alternative premises. Aspect Co paid rent of $46,000 in 20X4. Commercial rents for equivalent office space would cost $120,000.

(iv)  The following is a list of comparable industry average key performance indicators (KPIs) for 20X4:

|  | KPI |
|---|---|
| Gross profit margin | 45% |
| Operating profit margin | 28% |
| Receivables collection period | 41 days |
| Current ratio | 1.6:1 |
| Acid test (quick) ratio | 1.4:1 |
| Gearing (debt/equity) | 240% |

*Required:*

(a)  Redraft Aspect Co's statement of profit or loss for 20X4 to adjust for the disposal of the non-core division in note (i) and the management and rent charges which would be imposed per notes (ii) and (iii) if Aspect Co was acquired by Funject Co. **(5 marks)**

(b)  Calculate the 20X4 ratios for Aspect Co equivalent to those shown in note (iv) based on the restated financial information calculated in part (a).

**Note:** You should assume that any increase or decrease in profit as a result of your adjustments in part (a) will also increase or decrease cash. **(5 marks)**

(c)  Using the ratios calculated in part (b), comment on Aspect Co's 20X4 performance and financial position compared to the industry average KPIs provided in note (iv). **(10 marks)**

**(20 marks)**

# 222 Harbin Co

**36 mins**

Shown below are the recently issued (summarised) financial statements of Harbin Co, a listed company, for the year ended 30 September 20X7, together with comparatives for 20X6 and extracts from the chief executive's report that accompanied their issue.

STATEMENT OF PROFIT OR LOSS

|  | 20X7 | 20X6 |
|---|---|---|
|  | $'000 | $'000 |
| Revenue | 250,000 | 180,000 |
| Cost of sales | (200,000) | (150,000) |
| Gross profit | 50,000 | 30,000 |
| Operating expenses | (26,000) | (22,000) |
| Finance costs | (8,000) | (nil) |
| Profit before tax | 16,000 | 8,000 |
| Income tax expense (at 25%) | (4,000) | (2,000) |
| Profit for the year | 12,000 | 6,000 |

STATEMENT OF FINANCIAL POSITION

|  | 20X7 | 20X6 |
|---|---|---|
|  | $'000 | $'000 |
| *Non-current assets* |  |  |
| Property, plant and equipment | 210,000 | 90,000 |
| Goodwill | 10,000 | nil |
|  | 220,000 | 90,000 |
| *Current assets* |  |  |
| Inventories | 25,000 | 15,000 |
| Trade receivables | 13,000 | 8,000 |
| Cash and cash equivalents | nil | 14,000 |
|  | 38,000 | 37,000 |
| Total assets | 258,000 | 127,000 |
|  |  |  |
| *Equity and liabilities* |  |  |
| Equity shares of $1 each | 100,000 | 100,000 |
| Retained earnings | 14,000 | 12,000 |
|  | 114,000 | 112,000 |
| *Non-current liabilities* |  |  |
| 8% loan notes | 100,000 | nil |
| *Current liabilities* |  |  |
| Bank overdraft | 17,000 | nil |
| Trade payables | 23,000 | 13,000 |
| Current tax payable | 4,000 | 2,000 |
|  | 44,000 | 15,000 |
| Total equity and liabilities | 258,000 | 127,000 |

Extracts from the chief executive's report:

'Highlights of Harbin Co's performance for the year ended 30 September 20X7:

An increase in sales revenue of 39%

Gross profit margin up from 16.7% to 20%

A doubling of the profit for the period

In response to the improved position, the board paid a dividend of 10 cents per share in September 20X7 an increase of 25% on the previous year.'

You have also been provided with the following further information.

On 1 October 20X6 Harbin Co purchased the whole of the net assets of Fatima Co (previously a privately owned entity) for $100 million, financed by the issue of $100,000 8% loan notes. The contribution of the purchase to Harbin Co's results for the year ended 30 September 20X7 was:

|  | $'000 |
|---|---|
| Revenue | 70,000 |
| Cost of sales | (40,000) |
| Gross profit | 30,000 |
| Operating expenses | (8,000) |
| Profit before tax | 22,000 |

There were no disposals of non-current assets during the year.

The following ratios have been calculated for Harbin Co for the year ended 30 September.

|  | 20X6 |
|---|---|
| Return on year-end capital employed | 7.1% |
| (profit before interest and tax over total assets less current liabilities) |  |
| Net asset (equal to capital employed) turnover | 1.6 |
| Net profit (before tax) margin | 4.4% |
| Current ratio | 2.5 |
| Closing inventory holding period (in days) | 37 |
| Trade receivables' collection period (in days) | 16 |
| Trade payables' payment period (based on cost of sales) (in days) | 32 |
| Gearing (debt over debt plus equity) | nil |

*Required*

(a) Calculate equivalent ratios for Harbin Co for 20X7 **(5 marks)**

(b) Assess the financial performance and position of Harbin Co for the year ended 30 September 20X7 compared to the previous year. Your answer should refer to the information in the chief executive's report and the impact of the purchase of the net assets of Fatima. **(15 marks)**

**(Total = 20 marks)**

# 223 Quartile (Dec12 amended)                                     36 mins

Quartile Co sells jewellery through stores in retail shopping centres throughout the country. Over the last two years it has experienced declining profitability and is wondering if this is related to the sector as a whole. It has recently subscribed to an agency that produces average ratios across many businesses. Below are the ratios that have been provided by the agency for Quartile Co's business sector based on a year end of 30 June 20X2.

|  | Sector average |
|---|---|
| Return on year-end capital employed (ROCE) | 16.8% |
| Net asset (total assets less current liabilities) turnover | 1.4 times |
| Gross profit margin | 35% |
| Operating profit margin | 12% |
| Current ratio | 1.25:1 |
| Average inventory turnover | 3 times |
| Trade payables' payment period | 64 days |
| Debt to equity | 38% |

The financial statements of Quartile Co for the year ended 30 September 20X2 are:

STATEMENT OF PROFIT OR LOSS

|  | $'000 | $'000 |
|---|---|---|
| Revenue |  | 56,000 |
| Opening inventory | 8,300 |  |
| Purchases | 43,900 |  |
| Closing inventory | (10,200) |  |
| Cost of sales |  | (42,000) |
| Gross profit |  | 14,000 |
| Operating costs |  | (9,800) |
| Finance costs |  | (800) |
| Profit before tax |  | 3,400 |
| Income tax expense |  | (1,000) |
| Profit for the year |  | 2,400 |

STATEMENT OF FINANCIAL POSITION

|  | $'000 |
|---|---|
| ASSETS |  |
| Non-current assets |  |
| Property and shop fittings | 25,600 |
| Deferred development expenditure | 5,000 |
|  | 30,600 |
| Current assets |  |
| Inventories | 10,200 |
| Cash and cash equivalents | 1,000 |
|  | 11,200 |
| Total assets | 41,800 |
| EQUITY AND LIABILITIES |  |
| Equity |  |
| Equity shares of $1 each | 15,000 |
| Property revaluation reserve | 3,000 |
| Retained earnings | 8,600 |
|  | 26,600 |
| Non-current liabilities |  |
| 10% loan notes | 8,000 |
| Current liabilities |  |
| Trade payables | 5,400 |
| Current tax payable | 1,800 |
|  | 7,200 |
| Total equity and liabilities | 41,800 |

The deferred development expenditure relates to an investment in a process to manufacture artificial precious gems for future sale by Quartile Co in the retail jewellery market.

Required

(a)   Prepare for Quartile Co the equivalent ratios to those provided by the agency.                        (6 marks)
(b)   Assess the financial and operating performance of Quartile Co in comparison to its sector averages.

(10 marks)
(c)   Explain four possible limitations on the usefulness of the above comparison.                          (4 marks)

(Total = 20 marks)

# Section A

# Consolidated statement of financial position

224    Witch Co acquired 70% of the 200,000 equity shares of Wizard, its only subsidiary, on 1 April 20X8 when the retained earnings of Wizard Co were $450,000. The carrying amounts of Wizard Co's net assets at the date of acquisition were equal to their fair values apart from a building which had a carrying amount of $600,000 and a fair value of $850,000. The remaining useful life of the building at the acquisition date was 40 years.

Witch Co measures non-controlling interest at fair value, based on share price. The market value of Wizard Co shares at the date of acquisition was $1.75.

At 31 March 20X9 the retained earnings of Wizard Co were $750,000. At what amount should the non-controlling interest appear in the consolidated statement of financial position of Witch Co at 31 March 20X9?

$ ⬚                                                                                            (2 marks)

225    Cloud Co obtained a 60% holding in the 100,000 $1 shares of Mist Co on 1 January 20X8, when the retained earnings of Mist Co were $850,000. Consideration comprised $250,000 cash, $400,000 payable on 1 January 20X9 and one share in Cloud Co for each two shares acquired. Cloud Co has a cost of capital of 8% and the market value of its shares on 1 January 20X8 was $2.30.

Cloud Co measures non-controlling interest at fair value. The fair value of the non-controlling interest at 1 January 20X8 was estimated to be $400,000.

What was the goodwill arising on acquisition?

A    $139,370
B    $169,000
C    $119,370
D    $130,370                                                                                  (2 marks)

226    On 1 June 20X1 Premier Co acquired 80% of the equity share capital of Sandford Co. At the date of acquisition the fair values of Sandford Co's net assets were equal to their carrying amounts with the exception of its property. This had a fair value of $1.2 million **BELOW** its carrying amount. The property had a remaining useful life of eight years.

What effect will any adjustment required in respect of the property have on group retained earnings at 30 September 20X1?

$ ☐☐☐☐ Increase / decrease          **(2 marks)**

---

227    On 1 August 20X7 Patronic Co purchased 18 million of the 24 million $1 equity shares of Sardonic Co. The acquisition was through a share exchange of two shares in Patronic Co for every three shares in Sardonic Co. The market price of a share in Patronic Co at 1 August 20X7 was $5.75. Patronic Co will also pay in cash on 31 July 20X9 (two years after acquisition) $2.42 per acquired share of Sardonic Co. Patronic Co's cost of capital is 10% per annum.

What is the amount of the consideration attributable to Patronic Co for the acquisition of Sardonic Co?

A    $105 million
B    $139.5 million
C    $108.2 million
D    $103.8 million          **(2 marks)**

---

228    On 1 April 20X0 Picant Co acquired 75% of Sander Co's equity shares by means of a share exchange and an additional amount payable on 1 April 20X1 that was contingent upon the post-acquisition performance of Sander Co. At the date of acquisition Picant Co assessed the fair value of this contingent consideration at $4.2 million but by 31 March 20X1 it was clear that the amount to be paid would be only $2.7 million.

Using the drag and drop options below, demonstrate how Picant Co would account for this $1.5 million adjustment in its financial statements as at 31 March 20X1?

Account

| Debit | ▨▨▨▨ | Current liabilities |
| Credit | ▨▨▨▨ | Goodwill |
| | | Retained earnings |

**(2 marks)**

---

229    Crash Co acquired 70% of Bang Co's 100,000 $1 ordinary shares for $800,000 when the retained earnings of Bang Co were $570,000 and the balance in its revaluation surplus was $150,000. Bang Co also has an internally developed customer list which has been independently valued at $90,000. The non-controlling interest in Bang Co was judged to have a fair value of $220,000 at the date of acquisition.

What was the goodwill arising on acquisition?

A    $200,000
B    $163,000
C    $226,000
D    $110,000          **(2 marks)**

230 Phantom Co acquired 70% of the $100,000 equity share capital of Ghost Co, its only subsidiary, for $200,000 on 1 January 20X9 when the retained earnings of Ghost Co were $156,000.

At 31 December 20X9 retained earnings are as follows.

|  | $ |
| --- | --- |
| Phantom Co | 275,000 |
| Ghost Co | 177,000 |

Phantom Co considers that goodwill on acquisition is impaired by 50%. Non-controlling interest is measured at fair value, estimated at $82,800.

Using the drop down box, select what are group retained earnings at 31 December 20X9?

**Picklist**

$262,900
$280,320
$289,700
$585,700

(2 marks)

231 Tazer Co, a parent company, acquired Lowdown Co, an unincorporated entity, for $2.8 million. A fair value exercise performed on Lowdown Co's net assets at the date of purchase showed:

|  | $'000 |
| --- | --- |
| Property, plant and equipment | 3,000 |
| Identifiable intangible asset | 500 |
| Inventories | 300 |
| Trade receivables less payables | 200 |
|  | 4,000 |

How should the purchase of Lowdown be reflected in Tazer Co's consolidated statement of financial position?

A Record the net assets at their values shown above and credit profit or loss with $1.2 million

B Record the net assets at their values shown above and credit Tazer Co's consolidated goodwill with $1.2 million

C Write off the intangible asset ($500,000), record the remaining net assets at their values shown above and credit profit or loss with $700,000

D Record the purchase as a financial asset investment at $2.8 million

(2 marks)

# Consolidated statement of profit or loss and other comprehensive income

232 Hillusion Co acquired 80% of Skeptik Co on 1 July 20X2. In the post-acquisition period Hillusion Co sold goods to Skeptik Co at a price of $12 million. These goods had cost Hillusion Co $9 million. During the year to 31 March 20X3 Skeptik Co had sold $10 million (at cost to Skeptik Co) of these goods for $15m million.

How will this affect group cost of sales in the consolidated statement of profit or loss of Hillusion Co for the year ended 31 March 20X3?

A Increase by $11.5 million
B Increase by $9.6 million
C Decrease by $11.5 million
D Decrease by $9.6 million

(2 marks)

233   On 1 July 20X7, Spider Co acquired 60% of the equity share capital of Fly Co and on that date made a $10 million loan to Fly Co at a rate of 8% per annum.

What will be the effect on group retained earnings at the year-end date of 31 December 20X7 when this intragroup transaction is cancelled?

A   Group retained earnings will increase by $400,000.
B   Group retained earnings will be reduced by $240,000.
C   Group retained earnings will be reduced by $160,000.
D   There will be no effect on group retained earnings.

(2 marks)

234   Wiley Co acquired 80% of Coyote Co on 1 January 20X8. At the date of acquisition Coyote Co had a building which had a fair value $22 million and a carrying amount of $20 million. The remaining useful life was 20 years.

Coyote Co's profit for the year to 30 June 20X8 was $1.6 million which accrued evenly throughout the year.

Wiley Co measures non-controlling interest at fair value. At 30 June 20X8 it estimated that goodwill in Coyote Co was impaired by $500,000.

What is the total comprehensive income attributable to the non-controlling interest at 30 June 20X8?

A   $40,000
B   $50,000
C   $187,500
D   $150,000

(2 marks)

235   Basil Co acquired 60% of Parsley Co on 1 March 20X9. In September 20X9 Basil Co sold $46,000 worth of goods to Parsley Co. Basil Co applies a 30% mark-up to all its sales. 25% of these goods were still held in inventory by Parsley Co at the end of the year.

An extract from the draft statements of profit or loss of Basil Co and Parsley Co at 31 December 20X9 is:

|  | Basil Co $ | Parsley Co $ |
|---|---|---|
| Revenue | 955,000 | 421,500 |
| Cost of sales | (407,300) | (214,600) |
| Gross profit | 547,700 | 206,900 |

All revenue and costs arise evenly throughout the year.

What will be shown as gross profit in the consolidated statement of profit or loss of Basil Co for the year ended 31 December 20X9?

$ [        ]

(2 marks)

236   Premier Co acquired 80% of Sanford Co on 1 June 20X1. Sales from Sanford Co to Premier Co throughout the year ended 30 September 20X1 were consistently $1 million per month. Sanford Co made a mark-up on cost of 25% on these sales. At 30 September 20X1 Premier Co was holding $2 million inventory that had been supplied by Sanford Co in the post-acquisition period.

By how much will the unrealised profit decrease the profit attributable to the non-controlling interest for the year ended 30 September 20X1?

$ [        ]

(2 marks)

237 Brigham Co has owned 70% of Dorset Co for many years. It also holds a $5 million 8% loan note from Dorset Co. One of Dorset Co's non-current assets has suffered an impairment of $50,000 during the year. There is a balance in the revaluation surplus of Dorset Co of $30,000 in respect of this asset. The impairment loss has not yet been recorded.

The entity financial statements of Dorset Co show a profit for the year of $1.3 million.

What is the amount attributable to the non-controlling interests in the consolidated statement of profit or loss?

$ [          ] **(2 marks)**

238 On 1 January 20X3 Westbridge Co acquired all of Brookfield Co's 100,000 $1 shares for $300,000. The goodwill acquired in the business combination was $40,000, of which 50% had been written off as impaired by 31 December 20X5. On 31 December 20X5 Westbridge Co sold all of Brookfield Co's shares for $450,000 when Brookfield Co had retained earnings of $185,000.

Using the drop down box, select which is the correct answer for the profit on disposal that should be included in the **CONSOLIDATED** financial statements of Westbridge Co?

[          ▼]

**Picklist**

$145,000
$165,000
$245,000
$330,000 **(2 marks)**

239 On 1 January 20X3 Westbridge Co acquired all of Brookfield Co's 100,000 $1 shares for $300,000. The goodwill acquired in the business combination was $40,000, of which 50% had been written off as impaired by 31 December 20X5. On 31 December 20X5 Westbridge Co sold all of Brookfield's shares for $450,000 when Brookfield had retained earnings of $185,000.

What is the profit on disposal that should be included in the **INDIVIDUAL ENTITY** financial statements of Westbridge Co?

$ [          ] **(2 marks)**

240 Alderminster Co acquired a 70% holding in Bidford Co on 1 January 20X4 for $600,000. At that date the fair value of the net assets of Bidford Co was $700,000. Alderminster Co measures non-controlling interest at its share of net assets.

On 31 December 20X6 Alderminster Co sold all its shares in Bidford Co for $950,000. At that date the fair value of Bidford Co's net assets was $850,000. Goodwill was not impaired.

What was the profit or loss on disposal to be recognised in the consolidated financial statements of Alderminster Co?

[          ▼] profit / loss

**Picklist**
$135,000
$200,000
$245,000
$355,000 **(2 marks)**

# Accounting for associates

241    On 1 October 20X8 Pacemaker Co acquired 30 million of Vardine Co's 100 million shares in exchange for 75 million of its own shares. The stock market value of Pacemaker Co's shares at the date of this share exchange was $1.60 each.

Vardine Co's profit is subject to seasonal variation. Its profit for the year ended 31 March 20X9 was $100 million. $20 million of this profit was made from 1 April 20X8 to 30 September 20X8.

Pacemaker Co has one subsidiary and no other investments apart from Vardine Co.

What amount will be shown as 'investment in associate' in the consolidated statement of financial position of Pacemaker Co as at 31 March 20X9?

    A    $144 million
    B    $150 million
    C    $78 million
    D    $126 million                                                                     (2 marks)

242    How should an associate be accounted for in the consolidated statement of profit or loss?

    A    The associate's income and expenses are added to those of the group on a line by line basis.
    B    The group share of the associate's income and expenses is added to the group figures on a line by line basis.
    C    The group share of the associate's profit after tax is recorded as a one-line entry.
    D    Only dividends received from the associate are recorded in the group statement of profit or loss.                                                                     (2 marks)

243    Jarvis Co owns 30% of McLintock Co. During the year to 31 December 20X4 McLintock Co sold $2 million of goods to Jarvis Co, of which 40% were still held in inventory by Jarvis at the year end. McLintock Co applies a mark-up of 25% on all goods sold.

What effect would the above transactions have on group inventory at 31 December 20X4?

    A    Debit group inventory $48,000
    B    Debit group inventory $160,000
    C    Credit group inventory $48,000
    D    No effect on group inventory                                                     (2 marks)

244    Ulysses Co owns 25% of Grant Co, which it purchased on 1 May 20X8 for $5 million. At that date Grant Co had retained earnings of $7.4 million. At the year-end date of 31 October 20X8 Grant Co had retained earnings of $8.5 million after paying out a dividend of $1 million. On 30 September 20X8 Ulysses Co sold $600,000 of goods to Grant Co, on which it made 30% profit. Grant Co had resold none of these goods by 31 October.

At what amount will Ulysses Co record its investment in Grant Co in its consolidated statement of financial position at 31 October 20X8?

    A    $5,000,000
    B    $5,275,000
    C    $5,230,000
    D    $4,855,000                                                                        (2 marks)

245    On 1 February 20X3 Pinot Co acquired 30% of the equity shares of Noir Co, its only associate, for $10 million in cash. The post-tax profit of Noir Co for the year to 30 September 20X3 was $6 million. Profits accrued evenly throughout the year. Noir Co made a dividend payment of $1 million on 1 September 20X3. At 30 September 20X3 Pinot Co decided that an impairment loss of $700,000 should be recognised on its investment in Noir Co.

What amount will be shown as 'investment in associate' in the statement of financial position of Pinot Co as at 30 September 20X3?

    $ [          ]                                                                          (2 marks)

246 An associate is an entity in which an investor has significant influence over the investee.

Which **TWO** of the following indicate the presence of significant influence?

☐ The investor owns 330,000 of the 1,500,000 equity voting shares of the investee.

☐ The investor has representation on the board of directors of the investee.

☐ The investor is able to insist that all of the sales of the investee are made to a subsidiary of the investor.

☐ The investor controls the votes of a majority of the board members. **(2 marks)**

247 Ruby Co owns 30% of Emerald Co and exercises significant influence over it. Emerald Co sold goods to Ruby Co for $160,000. Emerald Co applies a one-third mark-up on cost. Ruby Co still had 25% of these goods in inventory at the year end.

What amount should be deducted from consolidated retained earnings in respect of this transaction?

$ [        ] **(2 marks)**

# Presentation of published financial statements

248 Which of the following would not **NECESSARILY** lead to a liability being classified as a current liability?

A The liability is expected to be settled in the course of the entity's normal operating cycle.

B The liability has arisen during the current accounting period.

C The liability is held primarily for the purpose of trading.

D The liability is due to be settled within 12 months after the end of the reporting period. **(2 marks)**

249 Which of the following would be shown in the 'other comprehensive income' section of the statement of profit or loss and other comprehensive income?

A A revaluation gain on an investment property

B Profit on sale of an investment

C Receipt of a government grant

D Gain on revaluation of a factory building **(2 marks)**

250 Using the drop down box provided which of the following are **NOT** items required by IAS 1 *Presentation of Financial Statements* to be shown on the face of the statement of financial position?

[        ▼]

**Picklist**

Inventories
Provisions
Government grants
Intangible assets **(2 marks)**

251 How does IAS 1 define the 'operating cycle' of an entity?

A The time between acquisition of assets for processing and delivery of finished goods to customers

B The time between delivery of finished goods and receipt of cash from customers

C The time between acquisition of assets for processing and payment of cash to suppliers

D The time between acquisition of assets for processing and receipt of cash from customers **(2 marks)**

252 Where are equity dividends paid presented in the financial statements?

A As a deduction from retained earnings in the statement of changes in equity

B As a liability in the statement of financial position

C As an expense in profit or loss

D As a loss in 'other comprehensive income' **(2 marks)**

# Statement of cash flows

253 Extracts from the statements of financial position of Nedburg Co are as follows:

Statements of financial position as at 30 September:

|  | 20X2 $m | 20X1 $m |
|---|---|---|
| Ordinary shares of $1 each | 750 | 500 |
| Share premium | 350 | 100 |

On 1 October 20X1 a bonus issue of one new share for every ten held was made, financed from the share premium account. This was followed by a further issue for cash.

Using the drop down options available, what amount will appear under 'cash flows from financing activities' in the statement of cash flows of Nedburg Co for the year ended 30 September 20X2 in respect of share issues?

**Picklist**

$500 million
$450 million
$550 million
$250 million

**(2 marks)**

254 The statement of financial position of Pinto Co at 31 March 20X7 showed property, plant and equipment with a carrying amount of $1,860,000. At 31 March 20X8 it had increased to $2,880,000.

During the year to 31 March 20X8 plant with a carrying amount of $240,000 was sold at a loss of $90,000, depreciation of $280,000 was charged and $100,000 was added to the revaluation surplus in respect of property, plant and equipment.

What amount should appear under 'investing activities' in the statement of cash flows of Pinto Co for the year ended 31 March 20X8 as cash paid to acquire property, plant and equipment?

A $1,640,000
B $1,440,000
C $1,260,000
D $1,350,000

**(2 marks)**

255 The following information is available for the property, plant and equipment of Fry Co as at 30 September:

|  | 20X4 $'000 | 20X3 $'000 |
|---|---|---|
| Carrying amounts | 23,400 | 14,400 |

The following items were recorded during the year ended 30 September 20X4:

(i) Depreciation charge of $2.5 million
(ii) An item of plant with a carrying amount of $3 million was sold for $1.8 million
(iii) A property was revalued upwards by $2 million
(iv) Environmental provisions of $4 million relating to property, plant and equipment were capitalised during the year

What amount would be shown in Fry Co's statement of cash flows for purchase of property, plant and equipment for the year ended 30 September 20X4?

A $8.5 million
B $12.5 million
C $7.3 million
D $10.5 million

**(2 marks)**

256 The carrying amount of property, plant and equipment was $410 million at 31 March 20X1 and $680 million at 31 March 20X2. During the year, property with a carrying amount of $210 million was revalued to $290 million. The depreciation charge for the year was $115 million. There were no disposals.

What amount will appear on the statement of cash flows for the year ended 31 March 20X2 in respect of purchases of property, plant and equipment?

$ _____                                                                                    (2 marks)

---

257 Extracts from Deltoid Co's statements of financial position are as follows:

STATEMENT OF FINANCIAL POSITION AS AT 31 MARCH

|  | 20X1 $'000 | 20X0 $'000 |
|---|---|---|
| Non-current assets | | |
| Property, plant and equipment | | |
| Right-of-use asset | 6,500 | 2,500 |
| Non-current liabilities | | |
| Lease obligations | 4,800 | 2,000 |
| Current liabilities | | |
| Lease obligations | 1,700 | 800 |

During the year to 31 March 20X1 depreciation charged on leased plant was $1,800,000.

What amount will be shown in the statement of cash flows of Deltoid Co for the year ended 31 March 20X1 in respect of payments made under leases?

$ _____                                                                                    (2 marks)

# Section B

## Root and Branch OTQ case

**18 mins**

Information relevant to questions 258–262

On 1 April 20X7 Root Co acquired 116 million of Branch Co's 145 million ordinary shares for an immediate cash payment of $210 million and issued at par one 10% $100 loan note for every 200 shares acquired.

At the date of acquisition Branch Co owned a recently built property that was carried at its depreciated construction cost of $62 million. The fair value of this property at the date of acquisition was $82 million and it had an estimated remaining life of 20 years.

Branch Co also had an internally developed brand which was valued at the acquisition date at $25 million with a remaining life of 10 years.

The inventory of Branch Co at 31 March 20X9 includes goods supplied by Root Co for a sale price of $56 million. Root adds a mark-up of 40% on cost to all sales.

258 What is the total amount of the consideration transferred by Root Co to acquire the investment in Branch Co?

$ ☐ million

---

259 What will be the amount of the adjustment to group retained earnings at 31 March 20X9 in respect of the movement on the fair value adjustments?

    A    $7 million
    B    $3.5 million
    C    $5.6 million
    D    $2.8 million

---

260 What is the amount of the unrealised profit arising from intragroup trading?

$ ☐ million

---

261 Using the drag and drop options available, show how should the unrealised profit be posted?

Account

| Debit | ░░░░░░░ | Cost of sales |

| Credit | ░░░░░░░ | Inventories |

Non-controlling interest

Non-current assets

---

262 Branch Co has recently lost some large contracts and the directors of Root Co are wondering if Branch Co can be excluded from consolidation next year.

Which of the following situations would allow a subsidiary to be excluded from consolidation?

    A    The activities of the subsidiary are significantly different to the activities of the rest of the group.

    B    Control of the subsidiary has been lost.

    C    Control of the subsidiary is only intended to be temporary.

    D    The subsidiary operates under long-term restrictions which prevent it from transferring funds to the parent.

**(10 marks)**

# Port and Alfred OTQ case

**18 mins**

## Information relevant to questions 263–267

On 1 November 20X4 Port Co purchased 75% of the equity of Alfred Co for $650,000. The consideration was 35,000 $1 equity shares in Port Co with a fair value of $650,000.

Noted below are extracts from the draft statements of profit or loss for Port Co and its subsidiary Alfred Co for the year ending 31 December 20X4 along with the draft statements of financial position as at 31 December 20X4.

The profits of Alfred Co have been earned evenly throughout the year.

STATEMENTS OF PROFIT OR LOSS FOR THE YEAR ENDING 31 DECEMBER 20X4 (extract)

|  | Port Co $'000 | Alfred Co $'000 |
|---|---|---|
| Gross profit | 364 | 240 |
| Profit for the year | 330 | 96 |

STATEMENTS OF FINANCIAL POSITION AS AT 31 DECEMBER 20X4 (extracts)

|  | Port | Alfred |
|---|---|---|
| *Equity* | | |
| $1 Equity shares | 200 | 100 |
| Share premium | 500 | 85 |
| Retained earnings | 2,900 | 331 |
| Revaluation surplus | 30 | – |
|  | 3,630 | 516 |

Port Co has not accounted for the issue of its own shares or for the acquisition of the investment in Alfred Co.

263 Using the drag and drop options below, show the balances on the share capital and share premium accounts at 31 December 20X4.

*Share capital*
$

*Share premium*
$

| 235,000 |
|---|

| 335,000 |
|---|

| 585,000 |
|---|

| 1,115,000 |
|---|

---

264 What are the net assets of Alfred Co at acquisition?

$ [       ]

---

265 The accountant of Port Co is finalising the consolidated financial statements. Which **TWO** of the following statements are true regarding consolidated financial statements?

☐ The non-controlling interest share of profit is part of the consolidated statement of profit or loss.

☐ Goodwill on acquisition should be amortised over a period not exceeding 20 years.

☐ If a subsidiary is acquired during the year, its results are apportioned over the year of acquisition.

☐ Only the group share of the subsidiary's non-current assets is shown in the statement of financial position.

266 What is the amount of group gross profit for the year ended 31 December 20X4?

$ [          ]

267 What is group retained earnings at 31 December 20X4?

    A    $2,912,000
    B    $2,916,000
    C    $2,972,000
    D    $2,996,000

(10 marks)

# Polestar OTQ case

18 mins

**The following scenario relates to questions 136–140.**

On 1 April 20X3, Polestar Co acquired 75% of the 12 million 50 cent equity shares of Southstar Co. Southstar Co had been experiencing difficult trading conditions and making significant losses. Its retained earnings at the acquisition date were $14.3 million. In allowing for Southstar Co's difficulties, Polestar Co made an immediate cash payment of only $1.50 per share. In addition, Polestar Co will pay a further amount in cash on 30 September 20X4 if Southstar Co returns to profitability by that date. The value of this contingent consideration at the date of acquisition was estimated to be $1.8 million, but at 30 September 20X3 in the light of continuing losses, its value was estimated at only $1.5 million. The contingent consideration has not been recorded by Polestar Co. Overall, the directors of Polestar Co expect the acquisition to be a bargain purchase leading to negative goodwill.

At the date of acquisition shares in Southstar Co had a listed market price of $1.20 each.

The statements of profit or loss for the year ended 30 September 20X3 show revenue for Polestar Co and Southstar Co as $110m and $66m respectively. Revenue accrued evenly over the year.

Additional information:

(i)    At the date of acquisition, the fair values of Southstar Co's assets were equal to their carrying amounts with the exception of a leased property. This had a fair value of $2 million above its carrying amount and a remaining lease term of ten years at that date. All depreciation is included in cost of sales.

(ii)   Polestar transferred raw materials at their cost of $4 million to Southstar Co in June 20X3. Southstar Co processed all of these materials incurring additional direct costs of $1.4 million and sold them back to Polestar Co in August 20X3 for $9 million. At 30 September 20X3 Polestar Co had $1.5 million of these goods still in inventory. There were no other intragroup sales.

(iii)  Polestar Co's policy is to value the non-controlling interest at fair value at the date of acquisition. For this purpose, Southstar Co's share price at that date can be deemed to be representative of the fair value of the shares held by the non-controlling interest.

268 What was the fair value of Southstar Co's net assets at the acquisition date? Submit your answer to one decimal place.

$ [          ] million

269   What is consolidated revenue for the year ended 30 September 20X3?

    A    $130 million
    B    $143 million
    C    $163 million
    D    $156 million

270   The estimated value of the contingent consideration has fallen from $1.8m to $1.5m.

Using the drag and drop options below, show how this be accounted for in Polestar Co.

| Debit | | Account |
|---|---|---|
| | | Goodwill |
| Credit | | Liability |
| | | Profit or loss |

271   What is the amount of the adjustment to profit attributable to the non-controlling interest in respect of unrealised profit?

$ [            ]

272   Polestar Co measures the non-controlling interest in Southstar Co at fair value. Which of the following applies when non-controlling interest is measured at fair value?

    A    The non-controlling interest will be allocated their share of any negative goodwill.
    B    The non-controlling interest will be allocated the whole of the pre-acquisition profits.
    C    The non-controlling interest will be allocated their share of any goodwill impairment.
    D    If the subsidiary's share price falls, the non-controlling interest will be adjusted.

(Total = 10 marks)

# Plateau OTQ case                                                          18 mins

**The following information relates to questions 273–277.**

On 1 October 20X6 Plateau Co acquired the following non-current investments:

- Three million equity shares in Savannah Co by an exchange of one share in Plateau Co for every two shares in Savannah Co plus $1.25 per acquired Savannah Co share in cash. The market price of each Plateau Co share at the date of acquisition was $6 and the market price of each Savannah Co share at the date of acquisition was $3.25.

- 30% of the equity shares of Axle Co at a cost of $7.50 per share in cash.

Only the cash consideration of the above investments has been recorded by Plateau Co.

Extracts from the summarised draft statements of financial position of the three companies at 30 September 20X7 are:

| | Plateau Co $'000 | Savannah Co $'000 | Axle Co $'000 |
|---|---|---|---|
| Equity shares of $1 each | 10,000 | 4,000 | 4,000 |
| Retained earnings | | | |
| – at 30 September 20X6 | 16,000 | 6,000 | 11,000 |
| – for year ended 30 September 20X7 | 9,250 | 2,900 | 5,000 |
| | 35,250 | 12,900 | 20,000 |

The following information is relevant:

(i)     At the date of acquisition Savannah Co had five years remaining of an agreement to supply goods to one of its major customers. The agreement has been consistently renewed when it expires. The directors of Plateau Co estimate that the value of this customer based contract has a fair value of $1 million and an indefinite life and has not suffered any impairment.

(ii)    During the year ended 30 September 20X7 Savannah Co sold goods to Plateau Co for $2.7 million. Savannah Co had marked up these goods by 50% on cost. Plateau Co had a third of the goods still in its inventory at 30 September 20X7. There were no intragroup payables/receivables at 30 September 20X7.

(iii)   It is the group policy to value non-controlling interest at acquisition at full (or fair) value. For this purpose the share price of Savannah Co at the acquisition date should be used.

273    What is the total of the consideration paid by Plateau Co for Savannah Co?

A      $3,750,000
B      $9,750,000
C      $12,750,000
D      $21,750,000

274    How should the customer contract in note (i) be accounted for?

A      Should not be recognised as item is internally generated
B      Group share of 75% should be recognised and not amortised
C      Should be recognised at $1 million and not amortised
D      Should be recognised at $1 million and amortised over five years

275    What amount will be shown as non-controlling interest in the consolidated statement of financial position at 30 September 20X7?

A      $3,900,000
B      $3,250,000
C      $3,225,000
D      $3,975,000

276    What amount will be shown in the consolidated statement of financial position at 30 September 20X7 in respect of the investment in Axle Co?

$ _____

277    Plateau Co is negotiating a contract to supply goods to Axle Co in the coming year (ended 30 September 20X8) at 20% profit. How will the unrealised profit on the sale of these goods be adjusted in the consolidated financial statements for the year ended 30 September 20X8?

|  |  | Account |
| --- | --- | --- |
| Debit |  | Group inventory |
| Credit |  | Investment in associate |
|  |  | Share of profit of associate |

(10 marks)

# Pinto Co –OTQ case

**The following scenario relates to questions 278–282.**

Pinto Co is a publicly listed company. The following financial statements of Pinto Co are available:

STATEMENT OF PROFIT OR LOSS AND OTHER COMPREHENSIVE INCOME FOR YEAR ENDED 31 MARCH 20X8 (extract)

|  | $'000 |
|---|---|
| Profit before tax | 440 |
| Income tax expense | (160) |
| Profit for the year | 280 |
| Other comprehensive income | |
| Gains on property revaluation | 100 |
| Total comprehensive income | 380 |

STATEMENTS OF FINANCIAL POSITION (extracts) AS AT

|  | 31 March 20X8 | | 31 March 20X7 | |
|---|---|---|---|---|
|  | $'000 | $'000 | $'000 | $'000 |
| *Non-current assets* (note (i)) | | | | |
| Property, plant and equipment | | 2,880 | | 1,860 |
| Investment property | | 420 | | 400 |
| | | 3,300 | | 2,260 |
| *Current assets* | | 1,700 | | 1,400 |
| | | 5,000 | | 3,660 |
| *Equity and liabilities* | | | | |
| Equity shares of 20 cents each (note (iii)) | | 1,000 | | 600 |
| Share premium | 600 | | Nil | |
| Revaluation surplus | 150 | | 50 | |
| Retained earnings | 1,440 | 2,190 | 1,310 | 1,360 |
| | | 3,190 | | 1,960 |
| *Non-current liabilities* | | | | |
| 6% loan notes | nil | | 400 | |
| Deferred tax | 50 | 50 | 30 | 430 |
| *Current liabilities* | | | | |
| Trade payables | 1,410 | | 1,050 | |
| Bank overdraft | nil | | 120 | |
| Warranty provision | 200 | | 100 | |
| Current tax payable | 150 | 1,760 | nil | 1,270 |
| Total equity and liabilities | | 5,000 | | 3,660 |

The following supporting information is available:

(i)   An item of plant with a carrying amount of $240,000 was sold at a loss of $90,000 during the year. Depreciation of $280,000 was charged (to cost of sales) for property, plant and equipment in the year ended 31 March 20X8.

Pinto Co uses the fair value model in IAS 40 *Investment Property*. There were no purchases or sales of investment property during the year.

(ii)  A dividend of 3 cents per share was paid on 1 January 20X8.

(iii) $60,000 was included in Pinto's profit before tax for the year ended 31 March 20X8 in respect of income and gains on investment property.

You are preparing a statement of cash flows for Pinto Co for the year to 31 March 20X8.

278 What is the amount of tax that Pinto Co either received or paid during the year?

    A    $60,000 paid
    B    $60,000 received
    C    $10,000 paid
    D    $10,000 received

279 Pinto has spent $1,440,000 on purchase of plant. What is the net cash used in investing activities?

$ ☐

280 What was the amount of the dividend paid on 1 January 20X8?

    A    $150,000
    B    $300,000
    C    $240,000
    D    $120,000

281 Under which **TWO** classification(s) can dividends paid be shown in the statement of cash flows?

☐ Investing activities

☐ Financing activities

☐ Operating activities

☐ Movement in payables

282 Which of the following items will **NOT** be adjusted against Pinto Co's profit before tax in arriving at net cash from operating activities?

    A    The increase in trade payables
    B    The proceeds from sale of plant
    C    The increase in the warranty provision
    D    The investment income

**(10 marks)**

# Section C

## 283 Pedantic Co (Dec08 amended)                          36 mins

On 1 April 20X8, Pedantic Co acquired 60% of the equity share capital of Sophistic Co in a share exchange of two shares in Pedantic Co for three shares in Sophistic Co. At that date the retained earnings of Sophistic Co were $5 million. The issue of shares has not yet been recorded by Pedantic Co. At the date of acquisition shares in Pedantic Co had a market value of $6 each. Below are the summarised draft statements of financial position of both companies.

STATEMENTS OF FINANCIAL POSITION AS AT 30 SEPTEMBER 20X8

|                                      | Pedantic Co | Sophistic Co |
|--------------------------------------|------------:|-------------:|
| Assets                               | $'000       | $'000        |
| Non-current assets                   |             |              |
| Property, plant and equipment        | 40,600      | 12,600       |
| Current assets                       | 16,000      | 6,600        |
| Total assets                         | 56,600      | 19,200       |
|                                      |             |              |
| Equity and liabilities               |             |              |
| Equity shares of $1 each             | 10,000      | 4,000        |
| Retained earnings                    | 35,400      | 6,500        |
|                                      | 45,400      | 10,500       |
|                                      |             |              |
| Non-current liabilities              |             |              |
| 10% loan notes                       | 3,000       | 4,000        |
| Current liabilities                  | 8,200       | 4,700        |
| Total equity and liabilities         | 56,600      | 19,200       |

The following information is relevant:

(i)    At the date of acquisition, the fair values of Sophistic's assets were equal to their carrying amounts with the exception of an item of plant, which had a fair value of $2 million in excess of its carrying amount. It had a remaining life of five years at that date (straight-line depreciation is used). Sophistic Co has not adjusted the carrying amount of its plant as a result of the fair value exercise.

(ii)   Sales from Sophistic Co to Pedantic Co in the post-acquisition period were $8 million. Sophistic Co made a mark-up on cost of 40% on these sales. Pedantic Cohad sold $5.2 million (at cost to Pedantic Co) of these goods by 30 September 20X8.

(iii)  Sophistic Co's trade receivables at 30 September 20X8 include $600,000 due from Pedantic Co which did not agree with Pedantic Co's corresponding trade payable. This was due to cash in transit of $200,000 from Pedantic Co to Sophistic Co. Both companies have positive bank balances.

(iv)   Pedantic Co has a policy of accounting for any non-controlling interest at full fair value. The fair value of the non-controlling interest in Sophistic Co at the date of acquisition was estimated to be $5.9 million. Consolidated goodwill was not impaired at 30 September 20X8.

*Required*

(a)    Prepare the consolidated statement of financial position for Pedantic Coas at 30 September 20X8.

                                                                                        (16 marks)

(b)    Pedantic Co has been approached by a potential new customer, Trilby Co, to supply it with a substantial quantity of goods on three-month credit terms. Pedantic Co is concerned at the risk that such a large order represents in the current difficult economic climate, especially as Pedantic Co's normal credit terms are only one month's credit. To support its application for credit, Trilby has sent Pedantic Co a copy of Tradhat Co's most recent audited consolidated financial statements. Trilby Co is a wholly owned subsidiary within the Tradhat Co group. Tradhat Co's consolidated financial statements show a strong statement of financial position including healthy liquidity ratios.

       Comment on the importance that Pedantic Co should attach to Tradhat Co's consolidated financial statements when deciding on whether to grant credit terms to Trilby Co.                         (4 marks)

                                                                                  (Total = 20 marks)

# 284 Highveldt Co

Highveldt Co, a public listed company, acquired 75% of Samson Co's ordinary shares on 1 April 20X4. Highveldt Co paid an immediate $3.50 per share in cash and agreed to pay a further amount of $108 million on 1 April 20X5. Highveldt Co's cost of capital is 8% per annum. Highveldt Co has only recorded the cash consideration of $3.50 per share.

The summarised statements of financial position of the two companies at 31 March 20X5 are shown below:

| | Highveldt Co | | Samson Co | |
|---|---|---|---|---|
| | $m | $m | $m | $m |
| Property, plant and equipment (note (i)) | | 420 | | 320 |
| Development costs (note (iv)) | | nil | | 40 |
| Investments (note (ii)) | | 300 | | 20 |
| | | 720 | | 380 |
| Current assets | | 133 | | 91 |
| Total assets | | 853 | | 471 |
| **Equity and liabilities** | | | | |
| Ordinary shares of $1 each | | 270 | | 80 |
| Reserves: | | | | |
| Share premium | | 80 | | 40 |
| Revaluation surplus | | 45 | | nil |
| Retained earnings – 1 April 20X4 | 160 | | 134 | |
| – year to 31 March 20X5 | 190 | | 76 | |
| | | 350 | | 210 |
| | | 745 | | 330 |
| **Non-current liabilities** | | | | |
| 10% intragroup loan (note (ii)) | | nil | | 60 |
| Current liabilities | | 108 | | 81 |
| Total equity and liabilities | | 853 | | 471 |

The following information is relevant:

(i)     Highveldt Co has a policy of revaluing land and buildings to fair value. At the date of acquisition Samson Co's land and buildings had a fair value $20 million higher than their carrying amount and at 31 March 20X5 this had increased by a further $4 million (ignore any additional depreciation).

(ii)    Included in Highveldt Co's investments is a loan of $60 million made to Samson Co at the date of acquisition. Interest is payable annually in arrears. Samson Co paid the interest due for the year on 31 March 20X5, but Highveldt Co did not receive this until after the year end. Highveldt Co has not accounted for the accrued interest from Samson Co.

(iii)   Samson Co had established a line of products under the brand name of Titanware. Acting on behalf of Highveldt Co, a firm of specialists, had valued the brand name at a value of $40 million with an estimated life of ten years as at 1 April 20X4. The brand is not included in Samson Co's statement of financial position.

(iv)    Samson Co's development project was completed on 30 September 20X4 at a cost of $50 million. $10 million of this had been amortised by 31 March 20X5. Development costs capitalised by Samson Co at the date of acquisition were $18 million. Highveldt Co's directors are of the opinion that Samson Co's development costs do not meet the criteria in IAS 38 *Intangible Assets* for recognition as an asset.

(v)     Samson Co sold goods to Highveldt Co during the year at a profit of $6 million; one-third of these goods were still in the inventory of Highveldt Co at 31 March 20X5.

(vi)    An impairment test at 31 March 20X5 on the consolidated goodwill concluded that it should be written down by $20 million. No other assets were impaired.

(vii)   It is the group policy to measure non-controlling interest fair value. The fair value of the non-controlling interest in Samson Co at the acquisition date was $83 million.

## Required

Calculate the following figures as they would appear in the consolidated statement of financial position of Highveldt Co at 31 March 20X5:

| | | |
|---|---|---|
| (i) | Goodwill | **(8 marks)** |
| (ii) | Non-controlling interest | **(4 marks)** |
| (iii) | The following consolidated reserves: | |
| | share premium, revaluation surplus and retained earnings. | **(8 marks)** |

**(Total = 20 marks)**

# 285 Paradigm Co

**36 mins**

On 1 October 20X2, Paradigm Co acquired 75% of Strata Co's equity shares by means of a share exchange of two new shares in Paradigm Co for every five acquired shares in Strata Co. In addition, Paradigm Co issued to the shareholders of Strata Co a $100 10% loan note for every 1,000 shares it acquired in Strata Co. Paradigm Co has not recorded any of the purchase consideration, although it does have other 10% loan notes already in issue.

The market value of Paradigm Co's shares at 1 October 20X2 was $2 each.

The summarised statements of financial position of the two companies at 31 March 20X3 are:

| | Paradigm Co $'000 | Strata Co $'000 |
|---|---|---|
| **ASSETS** | | |
| *Non-current assets* | | |
| Property, plant and equipment | 47,400 | 25,500 |
| Financial asset: equity investments (note (i)) | 7,500 | 3,200 |
| | 54,900 | 28,700 |
| *Current assets* | | |
| Inventories (note (ii)) | 17,400 | 8,400 |
| Trade receivables (note (iii)) | 14,800 | 9,000 |
| Bank | 5,100 | – |
| Total assets | 92,200 | 46,100 |
| | | |
| **EQUITY AND LIABILITIES** | | |
| Equity | | |
| Equity shares of $1 each | 40,000 | 20,000 |
| Retained earnings/(losses) – at 1 April 20X2 | 19,200 | (4,000) |
| – for year ended 31 March 20X3 | 7,400 | 8,000 |
| | 66,600 | 24,000 |
| *Non-current liabilities* | | |
| 10% loan notes | 8,000 | – |
| | | |
| *Current liabilities* | | |
| Trade payables (note (iii)) | 17,600 | 13,000 |
| Bank overdraft | – | 9,100 |
| Total equity and liabilities | 92,200 | 46,100 |

The following information is relevant:

(i)   At the date of acquisition, Strata Co produced a draft statement of profit or loss which showed it had made a net loss after tax of $2 million at that date. Paradigm Co accepted this figure as the basis for calculating the pre- and post-acquisition split of Strata Co's profit for the year ended 31 March 20X3.

Also at the date of acquisition, Paradigm Co conducted a fair value exercise on Strata Co's net assets which were equal to their carrying amounts (including Strata Co's financial asset equity investments) with the exception of an item of plant which had a fair value of $3 million below its carrying amount. The plant had a remaining estimated useful life of three years at 1 October 20X2.

Paradigm Co's policy is to value the non-controlling interest at fair value at the date of acquisition. For this purpose, a share price for Strata Co of $1.20 each is representative of the fair value of the shares held by the non-controlling interest.

(ii) Each month since acquisition, Paradigm Co's sales to Strata Co were consistently $4.6 million. Paradigm Co had marked these up by 15% on cost. Strata Co had one month's supply ($4.6 million) of these goods in inventory at 31 March 20X3. Paradigm Co's normal mark-up (to third party customers) is 40%.

(iii) Strata Co's current account balance with Paradigm Co at 31 March 20X3 was $2.8 million, which did not agree with Paradigm Co's equivalent receivable due to a payment of $900,000 made by Strata Co on 28 March 20X3, which was not received by Paradigm Co until 3 April 20X3.

(iv) The financial asset equity investments of Paradigm Co and Strata Co are carried at their fair values as at 1 April 20X2. As at 31 March 20X3, these had fair values of $7.1 million and $3.9 million respectively.

(v) There were no impairment losses within the group during the year ended 31 March 20X3.

*Required*

Prepare the consolidated statement of financial position for Paradigm Co as at 31 March 20X3.

(20 marks)

# 286 Boo Co and Goose Co

**36 mins**

Boo Co acquired 80% of Goose Co's equity shares for $300,000 on 1 January 20X8. At the date of acquisition Goose Co had retained earnings of $190,000. On 31 December 20X8 Boo Co despatched goods which cost $80,000 to Goose Co, at an invoiced cost of $100,000. Goose Co received the goods on 2 January 20X9 and recorded the transaction then. The two companies' draft financial statements as at 31 December 20X8 are shown below.

STATEMENTS OF PROFIT OR LOSS AND OTHER COMPREHENSIVE INCOME
FOR THE YEAR ENDED 31 DECEMBER 20X8

| | Boo Co | Goose Co |
|---|---|---|
| | $'000 | $'000 |
| Revenue | 5,000 | 1,000 |
| Cost of sales | 2,900 | 600 |
| Gross profit | 2,100 | 400 |
| Other expenses | 1,700 | 320 |
| Profit before tax | 400 | 80 |
| Income tax expense | 130 | 30 |
| Profit for the year | 270 | 50 |
| Other comprehensive income: | | |
| Gain on revaluation of property | 20 | – |
| Total comprehensive income for the year | 290 | 50 |

STATEMENTS OF FINANCIAL POSITION AT 31 DECEMBER 20X8

| | $'000 | $'000 |
|---|---|---|
| *Assets* | | |
| *Non-current assets* | | |
| Property, plant and equipment | 1,940 | 200 |
| Investment in Goose Co | 300 | – |
| | 2,240 | 200 |
| *Current assets* | | |
| Inventories | 500 | 120 |
| Trade receivables | 650 | 40 |
| Cash and cash equivalents | 170 | 35 |
| | 1,320 | 195 |
| Total assets | 3,560 | 395 |

|  | $'000 | $'000 |
|---|---:|---:|
| *Equity and liabilities* | | |
| *Equity* | | |
| Share capital | 2,000 | 100 |
| Retained earnings | 500 | 240 |
| Revaluation surplus | 20 | – |
| | 2,520 | 340 |
| *Current liabilities* | | |
| Trade payables | 910 | 30 |
| Tax | 130 | 25 |
| | 1,040 | 55 |
| Total equity and liabilities | 3,560 | 395 |

*Required*

Prepare a draft consolidated statement of profit or loss and other comprehensive income and statement of financial position. It is the group policy to value the non-controlling interest at acquisition at fair value. The fair value of the non-controlling interest in Goose Co at the date of acquisition was $60,000. **(20 marks)**

---

# 287 Viagem Co (Dec12 amended)                      36 mins

On 1 January 20X2, Viagem Co acquired 90% of the equity share capital of Greca Co in a share exchange in which Viagem Co issued two new shares for every three shares it acquired in Greca Co. Additionally, on 31 December 20X2, Viagem Co will pay the shareholders of Greca Co $1.76 per share acquired. Viagem Co's cost of capital is 10% per annum.

At the date of acquisition, shares in Viagem Co and Greca Co had a stock market value of $6.50 and $2.50 each respectively.

STATEMENTS OF PROFIT OR LOSS FOR THE YEAR ENDED 30 SEPTEMBER 20X2

|  | *Viagem Co* | *Greca Co* |
|---|---:|---:|
|  | $'000 | $'000 |
| Revenue | 64,600 | 38,000 |
| Cost of sales | (51,200) | (26,000) |
| Gross profit | 13,400 | 12,000 |
| Distribution costs | (1,600) | (1,800) |
| Administrative expenses | (3,800) | (2,400) |
| Investment income | 500 | – |
| Finance costs | (420) | – |
| Profit before tax | 8,080 | 7,800 |
| Income tax expense | (2,800) | (1,600) |
| Profit for the year | 5,280 | 6,200 |
| Equity as at 1 October 20X1 | | |
| Equity shares of $1 each | 30,000 | 10,000 |
| Retained earnings | 54,000 | 35,000 |

The following information is relevant:

(i)     At the date of acquisition the fair values of Greca Co's assets were equal to their carrying amounts with the exception of two items:

1       An item of plant had a fair value of $1.8 million above its carrying amount. The remaining life of the plant at the date of acquisition was three years. Depreciation is charged to cost of sales.

2       Greca Co had a contingent liability which Viagem Co estimated to have a fair value of $450,000. This has not changed as at 30 September 20X2.

Greca Co has not incorporated these fair value changes into its financial statements.

(ii)   Viagem Co's policy is to value the non-controlling interest at fair value at the date of acquisition. For this purpose, Greca Co's share price at that date can be deemed to be representative of the fair value of the shares held by the non-controlling interest.

(iii)  Sales from Viagem Co to Greca Co throughout the year ended 30 September 20X2 had consistently been $800,000 per month. Viagem Co made a mark-up on cost of 25% on these sales. Greca Co had $1.5 million of these goods in inventory as at 30 September 20X2.

(iv)   Viagem Co's investment income is a dividend received from its investment in a 40% owned associate which it has held for several years. The underlying earnings for the associate for the year ended 30 September 20X2 were $2 million.

(v)    Although Greca Co has been profitable since its acquisition by Viagem Co, the market for Greca Co's products has been badly hit in recent months and Viagem Co has calculated that the goodwill has been impaired by $2 million as at 30 September 20X2.

*Required*

(a)    Calculate the goodwill arising on the acquisition of Greca Co                                    **(6 marks)**

(b)    Prepare the consolidated statement of profit or loss for Viagem Co for the year ended 30 September 20X2.

**(14 marks)**

**(Total = 20 marks)**

# 288 Prodigal Co (Jun11 amended)                                                         36 mins

On 1 October 20X0 Prodigal Co purchased 75% of the equity shares in Sentinel Co. The acquisition was through a share exchange of two shares in Prodigal Co for every three shares in Sentinel Co. The stock market price of Prodigal Co's shares at 1 October 20X0 was $4 per share. The summarised statements of profit or loss and other comprehensive income for the two companies for the year ended 31 March 20X1 are:

|                                             | Prodigal Co | Sentinel Co |
|---------------------------------------------|-------------|-------------|
|                                             | $'000       | $'000       |
| Revenue                                     | 450,000     | 240,000     |
| Cost of sales                               | (260,000)   | (110,000)   |
| Gross profit                                | 190,000     | 130,000     |
| Distribution costs                          | (23,600)    | (12,000)    |
| Administrative expenses                     | (27,000)    | (23,000)    |
| Finance costs                               | (1,500)     | (1,200)     |
| Profit before tax                           | 137,900     | 93,800      |
| Income tax expense                          | (48,000)    | (27,800)    |
| Profit for the year                         | 89,900      | 66,000      |
| Other comprehensive income                  |             |             |
| Gain on revaluation of land (note(i))       | 2,500       | 1,000       |
| Loss on fair value of investment in equity instrument | (700) | (400)  |
|                                             | 1,800       | 600         |
| Total comprehensive income for the year     | 91,700      | 66,600      |

The equity of Sentinel Co at 1 April 20X0 was:

|                                                        | $'000   |
|--------------------------------------------------------|---------|
| Equity shares of $1 each                               | 160,000 |
| Other equity reserve (re investment in equity instrument) | 2,200 |
| Retained earnings                                      | 125,000 |

The following information is relevant:

(i) Prodigal Co's policy is to revalue the group's land to market value at the end of each accounting period. Prior to its acquisition, Sentinel Co's land had been valued at historical cost. During the post-acquisition period Sentinel Co's land had increased in value over its value at the date of acquisition by $1 million. Sentinel Co has recognised the revaluation within its own financial statements.

(ii) Immediately after the acquisition of Sentinel Co on 1 October 20X0, Prodigal Co transferred an item of plant with a carrying amount of $4 million to Sentinel Co at an agreed value of $5 million. At this date the plant had a remaining life of two and a half years. Prodigal Co had included the profit on this transfer as a reduction in its depreciation costs. All depreciation is charged to cost of sales.

(iii) After the acquisition Sentinel Co sold goods to Prodigal Co for $40 million. These goods had cost Sentinel Co $30 million. $12 million of the goods sold remained in Prodigal Co's closing inventory.

(iv) Prodigal Co's policy is to value the non-controlling interest of Sentinel Co at the date of acquisition at its fair value which the directors determined to be $100 million.

(v) The goodwill of Sentinel Co has not suffered any impairment.

(vi) All items in the above statements of profit or loss and other comprehensive income are deemed to accrue evenly over the year unless otherwise indicated.

*Required*

(a) Calculate the goodwill on acquisition of Sentinel Co.                              **(4 marks)**

(b) Prepare the consolidated statement of profit or loss and other comprehensive income of Prodigal Co for the year ended 31 March 20X1.                              **(16 marks)**

**(Total = 20 marks)**

# 289 Plastik Co (Dec14 amended)                              36 mins

On 1 January 20X4, Plastik Co acquired 80% of the equity share capital of Subtrak Co. The consideration was satisfied by a share exchange of two shares in Plastik Co for every three acquired shares in Subtrak Co. At the date of acquisition, shares in Plastik Co and Subtrak Co had a market value of $3 and $2.50 each respectively. Plastik Co will also pay cash consideration of 27.5 cents on 1 January 20X5 for each acquired share in Subtrak Co. Plastik Co has a cost of capital of 10% per annum. None of the consideration has been recorded by Plastik Co.

Below are the summarised draft financial statements of both companies.

STATEMENTS OF PROFIT OR LOSS AND OTHER COMPREHENSIVE INCOME FOR THE YEAR ENDED 30 SEPTEMBER 20X4

|  | Plastik Co | Subtrak Co |
|---|---|---|
|  | $'000 | $'000 |
| Revenue | 62,600 | 30,000 |
| Cost of sales | (45,800) | (24,000) |
| Gross profit | 16,800 | 6,000 |
| Distribution costs | (2,000) | (1,200) |
| Administrative expenses | (3,500) | (1,800) |
| Finance costs | (200) | – |
| Profit before tax | 11,100 | 3,000 |
| Income tax expense | (3,100) | (1,000) |
| Profit for the year | 8,000 | 2,000 |
| Other comprehensive income: |  |  |
| Gain on revaluation of property | 1,500 | – |
| Total comprehensive income | 9,500 | 2,000 |

STATEMENTS OF FINANCIAL POSITION AS AT 30 SEPTEMBER 20X4

|  | Plastik Co $'000 | Subtrak Co $'000 |
|---|---|---|
| ASSETS | | |
| Non-current assets | | |
| Property, plant and equipment | 18,700 | 13,900 |
| Current assets | | |
| Inventories (note(ii)) | 4,300 | 1,200 |
| Trade receivables | 5,700 | 2,500 |
| Cash and cash equivalents | – | 300 |
| | 10,000 | 4,000 |
| Total assets | 28,700 | 17,900 |
| | | |
| EQUITY AND LIABILITIES | | |
| Equity | | |
| Equity shares of $1 each | 10,000 | 9,000 |
| Revaluation surplus (note(i)) | 2,000 | – |
| Retained earnings | 6,300 | 3,500 |
| | 18,300 | 12,500 |
| Non-current liabilities | | |
| 10% loan notes (note(ii)) | 2,500 | 1,000 |
| Current liabilities | | |
| Trade payables (note(iv)) | 3,400 | 3,600 |
| Bank | 1,700 | – |
| Current tax payable | 2,800 | 800 |
| | 7,900 | 4,400 |
| Total equity and liabilities | 28,700 | 17,900 |

The following information is relevant:

(i) At the date of acquisition, the fair values of Subtrak Co's assets and liabilities were equal to their carrying amounts with the exception of Subtrak Co's property which had a fair value of $4 million above its carrying amount. For consolidation purposes, this led to an increase in depreciation charges (in cost of sales) of $100,000 in the post-acquisition period to 30 September 20X4. Subtrak Co has not incorporated the fair value property increase into its entity financial statements.

The policy of the Plastik Co group is to revalue all properties to fair value at each year end. On 30 September 20X4, the increase in Plastik Co's property has already been recorded, however, a further increase of $600,000 in the value of Subtrak Co's property since its value at acquisition and 30 September 20X4 has not been recorded.

(ii) Sales from Plastik Co to Subtrak Co throughout the year ended 30 September 20X4 had consistently been $300,000 per month. Plastik Co made a mark-up on cost of 25% on all these sales. $600,000 (at cost to Subtrak Co) of Subtrak Co's inventory at 30 September 20X4 had been supplied by Plastik Co in the post-acquisition period.

(iii) Plastik Co's policy is to value the non-controlling interest at fair value at the date of acquisition. For this purpose Subtrak Co's share price at that date can be deemed to be representative of the fair value of the shares held by the non-controlling interest.

(iv) Due to recent adverse publicity concerning one of Subtrak Co's major product lines, the goodwill which arose on the acquisition of Subtrak Co has been impaired by $500,000 as at 30 September 20X4. Goodwill impairment should be treated as an administrative expense.

(v) Assume, except where indicated otherwise, that all items of income and expenditure accrue evenly throughout the year.

## Required

(a) Calculate the goodwill arising on the acquisition of Subtrak Co on 1 January 20X4. **(4 marks)**

(b) Calculate the following amounts for presentation in the consolidated statement of financial position:

    (i) Group retained earnings

    (ii) Non-controlling interest **(6 marks)**

(c) Prepare the consolidated statement of profit or loss and other comprehensive income for Plastik Co for the year ended 30 September 20X4. **(10 marks)**

**(Total = 20 marks)**

# 290 Laurel Co

**36 mins**

Laurel Co acquired 80% of the ordinary share capital of Hardy Co for $160m and 40% of the ordinary share capital of Comic Co for $70m on 1 January 20X7 when the retained earnings balances were $64m in Hardy Co and $24m in Comic Co. Laurel Co, Comic Co and Hardy Co are public limited companies.

The statements of financial position of the three companies at 31 December 20X9 are set out below:

|  | Laurel Co $m | Hardy Co $m | Comic Co $m |
|---|---|---|---|
| *Non-current assets* | | | |
| Property, plant and equipment | 220 | 160 | 78 |
| Investments | 230 | – | – |
| | 450 | 160 | 78 |
| *Current assets* | | | |
| Inventories | 384 | 234 | 122 |
| Trade receivables | 275 | 166 | 67 |
| Cash at bank | 42 | 10 | 34 |
| | 701 | 410 | 223 |
| | 1,151 | 570 | 301 |
| *Equity* | | | |
| Share capital – $1 ordinary shares | 400 | 96 | 80 |
| Share premium | 16 | 3 | – |
| Retained earnings | 278 | 128 | 97 |
| | 694 | 227 | 177 |
| *Current liabilities* | | | |
| Trade payables | 457 | 343 | 124 |
| | 1,151 | 570 | 301 |

You are also given the following information:

1 On 30 November 20X9 Laurel Co sold some goods to Hardy Co for cash for $32m. These goods had originally cost $22m and none had been sold by the year end. On the same date Laurel Co also sold goods to Comic Co for cash for $22m. These goods originally cost $10m and Comic Co had sold half by the year end.

2 On 1 January 20X7 Hardy Co owned some items of equipment with a Boo Cok value of $45m that had a fair value of $57m. These assets were originally purchased by Hardy Co on 1 January 20X5 and are being depreciated over six years.

3 Group policy is to measure non-controlling interests at acquisition at fair value. The fair value of the non-controlling interests in Hardy Co on 1 January 20X7 was calculated as $39m.

4 Cumulative impairment losses on recognised goodwill amounted to $15m at 31 December 20X9. No impairment losses have been necessary to date relating to the investment in the associate.

*Required*

Prepare a consolidated statement of financial position for Laurel Co and its subsidiary as at 31 December 20X9, incorporating its associate in accordance with IAS 28.

(20 marks)

# 291 Tyson Co

**36 mins**

Below are the statements of profit or loss and other comprehensive income of Tyson Co, its subsidiary Douglas Co and associate Frank Co at 31 December 20X8. Tyson Co, Douglas Coand Frank Co are public limited companies.

|  | Tyson Co | Douglas Co | Frank Co |
|---|---|---|---|
|  | $m | $m | $m |
| *Revenue* | 500 | 150 | 70 |
| Cost of sales | (270) | (80) | (30) |
| Gross profit | 230 | 70 | 40 |
| Other expenses | (150) | (20) | (15) |
| Finance income | 15 | 10 | – |
| Finance costs | (20) | – | (10) |
| *Profit before tax* | 75 | 60 | 15 |
| Income tax expense | (25) | (15) | (5) |
| PROFIT FOR THE YEAR | 50 | 45 | 10 |
| *Other comprehensive income:* |  |  |  |
| Gains on property revaluation, net of tax | 20 | 10 | 5 |
| TOTAL COMPREHENSIVE INCOME FOR THE YEAR | 70 | 55 | 15 |

You are also given the following information:

1    Tyson Co acquired 80m shares in Douglas Co for $188m three years ago when Douglas Co had a credit balance on its reserves of $40m. Douglas Co has 100m $1 ordinary shares.

2    Tyson Co acquired 40m shares in Frank Co for $60m two years ago when that company had a credit balance on its reserves of $20m. Frank Co has 100m $1 ordinary shares.

3    During the year Douglas Co sold some goods to Tyson Co for $66m (cost $48m). None of the goods had been sold by the year end.

4    Group policy is to measure non-controlling interests at acquisition at fair value. The fair value of the non-controlling interests in Douglas Co at acquisition was $40m. An impairment test carried out at the year end resulted in $15m of the recognised goodwill relating to Douglas Co being written off and recognition of impairment losses of $2.4m relating to the investment in Frank Co.

*Required*

Prepare the consolidated statement of profit or loss and other comprehensive income for the year ended 31 December 20X8 for Tyson Co, incorporating its associate.

(20 marks)

# 292 Paladin Co (Dec11 amended)

**36 mins**

On 1 October 20X0, Paladin Co secured a majority equity shareholding in Saracen Co on the following terms.

An immediate payment of $4 per share on 1 October 20X0; and a further amount deferred until 1 October 20X1 of $5.4 million.

The immediate payment has been recorded in Paladin Co's financial statements, but the deferred payment has not been recorded. Paladin Co's cost of capital is 8% per annum, giving the deferred payment a current cost at 1 October 20X0 of $5 million.

On 1 February 20X1, Paladin Co also acquired 25% of the equity shares of Augusta Co paying $10 million in cash.

The summarised statements of financial position of the three companies at 30 September 20X1 are:

|  | Paladin Co $'000 | Saracen Co $'000 | Augusta Co $'000 |
|---|---|---|---|
| *Assets* |  |  |  |
| *Non-current assets* |  |  |  |
| Property, plant and equipment | 40,000 | 31,000 | 30,000 |
| Intangible assets | 7,500 |  |  |
| Investments – Saracen Co (8 million shares at $4 each) | 32,000 |  |  |
| – Augusta Co | 10,000 | nil | nil |
|  | 89,500 | 31,000 | 30,000 |
| *Current assets* |  |  |  |
| Inventories | 11,200 | 8,400 | 10,000 |
| Trade receivables | 7,400 | 5,300 | 5,000 |
| Cash and cash equivalents | 3,400 | nil | 2,000 |
| Total assets | 111,500 | 44,700 | 47,000 |
| *Equity and liabilities* |  |  |  |
| *Equity* |  |  |  |
| Equity shares of $1 each | 50,000 | 10,000 | 10,000 |
| Retained earnings – at 1 October 20X0 | 25,700 | 12,000 | 31,800 |
| – for year ended 30 September 20X1 | 9,200 | 6,000 | 1,200 |
|  | 84,900 | 28,000 | 43,000 |
| *Non-current liabilities* |  |  |  |
| Deferred tax | 15,000 | 8,000 | 1,000 |
| *Current liabilities* |  |  |  |
| Bank | nil | 2,500 | nil |
| Trade payables | 11,600 | 6,200 | 3,000 |
| Total equity and liabilities | 111,500 | 44,700 | 47,000 |

The following information is relevant:

(i)     Paladin Co's policy is to value the non-controlling interest at fair value at the date of acquisition. The directors of Paladin Co considered the fair value of the non-controlling interest in Saracen Co to be $7 million.

(ii)    At the date of acquisition, the fair values of Saracen Co's property, plant and equipment was equal to its carrying amount with the exception of Saracen Co's plant which had a fair value of $4 million above its carrying amount. At that date the plant had a remaining life of four years. Saracen Co uses straight-line depreciation for plant assuming a nil residual value.

Also at the date of acquisition, Paladin Co valued Saracen Co's customer relationships as a customer base intangible asset at fair value of $3 million. Saracen Co has not accounted for this asset. Trading relationships with Saracen Co's customers last on average for six years.

(iii)   At 30 September 20X1, Saracen Co's inventory included goods bought from Paladin Co (at cost to Saracen Co) of $2.6 million. Paladin Co had marked up these goods by 30% on cost. Paladin Co's agreed current account balance owed by Saracen Co at 30 September 20X1 was $1.3 million.

(iv)    Impairment tests were carried out on 30 September 20X1 which concluded that consolidated goodwill was not impaired, but, due to disappointing earnings, the value of the investment in Augusta Co was impaired by $2.5 million.

(v)     Assume all profits accrue evenly through the year.

*Required*

Prepare the consolidated statement of financial position for Paladin Co as at 30 September 20X1.     **(20 marks)**

# 293 Dargent Co (Mar/Jun17)

**36 mins**

On 1 January 20X6, Dargent Co acquired 75% of Latree Co's equity shares by means of a share exchange of two shares in Dargent Co for every three Latree Co shares acquired. On that date, further consideration was also issued to the shareholders of Latree Co in the form of a $100 8% loan note for every 100 shares acquired in Latree Co. None of the purchase consideration, nor the outstanding interest on the loan notes at 31 March 20X6, has yet been recorded by Dargent Co. At the date of acquisition, the share price of Dargent Co and Latree Co is $3·20 and $1·80 respectively.

The summarised statements of financial position of the two companies as at 31 March 20X6 are:

|  | Dargent Co $'000 | Latree Co $'000 |
|---|---|---|
| **Assets** | | |
| *Non-current assets* | | |
| Property, plant and equipment (note (i)) | 75,200 | 31,500 |
| Investment in Amery Co at 1 April 20X5 (note (iv)) | 4,500 | – |
|  | 79,700 | 31,500 |
| *Current assets* | | |
| Inventory (note (iii)) | 19,400 | 18,800 |
| Trade receivables (note (iii)) | 14,700 | 12,500 |
| Bank | 1,200 | 600 |
|  | 35,300 | 31,900 |
| Total assets | 115,000 | 63,400 |
| **Equity and liabilities** | | |
| *Equity* | | |
| Equity shares of $1 each | 50,000 | 20,000 |
| Retained earnings – at 1 April 20X5 | 20,000 | 19,000 |
| – for year ended 31 March 20X6 | 16,000 | 8,000 |
|  | 86,000 | 47,000 |
| *Non-current liabilities* | | |
| 8% loan notes | 5,000 | nil |
| Current liabilities (note (iii)) | 24,000 | 16,400 |
|  | 29,000 | 16,400 |
| Total equity and liabilities | 115,000 | 63,400 |

The following information is relevant:

(i) At the date of acquisition, the fair values of Latree Co's assets were equal to their carrying amounts. However, Latree Co-operates a mine which requires to be decommissioned in five years' time. No provision has been made for these decommissioning costs by Latree Co. The present value (discounted at 8%) of the decommissioning is estimated at $4m and will be paid five years from the date of acquisition (the end of the mine's life).

(ii) Dargent Co's policy is to value the non-controlling interest at fair value at the date of acquisition. Latree Co's share price at that date can be deemed to be representative of the fair value of the shares held by the non-controlling interest.

(iii) The inventory of Latree Co includes goods bought from Dargent Co for $2·1m. Dargent Co applies a consistent mark-up on cost of 40% when arriving at its selling prices.

On 28 March 20X6, Dargent Co despatched goods to Latree Co with a selling price of $700,000. These were not received by Latree Co until after the year end and so have not been included in the above inventory at 31 March 20X6.

At 31 March 20X6, Dargent Co's records showed a receivable due from Latree Co of $3m, this differed to the equivalent payable in Latree Co's records due to the goods in transit.

The intra-group reconciliation should be achieved by assuming that Latree Co had received the goods in transit before the year end.

(iv)    The investment in Amery Co represents 30% of its voting share capital and Dargent Co uses equity accounting to account for this investment. Amery Co's profit for the year ended 31 March 20X6 was $6m and Amery Co paid total dividends during the year ended 31 March 20X6 of $2m. Dargent Co has recorded its share of the dividend received from Amery Co in investment income (and cash).

(v)     All profits and losses accrued evenly throughout the year.

(vi)    There were no impairment losses within the group for the year ended 31 March 20X6.

*Required:*

Prepare the consolidated statement of financial position for Dargent Co as at 31 March 20X6.

(20 marks)

# 294 Fresco Co (Jun12 amended)                     36 mins

The following trial balance relates to Fresco Co at 31 March 20X2:

|  | $'000 | $'000 |
|---|---|---|
| Equity shares of 50 cents each (note (i)) |  | 45,000 |
| Share premium (note (i)) |  | 5,000 |
| Retained earnings at 1 April 20X1 |  | 5,100 |
| Property (12 years) – at cost (note (ii)) | 48,000 |  |
| Plant and equipment – at cost (note (ii)) | 47,500 |  |
| Accumulated amortisation of leased property at 1 April 20X1 |  | 16,000 |
| Accumulated depreciation of plant and equipment at 1 April 20X1 |  | 33,500 |
| Inventories at 31 March 20X2 | 25,200 |  |
| Trade receivables (note (iii)) | 28,500 |  |
| Cash and cash equivalents |  | 1,400 |
| Deferred tax (note (iv)) |  | 3,200 |
| Trade payables |  | 27,300 |
| Revenue |  | 350,000 |
| Cost of sales | 298,700 |  |
| Lease payments (note (ii)) | 8,000 |  |
| Distribution costs | 16,100 |  |
| Administrative expenses | 26,900 |  |
| Bank interest | 300 |  |
| Current tax (note (iv)) | 800 |  |
| Suspense account (note (i)) |  | 13,500 |
|  | 500,000 | 500,000 |

The following notes are relevant:

(i)     The suspense account represents the corresponding credit for cash received for a fully subscribed rights issue of equity shares made on 1 January 20X2. The terms of the share issue were one new share for every five held at a price of 75 cents each. The price of the company's equity shares immediately before the issue was $1.20 each.

(ii)    Non-current assets:

To reflect a marked increase in property prices, Fresco Co decided to revalue its leased property on 1 April 20X1. The directors accepted the report of an independent surveyor who valued the leased property at $36 million on that date. Fresco Co has not yet recorded the revaluation. The remaining life of the leased property is eight years at the date of the revaluation. Fresco Co makes an annual transfer to retained profits to reflect the realisation of the revaluation surplus. In Fresco Co's tax jurisdiction the revaluation does not give rise to a deferred tax liability.

On 1 April 20X1, Fresco Co acquired an item of plant under a lease agreement that had an implicit finance cost of 10% per annum. The lease payments in the trial balance represent an initial deposit of $2 million paid on 1 April 20X1 and the first annual rental of $6 million paid on 31 March 20X2. The lease agreement requires further annual payments of $6 million on 31 March each year for the next four years. The present value of the minimum lease payments, which is equal to the initial measurement of the right-of-use asset, is $25 million.

Plant and equipment (other than the leased plant) is depreciated at 20% per annum using the reducing balance method.

No depreciation/amortisation has yet been charged on any non-current asset for the year ended 31 March 20X2. Depreciation and amortisation are charged to cost of sales.

(iii) In March 20X2, Fresco Co's internal audit department discovered a fraud committed by the company's credit controller who did not return from a foreign business trip. The outcome of the fraud is that $4 million of the company's trade receivables have been stolen by the credit controller and are not recoverable. Of this amount, $1 million relates to the year ended 31 March 20X1 and the remainder to the current year. Fresco Co is not insured against this fraud.

(iv) Fresco Co's income tax calculation for the year ended 31 March 20X2 shows a tax refund of $2.4 million. The balance on current tax in the trial balance represents the under/over provision of the tax liability for the year ended 31 March 20X1. At 31 March 20X2, Fresco Co had taxable temporary differences of $12 million (requiring a deferred tax liability). The income tax rate of Fresco Co is 25%.

*Required:*

(a) Prepare the statement of profit or loss and other comprehensive income for Fresco Co for the year ended 31 March 20X2.

**(8 marks)**

(b) Prepare the statement of financial position of Fresco Co as at 31 March 20X2.

**(12 marks)**

**(Total = 20 marks)**

# 295 Dexon plc

**36 mins**

Below is the summarised draft statement of financial position of Dexon plc, a publicly listed company, as at 31 March 20X8.

| | $'000 | $'000 | $'000 |
|---|---|---|---|
| ASSETS | | | |
| *Non-current assets* | | | |
| Property at valuation (land $20m; buildings $165m (note (i)) | | | 185,000 |
| Plant (note (i)) | | | 180,500 |
| Financial assets at fair value through profit or loss at 1 April 20X7 (note (ii)) | | | 12,500 |
| | | | 378,000 |
| *Current assets* | | | |
| Inventories | | 84,000 | |
| Trade receivables (note (iii)) | | 52,200 | |
| Cash and cash equivalents | | 3,800 | 140,000 |
| Total assets | | | 518,000 |
| EQUITY AND LIABILITIES | | | |
| *Equity* | | | |
| Ordinary shares of $1 each | | | 250,000 |
| Share premium | | 40,000 | |
| Revaluation surplus | | 18,000 | |
| Retained earnings  – At 1 April 20X7 | 12,300 | | |
| – For the year ended 31 March 20X8 | 96,700 | 109,000 | 167,000 |
| | | | 417,000 |
| *Non-current liabilities* | | | |
| Deferred tax – at 1 April 20X7 (note (iv)) | | | 19,200 |
| Current liabilities | | | 81,800 |
| Total equity and liabilities | | | 518,000 |

The following information is relevant:

(i)     The non-current assets have not been depreciated for the year ended 31 March 20X8.

Dexon plc has a policy of revaluing its land and buildings at the end of each accounting year. The values in the above statement of financial position are as at 1 April 20X7 when the buildings had a remaining life of 15 years. A qualified surveyor has valued the land and buildings at 31 March 20X8 at $180 million.

Plant is depreciated at 20% on the reducing balance basis.

(ii)    The financial assets at fair value through profit and loss are held in a fund whose value changes directly in proportion to a specified market index. At 1 April 20X7 the relevant index was 1,200 and at 31 March 20X8 it was 1,296.

(iii)   In late March 20X8 the directors of Dexon plc discovered a material fraud perpetrated by the company's credit controller that had been continuing for some time. Investigations revealed that a total of $4 million of the trade receivables as shown in the statement of financial position at 31 March 20X8 had in fact been paid and the money had been stolen by the credit controller. An analysis revealed that $1.5 million had been stolen in the year to 31 March 20X7 with the rest being stolen in the current year. Dexon plc is not insured for this loss and it cannot be recovered from the credit controller, nor is it deductible for tax purposes.

(iv)    During the year the company's taxable temporary differences increased by $10 million of which $6 million related to the revaluation of the property. The deferred tax relating to the remainder of the increase in the temporary differences should be taken to profit or loss. The applicable income tax rate is 20%.

(v)     The above figures do not include the estimated provision for income tax on the profit for the year ended 31 March 20X8. After allowing for any adjustments required in items (i) to (iii), the directors have estimated the provision at $11.4 million (this is in addition to the deferred tax effects of item (iv)).

(vi)    Dividends totalling $15.5 million were paid during the year.

*Required*

Taking into account any adjustments required by items (i) to (vi) above:

(a)     Prepare a statement showing the recalculation of Dexon plc's profit for the year ended 31 March 20X8.

**(8 marks)**

(b)     Redraft the statement of financial position of Dexon plc as at 31 March 20X8.

**(12 marks)**

Notes to the financial statements are not required.

**(Total = 20 marks)**

# 296 Xtol Co (Jun14 amended)                                                36 mins

The following trial balance relates to Xtol Co at 31 March 20X4:

|  | $'000 | $'000 |
|---|---|---|
| Revenue |  | 490,000 |
| Cost of sales | 290,600 |  |
| Distribution costs | 33,500 |  |
| Administrative expenses | 36,800 |  |
| Loan note interest and dividends paid (notes(iv) and (v)) | 13,380 |  |
| Bank interest | 900 |  |
| 20-year leased property at cost | 100,000 |  |
| Plant and equipment at cost (note (ii)) | 155,500 |  |

|  | $'000 | $'000 |
|---|---|---|
| Accumulated amortisation/depreciation at 1 April 20X3: | | |
|     Leased property | | 25,000 |
|     Plant and equipment | | 43,500 |
| Inventories at 31 March 20X4 | 61,000 | |
| Trade receivables | 63,000 | |
| Trade payables | | 32,200 |
| Bank | | 5,500 |
| Equity shares of 25 cents each (note (iii)) | | 56,000 |
| Share premium | | 25,000 |
| Retained earnings at 1 April 20X3 | | 26,080 |
| 5% convertible loan note (note (iv)) | | 50,000 |
| Current tax (note (vi)) | 3,200 | |
| Deferred tax (note (vi)) | | 4,600 |
| | 757,880 | 757,880 |

The following notes are relevant:

(i) Revenue includes an amount of $20 million for cash sales made through Xtol Co's retail outlets during the year on behalf of Francais. Xtol Co, acting as agent, is entitled to a commission of 10% of the selling price of these goods. By 31 March 20X4, Xtol Co had remitted to Francais $15 million (of the $20 million sales) and recorded this amount in cost of sales.

(ii) Plant and equipment is depreciated at 12½% per annum on the reducing balance basis. All amortisation and depreciation of non-current assets is charged to cost of sales.

(iii) On 1 August 20X3, Xtol Co made a fully subscribed rights issue of equity share capital based on two new shares at 60 cents each for every five shares held. The issue has been fully recorded in the trial balance figures.

(iv) On 1 April 20X3, Xtol Co issued a 5% $50 million convertible loan note at par. Interest is payable annually in arrears on 31 March each year. The loan note is redeemable at par or convertible into equity shares at the option of the loan note holders on 31 March 20X6. The interest on an equivalent loan note without the conversion rights would be 8% per annum.

The present values of $1 receivable at the end of each year, based on discount rates of 5% and 8%, are:

| | | 5% | 8% |
|---|---|---|---|
| End of year | 1 | 0.95 | 0.93 |
| | 2 | 0.91 | 0.86 |
| | 3 | 0.86 | 0.79 |

(v) An equity dividend of 4 cents per share was paid on 30 May 20X3 and, after the rights issue, a further dividend of 2 cents per share was paid on 30 November 20X3.

(vi) The balance on current tax represents the under/over provision of the tax liability for the year ended 31 March 20X3. A provision of $28 million is required for current tax for the year ended 31 March 20X4 and at this date the deferred tax liability was assessed at $8.3 million.

*Required*

(a) Prepare the statement of profit or loss for Xtol Co for the year ended 31 March 20X4 **(8 marks)**

(b) Prepare the statement of financial position for Xtol Co for the year ended 31 March 20X4 **(12 marks)**

**(Total = 20 marks)**

# 297 Atlas Co

**36 mins**

The following trial balance relates to Atlas Co at 31 March 20X3.

|  | $'000 | $'000 |
|---|---|---|
| Equity shares of 50 cents each |  | 50,000 |
| Share premium |  | 20,000 |
| Retained earnings at 1 April 20X2 |  | 11,200 |
| Land and buildings – at cost (land $10 million) (note (i)) | 60,000 |  |
| Plant and equipment – at cost (note (i)) | 94,500 |  |
| Accumulated depreciation at 1 April 20X2:  – buildings |  | 20,000 |
|                         – plant and equipment |  | 24,500 |
| Inventories at 31 March 20X3 | 43,700 |  |
| Trade receivables | 42,200 |  |
| Bank |  | 6,800 |
| Deferred tax (note (ii)) |  | 6,200 |
| Trade payables |  | 35,100 |
| Revenue |  | 550,000 |
| Cost of sales | 411,500 |  |
| Distribution costs | 21,500 |  |
| Administrative expenses | 30,900 |  |
| Dividends paid | 20,000 |  |
| Bank interest | 700 |  |
| Current tax (note (ii)) |  | 1,200 |
|  | 725,000 | 725,000 |

The following notes are relevant:

(i) Non-current assets:

On 1 April 20X2, the directors of Atlas Co decided that the financial statements would show an improved position if the land and buildings were revalued to market value. At that date, an independent valuer valued the land at $12 million and the buildings at $35 million and these valuations were accepted by the directors. The remaining life of the buildings at that date was 14 years. Atlas Co does not make a transfer to retained earnings for excess depreciation. Ignore deferred tax on the revaluation surplus.

Plant and equipment is depreciated at 20% per annum using the reducing balance method and time apportioned as appropriate. All depreciation is charged to cost of sales, but none has yet been charged on any non-current asset for the year ended 31 March 20X3.

(ii) Atlas Co estimates that an income tax provision of $27.2 million is required for the year ended 31 March 20X3 and at that date the liability to deferred tax is $9.4 million. The movement on deferred tax should be taken to profit or loss. The balance on current tax in the trial balance represents the under/over provision of the tax liability for the year ended 31 March 20X2.

*Required*

(a) Prepare the statement of profit or loss and other comprehensive income for Atlas Co for the year ended 31 March 20X3. **(8 marks)**

(b) Prepare the statement of financial position of Atlas Co as at 31 March 20X3. **(10 marks)**

(c) Calculate basic earnings per share for the year ended 31 March 20X3. **(2 marks)**

**(Total = 20 marks)**

# 298 Moby Co (Dec13 amended)

36 mins

The following trial balance relates to Moby Co as at 30 September 20X3.

|  | $'000 | $'000 |
|---|---|---|
| Revenue |  | 227,800 |
| Cost of sales | 164,500 |  |
| Long-term contract (note (i)) | 4,000 |  |
| Distribution costs | 13,500 |  |
| Administrative expenses | 16,500 |  |
| Bank interest | 900 |  |
| Dividend | 2,000 |  |
| Lease rental paid on 30 September 20X3 (note (ii)) | 9,200 |  |
| Land ($12 million) and building ($48 million) at cost (note (ii)) | 60,000 |  |
| Owned plant and equipment at cost (note (ii)) | 65,700 |  |
| Leased plant at initial carrying amount (note (ii)) | 35,000 |  |
| Accumulated depreciation at 1 October 20X2: |  |  |
|     Building |  | 10,000 |
|     Owned plant and equipment |  | 17,700 |
|     Leased plant |  | 7,000 |
| Inventories at 30 September 20X3 | 26,600 |  |
| Trade receivables | 38,500 |  |
| Bank |  | 5,300 |
| Insurance provision (note (iii)) |  | 150 |
| Deferred tax (note (iv)) |  | 8,000 |
| Lease obligation at 1 October 20X2 (note (ii)) |  | 29,300 |
| Trade payables |  | 21,300 |
| Current tax (note (iv)) |  | 1,050 |
| Equity shares of 20 cents each |  | 45,800 |
| Share premium |  | 3,200 |
| Loan note (note (v)) |  | 40,000 |
| Retained earnings at 1 October 20X2 | – | 19,800 |
|  | 436,400 | 436,400 |

The following notes are relevant:

(i)     The balance on the long-term contract is made up of the following items.

Cost incurred to date                                             $14 million
Value of invoices issued (work certified)                 $10 million

The contract commenced on 1 October 20X2 and is for a fixed price of $25 million. Performance obligations are satisfied over time. The costs to complete the contract at 30 September 20X3 are estimated at $6 million. Moby Co's policy is to recognise satisfaction of performance obligations (and therefore accrue profits) on such contracts based on a stage of completion given by the work certified as a percentage of the contract price.

(ii)    Non-current assets:

Moby Co decided to revalue its land and buildings for the first time on 1 October 20X2. A qualified valuer determined the relevant revalued amounts to be $16 million for the land and $38.4 million for the building. The building's remaining life at the date of the revaluation was 16 years. This revaluation has not yet been reflected in the trial balance figures. Moby Co does not make a transfer from the revaluation surplus to retained earnings in respect of the realisation of the revaluation surplus. Deferred tax is applicable to the revaluation surplus at 25%.

The leased plant was acquired on 1 October 20X1 under a five-year lease which has an implicit interest rate of 10% per annum. The rentals are $9.2 million per annum payable on 30 September each year.

Owned plant and equipment is depreciated at 12.5% per annum using the reducing balance method.

No depreciation has yet been charged on any non-current asset for the year ended 30 September 20X3. All depreciation is charged to cost of sales.

(iii) On 1 October 20X2 Moby Co received a renewal quote of $400,000 from the company's property insurer. The directors were surprised at how much it had increased and believed it would be less expensive for the company to 'self-insure'. Accordingly, they charged $400,000 to administrative expenses and credited the same amount to the insurance provision. During the year, the company incurred $250,000 of expenses relating to previously insured property damage which it has debited to the provision.

(iv) A provision for income tax for the year ended 30 September 20X3 of $3.4 million is required. The balance on current tax represents the under/over provision of the tax liability for the year ended 30 September 20X2. At 30 September 20X3 the tax base of Moby Co's net assets was $24 million less than their carrying amounts. This does not include the effect of the revaluation in note 2 above. The income tax rate of Moby Co is 25%.

(v) The $40 million loan note was issued at par on 1 October 20X2. No interest will be paid on the loan; however it will be redeemed on 30 September 20X5 for $53,240,000, which gives an effective finance cost of 10% per annum.

(vi) A share issue was made on 31 December 20X2 of 4 million shares for $1 per share. It was correctly accounted for.

*Required*

(a) Prepare the statement of profit or loss and other comprehensive income for Moby Co for the year ended 30 September 20X3. **(13 marks)**

(b) Prepare the statement of changes in equity for Moby Co for the year ended 30 September 20X3. **(7 marks)**

**(Total = 20 marks)**

# 299 Dickson Co                                        36 mins

Below are the statements of financial position of Dickson Co as at 31 March 20X8 and 31 March 20X7, together with the statement of profit or loss and other comprehensive income for the year ended 31 March 20X8.

|  | 20X8 $'000 | 20X7 $'000 |
|---|---|---|
| *Non-current assets* | | |
| Property, plant and equipment | 925 | 737 |
| Development expenditure | 290 | 160 |
| | 1,215 | 897 |
| *Current assets* | | |
| Inventories | 360 | 227 |
| Trade receivables | 274 | 324 |
| Investments | 143 | 46 |
| Cash and cash equivalents | 29 | 117 |
| | 806 | 714 |
| Total assets | 2,021 | 1,611 |
| *Equity* | $'000 | $'000 |
| Share capital – $1 ordinary shares | 500 | 400 |
| Share premium | 350 | 100 |
| Revaluation surplus | 160 | 60 |
| Retained earnings | 229 | 255 |
| | 1,239 | 815 |
| *Non-current liabilities* | | |
| 6% debentures | 150 | 100 |
| Lease liabilities | 100 | 80 |
| Deferred tax | 48 | 45 |
| | 298 | 225 |

| | 20X8 | 20X7 |
|---|---|---|
| *Current liabilities* | | |
| Trade payables | 274 | 352 |
| Lease liabilities | 17 | 12 |
| Current tax | 56 | 153 |
| Debenture interest | 5 | – |
| Bank overdraft | 132 | 54 |
| | 484 | 571 |
| Total equity and liabilities | 2,021 | 1,611 |

STATEMENT OF PROFIT OR LOSS AND OTHER COMPREHENSIVE INCOME

| | $'000 |
|---|---|
| Revenue | 1,476 |
| Cost of sales | (962) |
| Gross profit | 514 |
| Other expenses | (157) |
| Finance costs | (15) |
| Profit before tax | 342 |
| Income tax expense | (162) |
| Profit for the year | 180 |
| Other comprehensive income: | |
| Gain on revaluation of property, plant and equipment | 100 |
| Total comprehensive income for the year | 280 |

**Notes**

1    During 20X8, amortisation of $60,000 was charged on development projects.

2    During 20X8 items of property, plant and equipment with a carrying amount of $103,000 were sold for $110,000. Profit on sale was netted off against 'other expenses'.

     Depreciation charged in the year on property, plant and equipment totalled $57,000. Dickson Co acquired $56,000 of property, plant and equipment by means of leases, payments being made in arrears on the last day of each accounting period.

3    The current asset investments are government bonds and management has decided to class them as cash equivalents.

4    The new debentures were issued on 1 April 20X7. Finance cost includes debenture interest and lease finance charges only.

5    During the year Dickson Co made a 1 for 8 bonus issue, capitalising its retained earnings, followed by a rights issue.

*Required*

(a)    Prepare a statement of cash flows for Dickson Co in accordance with IAS 7 using the indirect method.

(b)    Prepare (additionally) net cash from operating activities using the direct method.    **(20 marks)**

# 300 Mocha Co (Dec11 amended)                                36 mins

(a)    The following information relates to the draft financial statements of Mocha Co:

SUMMARISED STATEMENTS OF FINANCIAL POSITION AS AT 30 SEPTEMBER

|  | 20X1 $'000 | 20X0 $'000 |
|---|---|---|
| ASSETS | | |
| *Non-current assets* | | |
| Property, plant and equipment (note (i)) | 32,600 | 24,100 |
| Financial asset: equity investments (note (ii)) | 4,500 | 7,000 |
| | 37,100 | 31,100 |
| *Current assets* | | |
| Inventories | 10,200 | 7,200 |
| Trade receivables | 3,500 | 3,700 |
| Cash and cash equivalents | nil | 1,400 |
| | 13,700 | 12,300 |
| Total assets | 50,800 | 43,400 |
| EQUITY AND LIABILITIES | | |
| *Equity* | | |
| Equity shares of $1 each (note (iii)) | 14,000 | 8,000 |
| Share premium (note (iii)) | nil | 2,000 |
| Revaluation reserve (note (iii)) | 2,000 | 3,600 |
| Retained earnings | 13,000 | 10,100 |
| | 29,000 | 23,700 |
| *Non-current liabilities* | | |
| Lease obligations | 7,000 | 6,900 |
| Deferred tax | 1,300 | 900 |
| *Current liabilities* | | |
| Tax | 1,000 | 1,200 |
| Bank overdraft | 2,900 | nil |
| Provision for product warranties (note (iv)) | 1,600 | 4,000 |
| Lease obligations | 4,800 | 2,100 |
| Trade payables | 3,200 | 4,600 |
| Total equity and liabilities | 50,800 | 43,400 |

SUMMARISED STATEMENTS OF PROFIT OR LOSS FOR THE YEARS ENDED 30 SEPTEMBER:

|  | 20X1 $'000 | 20X0 $'000 |
|---|---|---|
| Revenue | 58,500 | 41,000 |
| Cost of sales | (46,500) | (30,000) |
| Gross profit | 12,000 | 11,000 |
| Operating expenses | (8,700) | (4,500) |
| Investment income (note (ii)) | 1,100 | 700 |
| Finance costs | (500) | (400) |
| Profit before tax | 3,900 | 6,800 |
| Income tax expense | (1,000) | (1,800) |
| Profit for the year | 2,900 | 5,000 |

The following additional information is available.

(i)     Property, plant and equipment

|  | Cost | Accumulated depreciation | Carrying amount |
|---|---|---|---|
|  | $'000 | $'000 | $'000 |
| At 30 September 20X0 | 33,600 | (9,500) | 24,100 |
| Additions to right-of use assets | 6,700 |  | 6,700 |
| Purchase of new plant | 8,300 |  | 8,300 |
| Disposal of property | (5,000) | 1,000 | (4,000) |
| Depreciation for the year |  | (2,500) | (2,500) |
| At 30 September 20X1 | 43,600 | (11,000) | 32,600 |

The property disposed of was sold for $8.1 million.

(ii)    Investments/investment income:

During the year an investment that had a carrying amount of $3 million was sold for $3.4 million. No investments were purchased during the year.

Investment income consists of:

| Year to 30 September: | 20X1 | 20X0 |
|---|---|---|
|  | $'000 | $'000 |
| Dividends received | 200 | 250 |
| Profit on sale of investment | 400 | nil |
| Increases in fair value | 500 | 450 |
|  | 1,100 | 700 |

(iii)   On 1 April 20X1 there was a bonus issue of shares that was funded from the share premium and some of the revaluation reserve. This was followed on 30 April 20X1 by an issue of shares for cash at par.

(iv)    The movement in the product warranty provision has been included in cost of sales.

*Required*

Prepare a statement of cash flows for Mocha Co for the year ended 30 September 20X1, in accordance with IAS 7 *Statement of Cash Flows*, using the indirect method.                                    **(20 marks)**

# 301 Hassle Co

Hassle Co is a large public company that would like to acquire (100% of) a suitable private company. It has obtained the following draft financial statements for two companies, Astral Co and Breakout Co. They operate in the same industry, which is clothing manufacturing within the fashion sector. Both companies compete in the younger, high turnover, discount fashion markets.

## STATEMENTS OF PROFIT OR LOSS FOR THE YEAR ENDED 30 SEPTEMBER 20X8

|  | Astral Co | Breakout Co |
|---|---|---|
|  | $'000 | $'000 |
| Revenue | 12,000 | 20,500 |
| Cost of sales | (10,500) | (18,000) |
| Gross profit | 1,500 | 2,500 |
| Operating expenses | (240) | (500) |
| Finance costs – loan | (210) | (300) |
|     – overdraft | Nil | (10) |
|     – lease | Nil | (290) |
| Profit before tax | 1,050 | 1,400 |
| Income tax expense | (150) | (400) |
| Profit for the year | 900 | 700 |
|  |  |  |
| **Note.** Dividends were paid during the year | 250 | 700 |

## STATEMENTS OF FINANCIAL POSITION AS AT 30 SEPTEMBER 20X8

|  | Astral Co | Breakout Co |
|---|---|---|
|  | $'000 | $'000 |
| *Assets* |  |  |
| *Non-current assets* |  |  |
| Freehold factory (Note 1) | 4,400 | Nil |
| Owned plant (Note 2) | 5,000 | 2,200 |
| Leased plant (Note 2) | Nil | 5,300 |
|  | 9,400 | 7,500 |
|  |  |  |
| *Current assets* |  |  |
| Inventory | 2,000 | 3,600 |
| Trade receivables | 2,400 | 3,700 |
| Bank | 600 | Nil |
|  | 5,000 | 7,300 |
|  |  |  |
| Total assets | 14,400 | 14,800 |
|  |  |  |
| *Equity and liabilities* |  |  |
| Equity shares of $1 each | 2,000 | 2,000 |
| Property revaluation reserve | 900 | Nil |
| Retained earnings | 2,600 | 800 |
|  | 3,500 | 800 |
|  | 5,500 | 2,800 |
|  |  |  |
| *Non-current liabilities* |  |  |
| Lease obligations (Note 3) | Nil | 3,200 |
| 7% loan notes | 3,000 | Nil |
| 10% loan notes | Nil | 3,000 |
| Deferred tax | 600 | 100 |
| Government grants | 1,200 | Nil |
|  | 4,800 | 6,300 |

|  | Astral Co<br>$'000 | Breakout Co<br>$'000 |
|---|---|---|
| *Current liabilities* | | |
| Bank overdraft | Nil | 1,200 |
| Trade payables | 3,100 | 3,800 |
| Government grants | 400 | Nil |
| Finance lease obligations (Note 3) | Nil | 500 |
| Taxation | 600 | 200 |
| | 4,100 | 5,700 |
| *Total equity and liabilities* | 14,400 | 14,800 |

**Notes**

1     Both companies operate from similar premises.

2     Additional details of the two companies' plant are:

|  | Astral Co<br>$'000 | Breakout Co<br>$'000 |
|---|---|---|
| Owned plant – cost | 8,000 | 10,000 |
| Leased plant – original fair value | Nil | 7,500 |

There were no disposals of plant during the year by either company.

3     The interest rate implicit within Breakout Co's leases is 7.5% per annum. For the purpose of calculating ROCE and gearing, all lease obligations are treated as long-term interest bearing borrowings.

4     The following ratios have been calculated for Astral Co and can be taken to be correct:

| | |
|---|---|
| Return on year end capital employed (ROCE) | 14.8% |
| (capital employed taken as shareholders' funds plus long-term interest bearing borrowings – see Note 3 above) | |
| Pre-tax return on equity (ROE) | 19.1% |
| Net asset (total assets less current liabilities) turnover | 1.2 times |
| Gross profit margin | 12.5% |
| Operating profit margin | 10.5% |
| Current ratio | 1.2:1 |
| Closing inventory holding period | 70 days |
| Trade receivables' collection period | 73 days |
| Trade payables' payment period (using cost of sales) | 108 days |
| Gearing (see Note 3 above) | 35.3% |
| Interest cover | 6 times |
| Dividend cover | 3.6 times |

*Required*

(a)     Calculate for Breakout Co the ratios equivalent to all those given for Astral Co above. **(8 marks)**

(b)     Assess the relative performance and financial position of Astral Co and Breakout Co for the year ended 30 September 20X8 to inform the directors of Hassle Co in their acquisition decision. **(12 marks)**

# Answers

# Section A

## Conceptual framework

1    C    A resource controlled by an entity as a result of past events and from which future economic benefits are expected to flow to the entity

2    C    This is a valid liability.

             The licence payment could be avoided by ceasing manufacture.

             The fall in value of the investment is a loss chargeable to profit or loss.

             Planned expenditure does not constitute an obligation.

3    B    The amount that could be obtained from selling the asset, less any costs of disposal

4    A    The underlying assumption is going concern.

5    C    Comparability

             Disclosure of accounting policies is particularly important when comparing the results and performance of one entity against another which may be applying different policies.

6       To assist the IASB in the preparation and review of IFRS

             To assist auditors in forming an opinion on whether financial statements comply with IFRS

             To assist in determining the treatment of items not covered by an existing IFRS

             It is not to be authoritative where a specific IFRS conflicts with the *Conceptual Framework* as the Conceptual Framework will be overridden if there is a specific IFRS. Whenever there is a conflict between an IFRS and the *Conceptual Framework*, the IFRS takes precedence.

7    D    A receivable from a customer which has been sold (factored) to a finance company. The finance company has full recourse to the company for any losses.

             The receivable has been factored with recourse so should continue to be recognised as an asset. The other options do not meet the criteria to be recognised as an asset.

8    D    Applying an entity's current accounting policy to a transaction which an entity has not engaged in before

             As the transaction has not been engaged in before, comparability is not an issue.

## Regulatory framework

9    A    Publication of an Exposure Draft

             An Exposure Draft will be published following the review of Discussion Paper comments.

10    C    Accountants and auditors would have more defence in case of litigation.

             Accountants and auditors may have **less** defence in case of litigation as they will not be able to demonstrate that they followed some precise rule, but will instead have to defend their application of judgement.

11    A rules-based system will tend to give rise to a larger number of accounting standards than a principles-based system.

             A principles-based system requires the exercise of more judgement in application than a rules-based system.

# Accounting for inflation

**12    C    It avoids the overstatement of profit which can arise during periods of inflation**

Historical cost accounting does not avoid the overstatement of profit which arises during periods of inflation, which is why alternative models have been proposed.

**13    C    Reduced dividends to shareholders**

The other options are all likely consequences of overstatement of profits.

In the case of C, what tends to happen when profits are overstated is that **too much** cash is paid out in dividends to shareholders, depleting funds needed for investment.

**14    B    $320,000 Historical cost; $384,000 current cost**

|  | Historical cost $'000 | Current cost $'000 |
|---|---|---|
| Cost/valuation | 500 | 600 |
| Depreciation ((500,000 × 90%) /5) × 2 | (180) | |
| Depreciation ((600,000 × 90%) /5) × 2 | | (216) |
| Carrying amount | 320 | 384 |

**15    A    Current cost accounting**

The concept of 'physical capital maintenance' is applied in current cost accounting.

**16    B    Current purchasing power accounting**

Current purchasing power accounting adjusts for general price inflation.

**17    B    Replacement cost**

Under CCA goods sold are charged to profit or loss at replacement cost.

# Section B

# Lisbon Co OTQ case

**18    C    The *Conceptual Framework* requires information to be presented understandably, but without omitting complex issues.**

**19    A    Faithful representation. The substance of the transaction is likely to be that of a secured loan.**

**20    C    Relevance. The historical cost of the properties will be less relevant than their current value.**

**21    C    The financial statements should be prepared on a different basis. The basis of valuation of assets will be affected.**

**22    D    This is a change of accounting policy so the information will be amended retrospectively.**

# Section A

## Tangible non-current assets

| 23 | B | | $'000 |
|----|---|---|---|
| | | Land | 1,200 |
| | | Materials | 2,400 |
| | | Labour | 3,000 |
| | | Architects fees | 25 |
| | | Surveyors fees | 15 |
| | | Site overheads | 300 |
| | | Testing fire alarms | 10 |
| | | | 6,950 |

24  A  Weighted average capitalisation rate =

$(9\% \times 15 / 39) + (11\% \times 24 / 39) = 3.5\% + 6.8\% = 10.3\%$

| | | | $ |
|---|---|---|---|
| Borrowing costs = | | $6m × 10.3% × 9/12 | 463,500 |
| | + | $2m × 10.3% × 5/12 | 85,833 |
| | | | 549,333 |

25  A

| | $ |
|---|---|
| Borrowing costs March – December ($2.4m × 8% × 10 / 12) | 160,000 |
| Less investment income ($1m × 6% × 4/12) | (20,000) |
| | 140,000 |

26  C  A property held by Build Co as a right-of-use asset and leased out under a six-month lease

The property intended for sale and the property being constructed would be classified as inventory and WIP. The property leased out to a subsidiary would be regarded as an investment property in the single entity financial statements of Build Co but is treated as owner occupied in the **consolidated** financial statements.

27  A gain or loss arising from a change in the fair value of an investment property should be recognised in other comprehensive income.

The gain or loss arising from a change in the fair value of an investment property should be recognised in profit or loss.

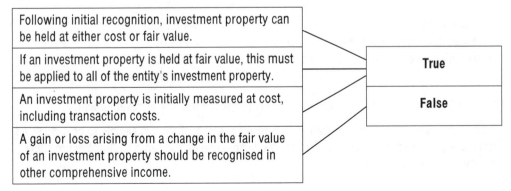

28  D  $2,200,000

Weighted capitalisation rate =

$(10\% \times 140 / 340) + (8\% \times 200 / 340) = 4.1\% + 4.7\% = 8.8\%$

$50 million × 8.8% × 6/ 12 = $2.2 million

29    $37,250

|                                                  | $'000  |
|--------------------------------------------------|--------|
| Machine ((500,000 – 20,000) / 10 × 9/12)         | 36,000 |
| Safety guard ((25,000/5) × 3 / 12)               | 1,250  |
|                                                  | 37,250 |

30    C    Capitalised and depreciated over the period to the next overhaul

The expenditure should be capitalised when it takes place and depreciated over the period to the next overhaul. It should not be provided for in advance because there is no obligation arising from a past event – the overhaul could be avoided by ceasing to operate the aircraft.

31    $4,765

The machine has been owned for 2 years 3 months, so the remaining useful life at 31 March 20X9 was 12 years 9 months.

Prior to revaluation it was being depreciated at $4,000 pa (60,000 / 15), so the charge for the first three months of 20X9 was $1,000.

The machine will now be depreciated over the remaining 12 years 9 months = 153 months. So the charge for the remaining 9 months of 20X9 is $3,765 ((64,000 / 153) × 9).

So total depreciation for the year ended 31.12.X9 is (1,000 + 3,765) = $4,765

32    $203,000

|                                                  | $         |
|--------------------------------------------------|-----------|
| Cost 1.1.X0                                      | 900,000   |
| Depreciation to 30.6.X8 (900,000 × 8.5 / 50)     | (153,000) |
| Carrying amount 30.6.X8                          | 747,000   |
| Revaluation surplus                              | 203,000   |
| Fair value 30.6.X8                               | 950,000   |

The increase of (1,200 – 950) = $250,000 arising between 30.6.X8 and 31.12.X8 will be credited to profit or loss in accordance with IAS 40.

# Intangible assets

33    D    In order for capitalisation to be allowed it is not necessary for development to be completed, patents to be registered or sales contracts signed. However, an intangible asset can only be recognised if its cost can be reliably measured.

34    C

|                                                  | $         |
|--------------------------------------------------|-----------|
| Research costs                                   | 1,400,000 |
| Expensed development Jan–Mar (800 × 3)           | 2,400,000 |
| Depreciation on capitalised amount b/f (20m × 20%) | 4,000,000 |
|                                                  | 7,800,000 |

Note that no depreciation is charged on the new project as it is still in development.

35    B    A pre-production prototype is classified as a development cost, so it is eligible to be capitalised. Internally generated customer lists and goodwill cannot be capitalised. IAS 38 does not allow capitalisation of research costs.

36    $12,500

|                                                        | $'000   |
|--------------------------------------------------------|---------|
| Recoverable amount – fair value less costs of disposal | 15,000  |
| Less depreciation 1.4.X9 – 30.9.X9 (15m / 3 × 6/12)    | ( 2,500) |
|                                                        | 12,500  |

37    $88,000

|                                                        | $      |
|--------------------------------------------------------|--------|
| Expenses 1 January to 1 March (40,000 × 2)             | 80,000 |
| 4 months capitalised and amortised                     |        |
| ((40,000 × 4) / 5 years × 3/12)                        | 8,000  |
|                                                        | 88,000 |

# Impairment of assets

38    C    $594,000

|                                      | $'000 |
|--------------------------------------|-------|
| Total impairment (1,010 – 750)       | 260   |
| Goodwill                             | (90)  |
| Damaged plant                        | (40)  |
| Balance to allocate                  | 130   |

The remaining $130,000 will be allocated pro rata as follows:

|            | Building | Plant  |
|------------|----------|--------|
|            | $'000    | $'000  |
|            | 700      | 160    |
| Impairment | (106)    | (24)   |
|            | 594      |        |

39    C    The higher of fair value less costs of disposal and value in use

40    $7,687

| Fair value less costs of disposal (78,000 – 2,500) | $75,500 |
|----------------------------------------------------|---------|

Value in use:     $30,000 × 1 / 1.08  = 27,778$
                  $30,000 × 1 / 1.08^2 = 25,720$
                  $30,000 × 1 / 1.08^3 = 23,815$     $77,313

Recoverable amount is $77,313 and carrying amount is $85,000, so impairment is $7,687.

41    An unusually significant fall in the market value of one or more assets
      An increase in the market interest rates used to calculate value in use of the assets

      The other options are internal indicators of impairment.

42    $350,000

|                                                       | $          |
|-------------------------------------------------------|------------|
| Fair value less costs of disposal (2.7m – 50,000)     | 2,650,000  |
| Value in use                                          | 2,600,000  |
|                                                       |            |
| Recoverable amount is therefore:                      | 2,650,000  |
| Impairment loss (β)                                   | 350,000    |
| Carrying amount                                       | 3,000,000  |

43    A    $8 million

|                      | $m  | $m   | $m  |
|----------------------|-----|------|-----|
| Goodwill             | 3   | (3)  | –   |
| Patent               | 5   | (3)  | 2   |
| Property             | 10  | (2)  | 8   |
| Plant and equipment  | 15  | (3)  | 12  |
| Current assets       | 2   | –    | 2   |
|                      | 35  | (11) | 24  |

The goodwill is written off, the patent is written down and the remaining $5m impairment is allocated
pro rata to the property and the plant.

**44    A    $17,785**

|  |  | $ |
|---|---|---:|
| Carrying amount (100,000 × 5/10) |  | 50,000 |
| Fair value less costs to sell |  | 30,000 |
| Value in use (8,500 × 3.79) |  | 32,215 |

Recoverable amount is $32,215 and impairment loss = 50,000 – 32,215 = $17,785

**45    A    $154,545**

|  | Net assets prior to impairment | Impairment | Impaired net assets |
|---|---:|---:|---:|
|  | $ | $ | $ |
| Property, plant and equipment | 200,000 | (45,455) | 154,545 |
| Goodwill | 50,000 | (50,000) | – |
| Product patent | 20,000 | (4,545) | 15,455 |
| Net current assets | 30,000 | – | 30,000 |
|  | 300,000 | (100,000) | 200,000 |

Goodwill is written off in full and the balance of the loss is pro-rated between PPE and the patent.

**46    D    The estimated net realisable value of inventory has been reduced due to fire damage although this value is greater than its carrying amount**

If the NRV of inventory is greater than its carrying amount, no impairment has arisen.

# Section B

# Plethora plc OTQ case

**47    $314,000**
*Building transferred to investment property*

|  | $'000 |
|---|---:|
| Original cost | 600 |
| Depreciation 1.1.X0 to 1.7.X9 ((600 / 50) × 9.5) | (114) |
| Carrying amount at 1.7.X9 | 486 |
| Revaluation surplus | 314 |
| Fair value | 800 |

**48    A    Credited to profit or loss**

The increase in value in this case of $190,000 (740,000 – 550,000) will be credited to profit or loss in accordance with IAS 40.

**49    Recoverable amount**

This is the higher of fair value less costs of disposal and value in use.

**50    B    $70,000**

The impairment loss is not allocated to current assets.

## 51    D    $825,000

|  | Prior to review $'000 | After review $'000 |
|---|---|---|
| Building | 900 | 825 |
| Plant and equipment | 300 | 275 |
| Inventories | 70 | 70 |
| Other current assets | 130 | 130 |
| Goodwill | 40 | – |
|  | 1,440 | 1,300 |
| Recoverable amount | (1,300) |  |
| Impairment loss | 140 |  |

The impairment loss is allocated first against goodwill and then pro rata against the tangible non-current assets. This means writing $75,000 off the carrying amount of the building and $25,000 off plant and equipment.

# Dearing Co OTQ case

## 52    B    $920,000
*Cost price*

|  | $ |
|---|---|
| Base price | 1,050,000 |
| Trade discount (1,050,000 × 20%) | (210,000) |
|  | 840,000 |
| Freight charges | 30,000 |
| Electrical installation cost | 28,000 |
| Pre-production testing | 22,000 |
|  | 920,000 |

## 53    A    Added to the carrying amount of the machine

They should be added to the carrying amount of the machine as they cannot be capitalised as a separate asset (per IAS 16 para.8 they should be capitalised with the relevant PPE to which they relate). Spare parts will normally be expensed, however, upgrades and major spare parts that will be used over more than one period should be capitalised. They would not be debited to accumulated depreciation as they increase the cost of the item, rather than reducing the depreciation to date.

## 54    C    The cost of the overhaul should be capitalised and amortised over the period to the next overhaul

Per IAS 16, para.8 any major upgrades or revisions to the capital items should be capitalised and depreciated over the useful life of the asset.

## 55    A    The economic performance of the machine had declined
The other options are **external** indicators of impairment.

## 56    B    $820,000

Fair value less costs of disposal

# Elite Leisure Co OTQ case

## 57    A    $279m

|  | Cost $m | Dep'n period | Dep'n to date | Carrying amount |
|---|---|---|---|---|
| Ships fabric | 300 | 8/25 | (96) | 204 |
| Cabins etc | 150 | 8/12 | (100) | 50 |
| Propulsion | 100 | 30/40 hrs | (75) | 25 |
|  |  |  |  | 279 |

## 58    A    $14m   (140m × 5,000/50,000)

## 59    $45m (Repainting $20m + Loss on disposal $25m)

60    D    Capitalise the cost when incurred and amortise over five years

IAS 16 paragraph 13-14 refers specifically to when assets may require substantial inspections and/or overhauls on a periodic basis ' When each major inspection is performed, its cost is recognised in the <u>carrying amount</u> of the item of property, plant and equipment as a replacement'(IAS 16, para.13)

61    $290,000

(250 + 40) At 55% losing the case is 'probable' so must be provided for.

# Dexterity Co OTQ case

62    A    Patent for new drug and licence for the new vaccine may be recognised under IAS 38 *Intangible Assets* as an internally generated assets.

The training courses should be charged to profit or loss.  IAS 38 states that training costs must be expensed as employees do not represent a resource controlled by the entity and therefore cannot recognise the training costs as an intangible asset (IAS 38, para.15)

63    D    The asset will generate probable future economic benefits

The asset does not need to be completed or the proceeds reliably measured.  Paragraph 57 of IAS 38 states that in order to recognise this as a development cost, and as an intangible asset, it must 'generate probable future economic benefits'.

64    C    The design of possible new or improved product or process alternatives

This activity is still at the research stage

65    B    $9,375,000

($10m − (($10m/8) × 6/12))

66    B    It should be capitalised and reviewed for impairment every year.

IAS 36 *Impairment of Assets* (para.10) requires that this type of intangible assets are tested for impairment on an annual basis, whether or not there is any indication of impairment.

# Advent Co OTQ case

67    A    $256m

|  |  | $m |
|---|---|---|
| Land |  | 85 |
| Building | 180 × 19/20 | 171 |
|  |  | 256 |

68    D    $35m

|  |  | $m |
|---|---|---|
| Existing plant | 150 × 20% | 30 |
| New plant | 50 × 10% | 5 |
|  |  | 35 |

69    B    Professional qualifications of valuer

There is no requirement to disclose the professional qualifications of the valuer.

70    $140m

|  | $m |
|---|---|
| Balance 1.10.X8 | 270 |
| Depreciation to 30.9.X9 | (30) |
|  | 240 |
| Impairment loss (β) | (140) |
| Recoverable amount | 100 |

71    A    Higher of fair value less costs of disposal and value in use

As stated in IAS 36 *Impairment of Assets*, para.22.  The other options are not in line with the accounting standard.

# Systria Co OTQ case

72    $40,000

|                       | Original $'000 | Impairment $'000 |                |
|-----------------------|----------------|------------------|----------------|
| Goodwill              | 50             | (50)             |                |
| Patent                | 10             | (10)             |                |
| Land and buildings    | 100            | (20)             | Remaining 30   |
| Plant and machinery   | 50             | (10)             | pro rata       |
| Net current assets    | 10             | –                |                |
|                       |                | (90)             |                |

73    There are adverse changes to the use to which the asset is put.

The operating performance of the asset has declined.

Depreciation is irrelevant and the other options is an **external** indicator of impairment.

74    $1.5 million

Recoverable amount is $6 million, leaving an impairment loss of $4 million.
$2.5 million will be allocated to the destroyed assets and the remaining $1.5 million written off against goodwill.
$3 million – $1.5 million = $1.5 million.

75

|                          | Debit     | Credit    |
|--------------------------|-----------|-----------|
| Accumulated depreciation | $20,000   |           |
| Property at cost         | $30,000   |           |
| Revaluation surplus      |           | $50,000   |

The depreciation is written off and the balance added to the cost of the property.

76    C    $3,250

Depreciation to date of $20,000 means the property has 40 years of useful life left at the revaluation date. Depreciation will be $130,000/40.

# Section A

# Revenue

77    A    $271,000 contract asset

|                          | $           |
|--------------------------|-------------|
| Costs incurred to date   | 740,000     |
| Recognised profits (W)   | 231,000     |
| Amounts invoiced         | (700,000)   |
| Contract asset           | 271,000     |

|                          | $           |
|--------------------------|-------------|
| Working                  |             |
| Total contract revenue   | 2,800,000   |
| Costs to date            | (740,000)   |
| Costs to complete        | (1,400,000) |
| Total expected profit    | 660,000     |
| Profit to date (660,000 × 35%) | 231,000 |

| 78 | C | Set up the grant as deferred income |
| | | Deduct the grant from the carrying amount of the asset |

The grant can be treated as deferred income or deducted from the carrying amount of the asset. It cannot be credited directly to profit or loss.

| 79 | A | | $'000 |
|---|---|---|---|
| | | Total contract revenue | 50,000 |
| | | Costs to date | (12,000) |
| | | Specialist plant | (8,000) |
| | | Costs to complete | (10,000) |
| | | Total profit on contract | 20,000 |

Profit to date = $20m × 22 / 50 = $8,800,000

| 80 | A | $8,400 | $ |
|---|---|---|---|
| | | Costs incurred to date | 48,000 |
| | | Recognised profits (W) | 10,800 |
| | | Amounts invoiced | (50,400) |
| | | Contract asset | 8,400 |

*Working*
| | |
|---|---|
| Total contract revenue | 120,000 |
| Costs to date | (48,000) |
| Costs to complete | (48,000) |
| Total expected profit | 24,000 |
| Profit to date (24,000 × 45%) | 10,800 |

| 81 | B | The seller has no further exposure to the risks of ownership |

This feature suggests that the transaction is a genuine sale.

If the seller retains the right to use the asset or it remains on his premises, then the risks and rewards have not been transferred, so control of the asset has not been transferred. If the sale price does not equal market value, then the transaction is likely to be a secured loan.

| 82 | A | $1 million contract liability |

| | $m |
|---|---|
| Contract price | 12 |
| Total costs (6 + 9) | (15) |
| Foreseeable loss | (3) |

| | |
|---|---|
| Costs to date | 6 |
| Foreseeable loss | (3) |
| Amounts invoiced | (4) |
| Contract liability | (1) |

| 83 | D | Do not include anything in revenue for the year |
| | | Show $90,000 as a current liability |

No sale has taken place as control of the goods has not been transferred, but Cambridge Co must show that it is holding $90,000 which belongs to Circus Co.

| 84 | C | Sales of $150,000 on 30 September 20X4. The amount invoiced to and received from the customer was $180,000, which included $30,000 for ongoing servicing work to be done by Repro Co over the next two years. |

The amount to recognise in revenue is $150,000 as the servicing amount of $30,000 has not yet been earned. This would be recognised as deferred income.

85    B    $160,000

Expected profit = ($5m − ($2.4m + $1.6m)) = $1m
Profit to date = ($1m × (1.8m/5)) = $0.36m

Contract asset:

|  | $'000 |
|---|---|
| Costs to date | 1,600 |
| Profit to date | 360 |
| Less amounts invoiced | (1,800) |
|  | 160 |

86        Manufacturer can require dealer to return the inventory
Manufacturer bears obsolescence risk

These both indicate that the manufacturer retains ownership of the inventory. The other options
would indicate that the risks and rewards have been transferred to the dealer.

87        $75,000

|  | $ |
|---|---|
| Grant received 1.4.X6 | 400,000 |
| Recognised year to 31.3.X7 (400,000 × 25%) | (100,000) |
| Balance 31.3.X7 | 300,000 |
| Recognised year to 31.3.X8 (300,000 × 25%) | 75,000 |

88        $24,920,000

|  | $'000 |
|---|---|
| Revenue per draft profit or loss | 27,000 |
| Servicing costs (800 × 2 × 130%) | (2,080) |
|  | 24,920 |

# Introduction to groups

89    D    There is no basis on which a subsidiary may be excluded from consolidation.

90    C    Credited to profit or loss

IFRS 3 requires a bargain purchase to be credited to profit or loss as it is an economic gain. If the
consideration is higher than the net assets being purchased, that would constitute goodwill (not
taking the debit to the profit and loss). By taking the bargain purchase to the profit and loss
immediately, IFRS 3 aims to restrict any excess being carried forwards.

91    C    Existence of significant influence.

The other options indicate control over a subsidiary as set out by IAS 27 *Consolidated and Separate
Financial Statements.*

92        A subsidiary with a different reporting date may prepare additional statements up to the group
reporting date for consolidation purposes.

Where a subsidiary's financial statements are drawn up to a different reporting date from those of the
parent, adjustments should be made for significant transactions or events occurring between the two
reporting dates.

The allowable gap between reporting dates is three months, not five. IAS 27 allows subsidiaries to
have non-coterminous year ends, provided several criteria are met, including stating reasons why the
financial year end is different to the parent.

93    B    The price paid to acquire the asset.

94    B    The power to participate in the financial and operating policies of the investee

This is the definition of **significant influence**, not control.

95  D  Gamma Co is located in a country where a military coup has taken place and Petre Co has lost control of the investment for the foreseeable future

Consolidation is not appropriate in this case as the parent has lost control.

# Financial instruments

96  B  $1,524,000

|  | $'000 |
|---|---|
| Interest years 1–3 (30m × 8% × 2.49) | 5,976 |
| Repayment year 3 (30m × 0.75) | 22,500 |
| Debt component | 28,476 |
| Equity option (β) | 1,524 |
|  | 30,000 |

97  D  $21,495,000

|  | $'000 |
|---|---|
| Proceeds (20m – 0.5m) | 19,500 |
| Interest 10% | 1,950 |
| Interest paid (20m × 5%) | (1,000) |
| Balance 30 March 20X1 | 20,450 |
| Interest 10% | 2,045 |
| Interest paid (20m × 5%) | (1,000) |
|  | 21,495 |

98

| Fair value | with changes going through | profit or loss |
|---|---|---|

Fair value through OCI would be correct if an election had been made to recognise changes in value through other comprehensive income. Amortised cost is used for debt instruments, not equity instruments.

99  A  $514,560

|  | $ |
|---|---|
| 1 January 20X1 | 500,000 |
| Interest 8% | 40,000 |
| Interest received (550,000 × 6%) | (33,000) |
| 31 December 20X1 | 507,000 |
| Interest 8% | 40,560 |
| Interest received | (33,000) |
| 31 December 20X2 | 514,560 |

100  B  Intangible assets.

These do not give rise to a present right to receive cash or other financial assets. The other options are financial instruments.

101  $1,000,000

|  | $'000 |
|---|---|
| $12,500 × 1,296 / 1,200 | 13,500 |
| Carrying amount | (12,500) |
| Gain | 1,000 |

102  $240,000

|  | $ |
|---|---|
| 40,000 shares @ $6 | 240,000 |

Transaction costs are added to the initial cost but omitted from subsequent measurement.

# Leasing

**103**    C    $1,872,000

|  | $,000 |
|---|---|
| Right of Use Asset | |
| PV of future cashflows | 2,426 |
| Non refundable deposit | 700 |
| Right of Use asset | 3,126 |

|  |  |
|---|---|
| Lease liability (3,126-700) b/d 1.1.X6 | 2,426 |
| Interest at 6% | 146 |
| Balance of lease liability at 31 Dec 20X6 | 2,572 |

|  |  |
|---|---|
| Current | 700 |
| Non-current | 1,872 |
|  | 2,572 |

**104**    D    If it suits them to do so, the lessor can substitute an identical asset

The lessee does not have right of use of an identified asset as the lessor has substitution rights.

**105**    A    $5,132,000

|  | $'000 |
|---|---|
| Initial liability | 15,600 |
| Interest 8% | 1,248 |
| Payment | (6,000) |
| Total lease liability at 31.3.X8 | 10,848 |

To calculate the current lease liability as at 31.3.X7, take the total lease liability ($10,848,000), less the non-current portion.

To work out the non-current portion, continue the calculation to work out the liability at 31.3.X9:

|  |  |
|---|---|
| Lease liability at 31.3.X8 | 10,848 |
| Interest 8% | 868 |
| Payment | (6,000) |
| Balance 31.3.X9 | 5,716 |

Current liability = 10,848 – 5,716 = 5,132

**106**    C    Lease liability + other direct costs + prepayments – incentives

**107**    D    $3,850,000

|  | $'000 |
|---|---|
| Present value of future cashflows | 25,000 |
| Initial payment at commencement of lease | 2,000 |
| Right in use asset value | 27,000 |
| Cash payment at commencement of lease | (2,000) |
| Lease liability | 25,000 |
| Interest 10% (25,000 x 10% for the year end 30.9.X4) | 2,500 |
| Payment in arrears 30.9.X4 | (6,000) |
| Liability bfwd 1.10.X4 | 21,500 |
| Interest 10% (21,500 x 10% for the year end 30.9.X5) | 2,150 |
| Parent in arrears 30.9.X5 | (6,000) |
| Lease liability cfwd at 1.10.X5 | 17,650 |

To work out the non-current portion of the liability at 30/9/X4, we must take the calculation forward another year. The non-current portion of the year end liability of $21,500 is $17,650.

108 The lessee has the right to substantially all the economic benefits from use of the asset.

The agreement concerns an identified asset which cannot be substituted.

The lease term does not have to be for substantially all of the estimated useful life of the asset. If the lessor has the right to direct the use of the asset, the lessee does not have right of use, so it is not a lease within the scope of IFRS 16.

109 Nil

Tourmalet Co can direct the use of and obtain substantially all of the remaining benefits from the plant, so this does not meet the IFRS 15 criteria to be recognised as a sale. This is in substance a secured loan, so the asset will continue to be recognised at its carrying amount of $40m and a lease liability will be set up for $50m.

110 D Recognise proportion relating to right of use transferred.

111 $97,000

|  | $ |
| --- | --- |
| Lease interest ((340,000 – 90,000) × 10%) | 25,000 |
| Plant depreciation (340,000 / 5) | 68,000 |
| Short-term lease (18,000 × 2/9) | 4,000 |
| Total charge to profit or loss | 97,000 |

112 $20,256

|  | $ |
| --- | --- |
| Lease liability | 240,000 |
| Interest 12% | 28,800 |
| Payment | (100,000) |
| Balance 31.12.X6 | 168,800 |
| Interest to 31.12.X7 12% | 20,256 |

# Provisions and events after the reporting period

113 D $100,000

Loss of the case is not 'probable', so no provision is made, but the legal costs will have to be paid so should be provided for.

114 A Provision $2 million and $2 million capitalised as part of cost of mine

$2 million should be provided for and capitalised as part of the cost of the mine. It will then be depreciated over the useful life.

115 D Dudley Co has acquired a machine which requires a major overhaul every three years. The cost of the first overhaul is reliably estimated at $120,000

The cost of the overhaul will be capitalised when it takes place. No obligation exists before the overhaul is carried out. The other options would all give rise to valid provisions.

116 C Two lines of inventory held at the year end were discovered to have faults rendering them unsaleable

We can assume that these faults also existed at the year end, so this is the only option which would require adjustment. The others have all taken place after the year end.

117 B Provisions should be made for both constructive and legal obligations
Discounting may be used when estimating the amount of a provision
A restructuring provision may only be made when a company has a detailed plan for the restructuring and has communicated to interested parties a firm intention to carry it out

A restructuring provision must not include the costs of retraining or relocating staff.

118 The signing of a non-cancellable contract in September 20X4 to supply goods in the following year on which, due to a pricing error, a loss will be made.

An amount of deferred tax relating to the gain on revaluation of a property during the current year. Tynan Co has no intention of selling the property in the foreseeable future.

The reorganisation does not meet the criteria for a provision and a provision is no longer needed for the warranties.

**119**   $24,532,000

|                                          | $'000  |
|------------------------------------------|--------|
| Restoration of seabed (10,000 × 250)     | 2,500  |
| Dismantling of equipment (30m × 0.68)    | 20,400 |
| Unwinding of discount (20,400 × 8%)      | 1,632  |
|                                          | 24,532 |

**120**   $0.6 million

|                     | $m  |
|---------------------|-----|
| $2 million × 15%    | 0.3 |
| $6 million × 5%     | 0.3 |
|                     | 0.6 |

**121**   The discovery of a fraud which occurred during the year

The determination of the sale proceeds of an item of plant sold before the year end

These both provide evidence of conditions that existed at the end of the reporting period. The other options refer to conditions which arose after the reporting period and are therefore non-adjusting events according to IAS 10 *Events After the Reporting Period*.

# Inventories and biological assets

**122**   C   $95,100

| Product        | $      |
|----------------|--------|
| A   1,000 × 40 | 40,000 |
| B   2,500 × 15 | 37,500 |
| C     800 × 22 | 17,600 |
|                | 95,100 |

**123**   C   The item is becoming obsolete

As the item becomes obsolete we can expect its market price to fall – and eventually fall below cost. The other options would all maintain or improve the net realisable value of the item.

**124**   D   Fair value less estimated costs to sell

IAS 41 *Agriculture* requires biological assets to be measured on initial recognition at fair value less estimated costs to sell.

**125**   B   Harvest

Harvest is an intervention, not a biological process. Growth, procreation and degeneration are natural biological processes.

**126**   A   Included in profit or loss for the year

A gain or loss on a biological asset is included in profit or loss for the year.

**127**   D   None of them

Production overheads are allocated on the basis of a company's **normal** level of activity. Settlement discounts are not deducted to arrive at NRV. The LIFO formula is not allowed under IAS 2 *Inventories*. Valuation of finished goods should include production overheads.

**128**   A   IAS 10 *Events After the Reporting Period*

This may be relevant as agricultural produce is perishable and if prices have to be reduced after the year end, this will affect the year end valuation.

**129** $39.3 million

|  | $m |
|---|---|
| Per inventory count | 36.0 |
| Received after year end | (2.7) |
| Sold after year end (7.8m / 1.3) | 6.0 |
|  | 39.3 |

**130** $55,080    NRV − (12,000 × (5.4 × 85%)) = $55,080

# Accounting for taxation

**131**  C    $16.8million

|  | $'000 |
|---|---|
| Charge for year | 16,200 |
| Underprovision | 2,100 |
| Adjust deferred tax (W) | (1,500) |
| Profit or loss charge | 16,800 |

*Working*

|  | $'000 |
|---|---|
| Provision needed (13m × 30%) | 3,900 |
| Provision b/f | (5,400) |
| Reduce provision | (1,500) |

**132**  C    $1.2million

|  | $'000 |
|---|---|
| Prior year underprovision | 700 |
| Current provision | 4,500 |
| Movement of deferred tax (8.4 − 5.6) | (2,800) |
| Deferred tax on revaluation surplus | (1,200) |
| Tax liability for the year | 1,200 |

**133**  D    $345,000

|  | $'000 |
|---|---|
| B/f | 850 |
| Year to 31.12.X8 (500 − 450) | 50 |
| Revaluation surplus | 250 |
|  | 1,150 |
| × 30% | 345 |

**134**    $130 million

|  | $m |
|---|---|
| B/f (140 + 160) | 300 |
| Charge for year | 270 |
| C/f (310 + 130) | (440) |
| Tax paid | 130 |

**135**    $19 million

|  | $'000 |
|---|---|
| Current charge | 19,400 |
| Over-provision | (800) |
| Deferred tax (W) | 400 |
|  | 19,000 |

*Working*

|  | $'000 |
|---|---|
| Required provision | 6,750 |
| Less revaluation | (3,750) |
|  | 3,000 |
| Balance b/f | (2,600) |
| Charge to income tax | 400 |

# Section B

## Derringdo Co OTQ case

**136  C  $22,000**

| | $ |
|---|---:|
| *Operating expenses* | |
| Depreciation charge (800,000 × 85% × 10% × 6/12) | 34,000 |
| Release of grant (240,000 × 10% × 6/12) | (12,000) |
| | 22,000 |

**137  D  $204,000**

| | $ |
|---|---:|
| *Deferred income* | |
| Grant received ($800,000 × 30%) | 240,000 |
| Release for this year ($240,000 × 10% × 6/12) | (12,000) |
| Total balance at year end | 228,000 |
| | |
| *Presentation* | |
| Current liability ($240,000 × 10%) | 24,000 |
| Non-current liability (balance) | 204,000 |
| | 228,000 |

**138  A  $439**

| | $ |
|---|---:|
| *Year 1* | |
| Laptop (W) | 158 |
| Broadband (562 (W) /2) | 281 |
| | 439 |

*Working*

| | | | |
|---|---:|---:|---:|
| Laptop | 200 | 22% | 158 |
| Broadband (30 × 12 × 2) | 720 | 78% | 562 |
| | 920 | 100% | 720 |

**139  B**  Recognising revenue when a performance obligation is satisfied.

**140  B**  Derringdo Co is not exposed to credit risk for the amount due from the customer

The other options would all suggest that Derringdo Co was the principal.

## Bridgenorth Co OTQ Case

**141  $240,000**

| | $ |
|---|---:|
| Revenue   40% × 5,000,000 = | 2,000,000 |
| Expenses  40% × (2,300,000 + 2,100,000) = | (1,760,000) |
| | 240,000 |

**142  $500,000**   Work invoiced less cash received

**143  $1,125,000**

| | $ |
|---|---:|
| Costs to date | 3,600,000 |
| Profit to date ((5,000,000 − 4,300,000) × 75%) | 525,000 |
| | 4,125,000 |
| Less amounts invoiced | (3,000,000) |
| | 1,125,000 |

**144**  Costs incurred as a percentage of total expected costs

Work invoiced to date as a percentage of the total contract price

These are valid measures of the inputs expended to satisfy the performance obligation.

145  $400,000

Bridgenorth Co can recognise revenue to the extent of costs incurred to date.

# Apex Co OTQ case

146  D  An asset that takes a substantial period of time to get ready for use or sale

A qualifiying asset is defined as 'an asset that necessaily takes a substantial period of time to get ready for its intended use or sale' (IAS 23, para.5)

147  C  Physical construction of the asset is nearing completion

IAS 23 has no requirements in respect of the stage of completion of the asset

148  A  $625,000 (($10m 7.5%) × 10/12)

149  D  9.25%

|  | % |
|---|---|
| 10% × 50/80 | 6.25 |
| 8% × 30/80 | 3.00 |
|  | 9.25 |

150  C  Recognised as investment income in the statement of profit or loss

The investment proceeds were earned before construction began, so are not deducted from the borrowing costs which are being capitalised.

# Bertrand Co OTQ case

151  B  As debt and equity

152  C  $735,000

|  | $'000 |
|---|---|
| Interest payable ($10m × 5% × 2.58*) | 1,290 |
| Capital repayable ($10m × 0.79) | 7,900 |
| Debt element | 9,190 |
| Finance costs for year = 9,190 × 8% | 735 |

153  A  $9,425,000

|  | $'000 |
|---|---|
| 1 October 20X0 | 9,190 |
| Finance charge 8% | 735 |
| Interest paid (10,000 × 5%) | (500) |
| Balance 30 September 20X1 | 9,425 |

154  B  Deducted from the proceeds of the loan notes.

The effective interest rate is then applied to the net amount.

155  D  As a financial asset at amortised cost

# Fino Co OTQ case

**156** D From the commencement of the lease to the shorter of the end of the lease term and the end of the useful life of the plant

**157** D $478,000

|  | $'000 |
|---|---|
| Present value of future cash flows | 350 |
| Payments made at the commencement of the lease | 100 |
| Initial direct costs | 20 |
| Dismantling costs | 15 |
| Lease incentives | (7) |
| Right of Use Asset measurement | 478 |

**158** B The lease is for less than 12 months
The asset has a low underlying value

Where the agreement is for less than 12 months or the underlying asset is of low value, lease payments can be charged directly to profit or loss, in accordance with IFRS 15 *Leases*.

**159** A $247,380

|  | $ |
|---|---|
| Right of Use asset calculation | 478,000 |
| Less non-refundable deposit on 1.4.X7 | (100,000) |
| Lease liability | 378,000 |
| Interest accrued 1.4.X7-31.3.X8 ($378,000 × 10%) | 37,800 |
| Lease liability as at 31.3.X8 | 415,800 |
| Payment made 1.4.X8 | (100,000) |
| Interest accrued 1.4.X8-31.3.X9 (315,800 × 10%) | 31,580 |
| Lease liability as at 31.3.X9 | 347,380 |
|  |  |
| Current liabilities as at 31.3.X9 | 100,000 |
| Non-current liabilities as at 31.3.X9 | 247,380 |
|  | 347,380 |

**160** D $((9,000/10) \times 6) = \$5,400$

# Rainbird Co OTQ case

**161** D Neither the reorganisation nor the staff training

The reorganisation cannot be provided for because it has only gone as far as a feasibility study.

Staff training is not a valid provision as IAS 37 paragraph 81 specifically forbids costs relating to retraining or relocating staff to be provided for in restructing provisions.

**162** A contingent liability.

The outcome is probable but cannot be reliably measured.

**163** B $1,811,250
Total returns = 525,000 × 12% = 63,000
Expected cost:

|  | $ |
|---|---|
| 63,000 × 95% × 30 | 1,795,500 |
| 63,000 × 5% × 5 | 15,750 |
|  | 1,811,250 |

**164** D $2.63 million × 108% = $2,840,400. This is the unwinding of the discount.

BPP
LEARNING MEDIA

165    C     This is a favourable event after the reporting period because it provides evidence regarding conditions that existed at the end of the reporting period ie the legal case that was ongoing.

The other events have all taken place after the reporting period.

# Julian Co OTQ case

166    C     The amount attributed to an asset or liability for tax purposes

167

Property, plant and equipment

$190,000

Development expenditure

$60,000

PPE ($460,000 – $270,000). Development expenditure is in line with IAS 38 and is per the question.

168    D     $27,000 will go to the revaluation surplus.

Workings: $90,000 \times 30\%$

169    A     $45,000. The tax charge for the year.

170    C     Accrued expenses which have already been deducted for tax purposes

They will not give rise to a temporary difference.

# Section A

## Reporting financial performance

171    A    A change in valuation of inventory from a weighted average to a FIFO basis

A change of depreciation method is treated as a change of accounting estimate. Adoption of the revaluation method is dealt with under IAS 16. Application of a new accounting policy (such as capitalisation of borrowing costs) for transactions that did not previously occur is not a change in accounting policy according to IAS 8.

172    B    A buyer must have been located for the asset

It is not necessary for a buyer to have been located for the asset, only that the sale is 'highly probable' and a buyer is being actively sought by organisation (IFRS 5, para.8)

173    A    Lower of carrying amount and fair value less costs of disposal.

As the assets are to be sold, value in use is not relevant and recoverable amount will be fair value less costs of disposal.

174    B    A change in reporting depreciation charges as cost of sales rather than as administrative expenses
This is a change in presentation which will affect calculation of gross profit and will be retrospectively adjusted when presenting comparatives. A and D are simply adjustments made during preparation of the financial statements, C is a change of accounting estimate.

175    A    Classifying commission earned as revenue in the statement of profit or loss, having previously classified it as other operating income   This is a change in presentation so qualifies as a change in accounting policy.

176    C    $36.8 million

Selling price × 90% minus selling costs.

177      $147,059      €125,000 / 0.85

178      Rate at the date of transaction

179      $98 loss

| Date | Rate | $ | € | Gain/(loss) |
|------|------|------|------|------|
| 1/11 | 1.63 | 30,675 | 50,000 | |
| 1/12 | 1.61 | (15,528) | (25,000) | (191) |
| 31/12 | 1.64 | 15,244 | 25,000 | 93 |
| | | | | 98 |

## Earnings per share

180    A    $0.167

| | $'000 |
|------|------|
| Earnings on dilution: | |
| Basic | 1,850 |
| Add back interest (2,000 × 6% × 70%) | 84 |
| | 1,934 |

| | '000 |
|------|------|
| Shares on dilution: | |
| Existing | 10,000 |
| Conversion (2m × 4/5) | 1,600 |
| | 11,600 |

Basic EPS = 1,850 / 10,000 = $0.185

Diluted EPS = 1,934 / 11,600 = $0.167

181

|  | Share capital $'000 | Share premium $'000 |
|---|---|---|
|  | $40,000 | $4,000 |

|  | Share capital $'000 | Share premium $'000 |
|---|---|---|
| Balance 30 September X2 (250m shares) | 50,000 | 15,000 |
| Rights issue: |  |  |
| Share capital (50m × 20c) | (10,000) |  |
| Share premium (50m × 22c) | – | (11,000) |
| Balance 30 September X1 (200m shares) | 40,000 | 4,000 |

182   C   The issue during the year of a convertible (to equity shares) loan note
The granting during the year of directors' share options exercisable in three years' time

The convertible loan note and the share options should be taken into account when calculating diluted EPS.

183   B   EPS takes into account the additional resources made available to earn profit when new shares are issued for cash, whereas net profit does not.

184   A   $1.35

TERP

$5 \times 1.8 = 9.0$
$1 \times 1.5 = 1.5$
              $10.5 / 6 = $1.75$

| Shares | '000 |
|---|---|
| $5,000 \times 5/12 \times 1.8 / 1.75$ | 2,143 |
| $6,000 \times 7/12$ | 3,500 |
|  | 5,643 |

EPS = 7,600 / 5,643 = $1.35

185   $0.50

| | Shares '000 |
|---|---|
| B/f (7,500 / 0.5) | 15,000 |
| Full market price issue (4,000 × 9/12) | 3,000 |
| Bonus issue (18,000 / 3) | 6,000 |
|  | 24,000 |

EPS = 12 / 24 = $0.50

186   $0.72 / $0.56

| | Shares '000 |
|---|---|
| B/f | 4,000 |
| Bonus issue | 1,000 |
|  | 5,000 |

EPS 20X8 = 3.6 / 5 = $0.72
EPS 20X7 = $0.70 × 4,000 / 5,000 = $0.56

# Section B

# Tunshill Co (Dec10) OTQ case

187 D    Change of accounting estimate: Prospective application

This is a change of accounting estimate so does not need to be retrospectively applied.

188    $10,000,000

|  | $m |
|---|---|
| Original cost 1 October 20X0 | 20 |
| Two years depreciation ((20/5) × 2) | (8) |
| Carrying amount at 1 October 20X2 | 12 |
| Depreciation to 30 September 20X3 (12/6) | (2) |
| Carrying amount at 30 September 20X3 | 10 |

189 C    Tunshill Co has reclassified development costs from other operating expenses to cost of sales.

This is a change in presentation so it is a change of accounting policy.

190 B    Reduced by $400,000

|  | FIFO | AVCO | Current year profit |
|---|---|---|---|
|  | $m | $m | $m |
| Year to 30 September 20X2 | 15 | 13.4 | (1.6) |
| B/f 1 October 20X2 |  |  | 1.6 |
| Year to 30 September 20X3 | 20 | 18 | ( 2.0) |
| At 30 September 20X3 |  |  | (0.4) |

The net effect at 30 September 20X3 of this proposal will be to reduce current year profits by $400,000.

191

| Debit | | Cost of sales |
|---|---|---|

| Credit | | Inventory |
|---|---|---|

The credit entry reduces inventory

# Section A

# Calculation and interpretation of accounting ratios and trends

192  D  A manufacturer

The low asset turnover suggests a capital-intensive industry. This rules out the estate agency or architectural practice. Supermarkets can also be capital-intensive but tend to operate on low profit margins.

193  Reducing the **payables payment period** will increase the length of a company's operating cycle.

This will reduce working capital and means that it will take longer to build up working capital needed for production. The other options will all speed up the operating cycle.

194  D  4.1%

Working: (Dividends (3.4 + 11.1) / Share price) × 100 = 14.5 / 350 × 100 = 4.1%

195  A  3.9%

Profit margin is a component of ROCE: Profit margin × Asset turnover = ROCE

Working: 16.3% / 4.19 = 3.9%

196  7.5

Working: EPS = 800 / 4,000 = $0.20. P/E ratio = 150 / 20 = 7.5

197  5.1%

|  | $'000 |
|---|---|
| Profit before interest and tax | 230 % |
| Capital employed (3,500 + 1,000) | 4,500 |
|  | = 5.1% |

# Limitations of financial statements and interpretation techniques

198  The effect of this impairment will **increase** the ROCE ratio of Cyan Co, and **increase** its gearing ratio.

Capital employed (assets) would decrease, increasing ROCE. The impairment loss will reduce equity (revaluation surplus) and so increase gearing.

199  A  The value of the inventory will be added to both current assets and current liabilities. It will add proportionately more to liabilities and so reduce the current ratio. The effect on the quick ratio will be even greater as inventory is excluded from assets.

200

| Operating profit margin | ROCE |
|---|---|
| Decrease | Increase |

The new product will have an operating profit of 120 / 1,600 = 7.5%, so will reduce the current margin. It will have an ROCE of 120 / 500 = 24%, higher than the current 20%.

201  C  Obsolete inventory lines

Obsolete goods can lead to a build-up of unsold inventory, thereby increasing the holding period. A reduction in selling price or an increase in demand could increase sales leading to a fall in the holding period. Seasonal fluctuations will change the holding period throughout the year, but should not affect the year on year picture.

**202   B**   Overstatement of profits

The use of historical cost accounting during a period of inflation can lead to overstatement of profits. Non-current assets carried at historical cost may be presented at a value well below their fair value, leading to understated depreciation and consequently overstated profits. This can be compounded by the use of FIFO, if inventory is held at an original cost which is significantly below replacement cost. The charge to cost of sales will be understated and profit overstated.

The use of historical cost accounting will lead to understatement rather than overstatement of non-current asset values and will not affect interest costs. It is likely to lead to overstatement rather than understatement of ROCE.

**203   A**   Renegotiating a loan to secure a lower interest rate

This may save interest costs but will have no effect on gearing. The other options are methods that could be resorted to in order to reduce or avoid any increase in gearing.

**204   A**   Enter into a sale and short-term leaseback

This would be an unlikely transaction as it would remove the asset from the statement of financial position.

The deferral method of accounting for government grants leaves the carrying amount of the asset intact, rather than deducting the amount of the grant from the asset amount.

Revaluing assets is the obvious way of increasing the carrying amount of assets.

Under the reducing balance method, more depreciation is charged in the earlier years of the life of an asset, so a change to 10% straight line would reduce the depreciation charge for the first few years. Of course this effect is only temporary as the charge will catch up after a few years.

**205   D**   Trent factors with recourse the receivable of its largest customer

A receivable factored with recourse will still be included in trade receivables at the year end. Seasonal trading will create particular distortion if the busiest period is just before the year end. Cash sales will need to be removed from the calculation and an adjustment will have to be made for sales tax.

# Specialised, not-for-profit and public sector entities

**206   C**   Shareholders

Charities do not usually have shareholders, in the commercial sense of the term.

**207   B**   Accruals

Public sector accounting needs to move from cash-based accounting to application of the accruals concept.

**208   A**   Rent receipts outstanding, interest paid, interest received, interest cover, financial actuals against budget

A local council would not pay dividends and would be unlikely to measure ROCE, which deals with return to investors.

**209   D**   They have only a narrow group of stakeholders to consider

Charities have to consider a very wide group of shareholders, which can include donors, beneficiaries, volunteers, local organisations, government bodies and the public at large.

**210   B**   Funded by government

Public sector bodies have a major advantage not generally enjoyed by charities – government funding.

**211   C**   Disclosure of dividends per share

Not-for-profit entities do not have share capital so dividends per share is not relevant. The other requirements could be relevant to a not-for-profit entity.

212 There is no requirement to calculate an earnings per share figure as it is not likely to have shareholders who need to assess its earnings performance.

It prioritising non-financial KPIs over financial targets.

The objectives of a not-for-profit entity do not include making a profit so it would not calculate earnings per share or report to shareholders. However, it is likely to have to account to the trustees of the Board of the charity or entity using non-financial KPIs. For example, a hospital may account for mortality rates, or a childrens' charity show the numbers of children assisted during the period.

# Section B

# Sandbag plc OTQ case

213 B 1.29

Current ratio = current assets/current liabilities = 133/103 = 1.29

214 C Make a rights issue of ordinary shares

This would increase both cash and share capital, increasing current assets without incurring any additional liabilities.

Offering a settlement discount to customers would make cash received lower than receivables which would decrease the current ratio.

Making a bonus issue of shares would generate no cash at all and would not affect the current ratio.

Selling current asset investments would simply replace one current asset with another, at the same amount.

215 0.36

Acid test ratio = (current assets − inventories)/current liabilities = (133 − 96)/103 = 0.36

216 D Proposal 1 – decrease ratio / Proposal 2 – increase ratio

Proposal 1 will cause the acid test ratio to fall because, although receivables will convert into cash more quickly, the amount of cash received will be less than the amount of the receivables. Current assets will fall without any change in current liabilities, so the acid test ratio will fall.

Proposal 2 will cause the acid test ratio to rise, by delaying the reduction in cash that would occur by paying suppliers. Since the acid test ratio is less than 1, anything that prevents an equal fall in current assets and current liabilities will boost the ratio.

217 C Non-current asset turnover

A manufacturing company will have high non-current assets (factory, plant and machinery), so this ratio will measure how efficiently it is using its non-current assets to generate revenue.

The P/E ratio is a measure of market confidence in the future of the entity. Gearing relates to long-term solvency and the current ratio relates to liquidity.

# Section C

# 218 Bengal Co (Jun 11 amended)

> **Text references**. Chapters 19 and 20.
>
> **Top tips**. Note that only five marks are available for ratios – the rest is for your analysis, so it needs to make sense. Review the information you have in the context of profitability, gearing and liquidity. This will tell you which ratios need to be included.
>
> **Easy marks**. Most marks here are for reviewing all the information and making as many useful points as you can, not just calculating loads of ratios. Try to bear in mind the shareholder's comments and arrive at a conclusion.
>
> **Examining Team's comments**. Most did well on the ratios but not so well on the performance analysis, often failing to see that the decline in profit was due to the finance costs and the tax charge.

## Marking scheme

|  | Marks |
|---|---|
| 1 mark per valid point (including up to 5 points for ratios) | <u>20</u> |

(a)  It is correct that revenue has increased by 48% while profit for the year has only increased by 20%. However, on closer inspection, we can see that this is to a large degree attributable to the tax charge for the year. The tax charge was 28.6% of the profit before tax in the year ended 31.3.20X0 and 42.8% of the profit before tax in the year ended 31.3.20X1. We do not have a breakdown of the tax charge but it could include underpayments in previous years, which distorts the trading results.

A better comparison between the two years is the profit before tax % and the gross profit %. Both of these are higher in 20X1 than in 20X0. The shareholders will also be interested in the ROCE. There has been a significant increase in capital employed during the year ended 31.3. 20X1. Bengal Co has acquired nearly $13m in tangible and intangible assets, financed from cash reserves and a new issue of 8% loan notes. An additional $2m of non-current assets have been reclassified as held for sale. This suggests that Bengal Co has taken over the trade of another business and is disposing of the surplus assets. This is a long-term project which may take time to show a return and the ROCE does show a significant drop in 20X1. However, if we disregard the loan capital and look at the ROE we can see a considerable increase in 20X1.

The increase in loan capital does have significance for shareholders. The interest charge has increased from $100,000 to $650,000, which reduces the amount available for dividend. Gearing has increased significantly. The rate that Bengal Co has to offer to loan note holders has already increased from 5% to 8%. If it required further borrowing, with this high gearing, it would have to pay substantially more. Shares in Bengal Co have become a riskier investment. One indicator of this is the interest cover, which has fallen from 36 times to 9 times. The acquisition could presumably have been financed from a share issue or share exchange, rather than loan capital. However, this would have diluted the return available to shareholders.

The area in which there is most cause for concern is liquidity. As we can see from the statement of cash flows, cash and cash equivalents have fallen by $4.2m and the company is now running an overdraft. It has tax to pay of $2.2m and this will incur penalties if it is not paid on time. The current ratio has declined from 2.1:1 to 1.5:1 and this is including the non-current assets held for sale as part of non-current assets. The quick ratio, excluding inventory and non-current assets held for sale, indicates the immediate cash situation and this shows a fall from 1.6:1 to 0.46:1. Bengal Co needs to remedy this by disposing of the non-current assets held for sale as soon as possible and selling off surplus inventory, which may have been acquired as part of the acquisition.

Overall, the shareholder should be reassured that Bengal Co is profitable and expanding. The company has perhaps overstretched itself and significantly raised its gearing, but it is to be hoped that the investment will bring in future returns. This is no doubt the picture the company wants to give to shareholders, which is why it has paid a dividend in spite of having very little cash with which to do so.

(b)  While ratio analysis is a useful tool, it has a number of limitations, particularly when comparing ratios for different companies.

Some ratios can be calculated in different ways. For instance, gearing can be expressed using debt as a proportion of debt and equity or simply debt as a proportion of equity. Ratios can be distorted by inflation, especially where non-current assets are carried at original cost.

Ratios are based upon financial statements which may not be comparable due to the adoption of different accounting policies and different estimation techniques. For instance, whether non-current assets are carried at original cost or current value will affect ROCE, as will the use of different depreciation rates. In addition, financial statements are often prepared with the key ratios in mind, so may have been subject to creative accounting. The year-end values also may not be representative of values during the year, due to seasonal trading.

**Appendix: Ratios**

|  |  | 20X1 | 20X0 |
|---|---|---|---|
| Net profit % | (3,000 / 25,500) / (2,500 / 17,250) | 11.8% | 14.5% |
| Net profit % (pre-tax) | (5,250 / 25,500) / (3,500 / 17,250) | 20.6% | 20.3% |
| Gross profit % | (10,700 / 25,500) / (6,900 / 17,250) | 42% | 40% |
| ROCE | (5,900 / 18,500) / (3,600 / 9,250) | 31.9% | 38.9% |
| ROE | (3,000 / 9,500) / (2,500 / 7,250) | 31.6% | 34.5% |
| Gearing | (9,000 / 9,500) / (2,000 / 7,250) | 94.7% | 27.6% |
| Interest cover | (5,900 / 650) / (3,600 / 100) | 9 times | 36 times |
| Current ratio | (8,000 / 5,200) / (7,200 / 3,350) | 1.5:1 | 2.1:1 |
| Quick ratio | (2,400 / 5,200) / (5,400 / 3,350) | 0.5:1 | 1.6:1 |

# 219 Woodbank Co (Jun 14 amended)

**Text reference.** Chapter 19.

**Top tips.** The question makes it very clear where your analysis should be heading – the effect of the purchase of Shaw Co – so concentrate on this and review the information from this angle.

**Easy marks.** The ratios were easy marks and a thorough reading of the question would have given you some obvious points to make.

**Examining Team's comments.** Many candidates paid too little attention to the incremental effect of the acquisition of Shaw Co and few commented on the fact that profit or loss only included the results of Shaw Co for three months. This led a lot of candidates to conclude that the acquisition was not advantageous, which is not the conclusion borne out by taking into account the expected profits of Shaw over 12 months.

**Marking scheme**

|  | Marks |
|---|---|
| 1 mark per valid point (including 9 for ratios) | <u>20</u> |

(a)  **Ratios for 20X4**

|  | 20X4 |
|---|---|
| Return on capital employed (ROCE) | 12% |
| (profit before interest and tax/year-end total assets less current liabilities) |  |
| Net asset (equal to capital employed) turnover | 1.0 times |
| Gross profit margin | 22% |
| Profit before interest and tax margin | 12% |
| Current ratio | 1.08:1 |
| Gearing (debt/(debt + equity)) | 36.7% |

(b) **Equivalent ratios for Woodbank Co without Shaw Co**

| | | |
|---|---|---|
| ROCE | $((18 - 5)/(150 - 50))$ | 13% |
| Net asset turnover | $((150 - 30)/100)$ | 1.2 times |
| Gross profit margin | $((33 - 9)/(150 - 30))$ | 20% |
| Profit before interest and tax % | $((18 - 5)/(150 - 30))$ | 10.8% |

(c) **Analysis of performance and position**

The acquisition of Shaw Co has materially affected the results of Woodbank Co for the year ended 31 March 20X4. In order to make a meaningful comparison of the performance of Woodbank Co during the year to 31 March 20X4 with its performance during the year to 31 March 20X3, it is necessary to isolate the effects of the acquisition and consider how Woodbank Co's performance would have looked without Shaw Co.

**Profitability**

Shaw Co has contributed significantly to profitability with its gross profit margin of 30% and PBIT% of 16.6%. However the $50 million of loan notes which financed the acquisition have increased capital employed and so exerted a downward pull on ROCE. With Shaw Co, ROCE is 12%. Without Shaw Co it would have been 13%. If we check the ROCE for Shaw Co alone we can see that it is only 10% (5,000/50,000). But this is based on the total net assets of Shaw Co and only three months profits. If 12 months' profits were used, we could expect the return to be correspondingly higher.

During the three months to 31 March 20X4 Shaw Co had a gross profit margin of 30%. Combined with Woodbank Co, it raises Woodbank Co's gross profit margin from 20% to 22%. Woodbank Co's individual gross profit has therefore declined by 2% since 20X3. While revenue has risen by 9%, cost of sales has increased by 11%. However, Woodbank Co has done well at keeping down expenses and its PBIT margin without Shaw Co (10.8%) would have been up on 20X3 (9.1%). It is important to remember that Shaw Co was only owned for the final three months of the financial year, not much time for the additional assets to show a return. It is likely that the acquisition will enhance profitability to a greater extent over the next 12 months.

**Liquidity**

The current ratio of Woodbank Co has fallen from 1.7:1 to 1.08:1. This is a steep drop. We can see immediately that cash reserves have declined by $4.5 million and trade payables have increased by $8 million. This suggests that Woodbank Co is having trouble paying its suppliers on time. Payables days have increased from 55 to 66. The retained earnings balance shows that Woodbank Co paid a dividend of $5.5 million during 20X4. This was perhaps unwise when working capital was needed to finance expansion and pay the additional loan interest. Had the dividend not been paid the current ratio for 20X4 would be 1.3:1 – still a fall from 20X3, but less alarming.

**Gearing**

Gearing has risen from 5.3% to 36.7%, attributable to an additional $50 million loan notes issued to finance the acquisition of Shaw Co. The interest payments each year will be $5.5 million – the amount of the dividend paid in 20X4. Shareholders may expect to receive less in future years as the servicing of the debt will take priority, but had the acquisition been funded by a share issue their returns would have been diluted. Gearing of 36.7% is still within acceptable limits and future good returns from the acquisition will build up retained earnings and keep gearing in check.

**Conclusion**

Woodbank Co's performance would have been broadly comparable to the previous year had no acquisition taken place. The acquisition of Shaw Co has had a detrimental effect on liquidity and gearing for 20X4 but appears from three months results to have the capacity to significantly increase profits for Woodbank Co. It seems likely that over a longer period this will also improve liquidity and gearing, giving an overall positive result for shareholders.

# 220 Greenwood Co

## Marking scheme

|  | Marks |
| --- | --- |
| Up to 6 marks for relevant ratios | 6 |
| Up to 5 marks for effect of disposal | 5 |
| Up to 1 mark per relevant interpretive comment | 9 |
| Maximum | 20 |
| Total for questions | |

The application of IFRS 5 *Non-current Assets Held for Sale and Discontinued Operations* makes it possible to separate out the results of continuing and discontinued operations. This is important for analysts as discontinued operations will not be contributing to future performance and non-current assets held for sale will be disposed of in the near future. As the disposal is treated as a discontinued operation and this was Greenwood Co's only subsidiary, the profits attributable to the non-controlling interest form part of the results of the discontinued operation.

We can see in comparing the statements of financial position for 20X6 and 20X7 that Deadwood Co had no property, plant or equipment, but it will have had some current assets and liabilities. The value disposed of will have been based on the group share of Deadwood Co's share capital and retained earnings, and the $1.5m goodwill. Looking at the analysis of discontinued operations for both years, it is likely that Deadwood Co did not have a large balance on retained earnings and the value of the goodwill is questionable on the same basis, so Greenwood Co probably did well to obtain $6m for its shareholding.

In the case of Greenwood Co we have excluded the results of the disposal and the disposal proceeds from ratios where applicable. Non-controlling interest is normally included in ROCE based on consolidated financial statements. It has been excluded here in order to facilitate comparison with the year of disposal.

Greenwood Co's ROCE based on continuing operations has declined from 32.6% to 29.7% between 20X6 and 20X7. Separating this ratio into its component parts, we can see that there has been a slight improvement in the profit before interest and tax ratio, from 17.7% to 17.8%. The problem therefore lies with the asset turnover, which has declined from 1.84 to 1.67. This means that Greenwood Co made less effective use of its assets in 20X7 than in 20X6. An additional $3m of loan notes were issued during the year, but this capital has not yet generated a commensurate return.

There has been a healthy increase in revenue in 20X7 and gross profit % has almost kept pace, but the margin has been eroded by an increase in operating expenses and finance costs which have increased by 140%. These are due to the additional $3m loan notes and the overdraft, on which Greenwood Co appears to be paying about 17% per annum (200/1,150 = 17.4%).

The analysis of discontinued operations demonstrates why Deadwood Co has been sold. A gross profit of $1m in 20X6 represented a return of 11%, compared with the 29% gross profit percentage on the continuing operations. In 20X6 the discontinued operation made a pre-tax profit of $450,000 which represents a ROCE of about 7% on its $6.3m assets. In 20X7 the ROCE was of course negative. The loss on disposal indicates that a goodwill impairment loss should probably have been recognised at the end of 20X6.

At first sight Greenwood Co's current ratio of 2.11 for 20X7 looks healthy, but this has been distorted by the assets relating to Deadwood Co. Adjusted for this, we get a current ratio of 0.77. This is alarming in itself and is a decline from 0.97 in 20X6. The quick ratio, similarly adjusted, stands at 0.62 in 20X6 and 0.44 in 20X7. During 20X7 Greenwood Co's cash balances have declined by $1.2m, despite the further $3m loan, and it has a tax bill of $950,000, which will presumably accrue interest if it is not paid by the due date.

What we cannot see from the consolidated financial statements is the level of intercompany trading as these transactions and balances will have been eliminated on consolidation. Greenwood Co could have been selling to Deadwood Co on favourable terms and providing management services free of charge in order to make the financial statements of Deadwood Co look better (or less disastrous) and boost the chances of a sale. Or it could have been using transfer pricing to move across profits from Deadwood Co in order to boost its own profits and be able to pay higher dividends to its own shareholders. We would need to have sight of the individual company financial statements of Greenwood Co and Deadwood Co in order to make a judgement about this.

Overall, Greenwood Co's results do not inspire confidence. Disposing of the unprofitable subsidiary was no doubt the correct action and management now needs to collect the proceeds and do whatever else can be done to handle the liquidity situation.

Appendix

| Ratios | 20X7 | 20X6 |
|---|---|---|
| ROCE – continuing operations | | |
| (4,500 + 400*)/(14,500 + 8,000 − 6,000**) | 29.7% | |
| (3,750/(12,750 + 5,000 − 6,250)) | | 32.6% |
| *Note that of the finance costs shown for 20X7 only $400,000 is loan note interest | | |
| ** Due on sale of subsidiary | | |
| Gross profit % – continuing operations | | |
| (8,000/27,500) | 29.1% | |
| (6,200/21,200) | | 29.2% |
| Net profit before interest and tax % | | |
| (4,900/27,500) | 17.8% | |
| (3,750/21,200) | | 17.7% |
| Asset turnover | | |
| (27,500/(14,500 + 8,000 − 6,000)) | 1.67 | |
| (21,200/(12750 + 5,000 − 6,250)) | | 1.84 |
| Current ratio | | |
| Including disposal assets (9,500/4,500) | 2.11 | |
| Excluding disposal assets (3,500/4,500) | 0.78 | |
| (3,700/3,800) | | 0.97 |
| Quick ratio (acid test) | | |
| Including disposal assets (8,000/4,500) | 1.78 | |
| Excluding disposal assets (2,000/4,500) | 0.44 | |
| (2,350/3,800) | | 0.62 |

# 221 Funject Co

**Text references.** Chapters 19 and 20

**Top tips.** Clearly laying out the calculations, especially for the ratios was vital in this question. Remember to state whether an adjustment makes an increase or decrease in profit (show decreases in brackets). Calculating the ratios in the correct way gained easy marks, but additional marks were given for adding comments relevant to the situation.

**Easy marks.** Calculation of ratios, remember to show your workings (as the revised figures were used, it was imperative to show the workings or zero marks were given). A mark was given for stating a conclusion, which the markers encouraged.

**Examining Team's comments.** Most answers confined themselves to giving a textbook based explanation of what the ratio told users and whether the company's ratio was higher or lower than the industry average. Some answers went on to suggest whether the company ratios were better or worse than the industry averages, but very few provided any further analysis. Better answers referred to the differing performance of the division disposed of and its impact on the company's results.

## Marking scheme

|     |                                                   |       | Marks |
| --- | ------------------------------------------------- | ----- | ----- |
| (a) | Adjustment to revenue and cost of sales           | 1     |       |
|     | Disposal of non-core division                     | 1     |       |
|     | Management charge (remove old, add new)           | 2     |       |
|     | Rent expense (remove current, add commercial)     | 1     |       |
|     |                                                   |       | 5     |
| (b) | Calculation of ratios                             |       | 5     |
| (c) | Profitability comments                            | 5     |       |
|     | Liquidity comments                                | 3     |       |
|     | Gearing comments                                  | 1     |       |
|     | Conclusion                                        | 1     |       |
|     |                                                   |       | 10    |
|     |                                                   |       | 20    |

(a)    Restated financial information

Statement of profit or loss

|                                             | 20X4      |
|---------------------------------------------|-----------|
|                                             | $'000     |
| Revenue (54,200-2,100 (note1))              | 52,100    |
| Cost of sales (21,500 -1,200 (note1)        | (20,300)  |
| Gross profit                                | 31,800    |
| Operating expenses (W1)                     | (12,212)  |
| Profit before tax                           | 19,588    |

| W1 Restatement of operating expenses                          |         |
|---------------------------------------------------------------|---------|
| As per question                                               | 11,700  |
| Less: expenses relating to non-core division                  | (700)   |
| loss on disposal of non-core division                         | (1,500) |
| Gamilton Group management charge (54,200 x1%)                 | (542)   |
| Add: Funject management charge (31,800 x10%)                  | 3,180   |
| Less: rent charged by Gamilton Group                          | (46)    |
| Add: commercial rent                                          | 120     |
|                                                               | 12,212  |

(b) Profit has decreased from $21,000,000 to $19,588,000 and the resulting journal entry will be ($'000s):

Dr Retained earnings (21,000-19,588)     $1,412

Cr Cash                                                    $1,412

**Ratio calculations**

|  | Workings | 20X4 |
|---|---|---|
| Gross profit margin | 31,800/52,000 × 100 | 61% |
| Operating profit margin | 19,588/52,100 × 100 | 38% |
| Receivables collection period (days) | (5,700/52,100) × 365 | 40 |
| Current ratio | $\frac{(12,900 - 1,412)}{(11,600)}$ | 1:1 |
| Acid test (quick) ratio | (12,900 – 4,900 – 1,412)/(11,600) | 0.57:1 |
| Gearing (debt/equity) | $\frac{16,700}{(9,000 - 1,412)}$ | 220% |

(c) **Commentary on performance**

**Profitability**

The discontinued operation had a gross profit % (GP%) of 43% (900/2,100 × 100) and an operating profit % (OP%) of 10% (200/2,100 × 100). Before adjusting for the disposal, Aspect Co has a GP% of 60%. After an adjustment has been made to reflect the disposal, Aspect Co's GP% is 61% which is higher than the industry average of 45%. Thus, it would appear that the disposal of the non-core division has had a positive impact on the GP% of Aspect Co. Such a positive comparison of the GP% to the industry average would suggest that Aspect Co has negotiated a very good deal with its suppliers for the cost of goods in comparison to its competitors; the GP% is 16% (61 – 45) higher than the industry average.

However, when considering the OP%, the financial statements have been adjusted to reflect: (i) the disposal of the discontinued operation;

(ii)    a new management charge which would be imposed by Funject Co; and

(iii)    commercial rent charges.

These adjustments result in an OP% of 38%. So, although the OP% is still 10% (38 – 28) higher than the industry average, it would appear that some of the advantage of having such a good deal with its suppliers is lost when operating costs are incurred. The OP% does not outperform the industry average to the same extent that GP% did. Although the management charge will be eliminated as an intra-group transaction on consolidation, it will still have an impact in the individual financial statements of Aspect Co. However, there is no indication of what this charge is for and whether or not it represents a market value for these costs. The rent of $120,000 is deemed to be a fair market value which would indicate that the previous rent charge of

$46,000 was artificially low. If Funject Co acquires Aspect Co, it may wish to capitalise on the relationship which Aspect Co has with its supplier of goods but it might also need to investigate the composition of operating costs other than those described above to see if any of these can be avoided/reduced.

**Liquidity**

Aspect Co's receivables collection period appears to be comparable with the KPIs provided (40 days in comparison to 41 days). Terms of trade of 30 days are quite reasonable (though this usually depends on the type of business) and so there are no causes for concern here.

Given that Aspect Co's receivables collection period is comparable to the industry average, the difference in the current ratio (1·1:1 in comparison to 1·6:1) can only be explained by either lower current assets other than receivables (for example, cash) or higher current liabilities. As Aspect Co's cash balance does not appear to be low ($2·3m), this suggests that its liabilities might be higher than average. Perhaps Aspect Co's favourable relationship with its suppliers also extends to longer than average credit terms. As Aspect Co's acid (quick) ratio (0·57:1) is much less than the industry average (1·4:1), this would also suggest that Aspect Co is holding a higher than average level of inventory. This may raise a concern about Aspect Co's ability to sell its inventory. There is also a current tax bill to consider. Indeed, if Aspect Co were asked to settle its current liabilities from merely its receivables and bank, it would be unable to do so. Perhaps Funject Co may wish to further investigate the procedures associated with the purchase and holding of Aspect Co's inventory prior to a takeover. As a parent company, Funject Co should be able to influence these procedures and have more control over the levels of inventory held.

### Gearing

Aspect Co appears to be highly geared but perhaps this is not a huge cause for concern because it appears to be a highly geared industry (220% compared to 240%). It may be that the proceeds from the sale of the non-core division can be/were used to pay down loans. As the gearing for the industry is higher than that of Aspect Co, it may be that Aspect Co could still increase borrowings in future. If so, Aspect Co may need to increase working capital efficiency and reduce costs in order to generate enough cash to service higher borrowings.

### Conclusion

Overall, Aspect's statement of financial position gives little cause for concern; the profitability margins appear to be healthy although further investigations of operating costs and working capital efficiency may be required. More information also needs to be obtained about the nature of the business and perhaps the financial statements of several years (as opposed to one) might also be beneficial

# 222 Harbin

**Text references**. Chapters 19 and 20.

**Top tips**. You have been given most of the ratios in this question. You can probably see that additional ratios are relevant here, to illustrate the effect of the purchase of Fatima Co. The examining team frequently points out that to compare two ratios and say something went up or down is not analysis. You must look behind the numbers and make some suggestion regarding why this has happened.

**Easy marks**. You were told that the purchase of Fatima Co was significant, so you must allow for this in looking at the ratios and compute additional ratios as needed. If you did this, the ratios gave you plenty to analyse.

**Examining Team's comments**. Unfortunately, the performance assessment in this question was quite poor. Some candidates did not even point out obvious issues arising from the purchase of Fatima Co.

### Marking scheme

|  | Marks |
| --- | --- |
| Ratios | 8 |
| Consideration of chief executive's report | 3 |
| Impact of purchase | 6 |
| Remaining issues – ½ mark per valid point | 3 |
|  | 20 |

(a) **Ratios for 20X7**

|  | 20X7 |
| --- | --- |
| Return on year-end capital employed | 11.2% |
| (profit before interest and tax over total assets less current liabilities) | |
| Net asset (equal to capital employed) turnover | 1.17 |
| Net profit (before tax) margin | 6.4% |
| Current ratio | 0.86:1 |
| Closing inventory holding period (in days) | 46 |
| Trade receivables' collection period (in days) | 19 |
| Trade payables' payment period (based on cost of sales) (in days) | 42 |
| Gearing (debt over debt plus equity) | 46.7% |

(b)    It is clear that the acquisition of Fatima Co has had a very positive impact on Harbin Co's results for the year ended 30 September 20X7. For this reason it is instructive to look at the 20X7 ratios which have been affected by the acquisition and see what they would have been without the addition of Fatima Co's results. The additional ratios are at the end of this report.

*Profitability*

It is immediately apparent that without the purchase of Fatima Co the chief executive's report would have looked very different. The increase in sales revenue of 39% would have disappeared. The sales revenue of Harbin Co is static. The increase in gross profit margin from 16.7% to 20% would have been a fall to 11.1%. The profit for the period would not have doubled. It would have gone from an $8m profit before tax in 20X6 to a $2m profit before tax in 20X7, assuming that the loan note interest would not have arisen. This would have given an ROCE of 2.05% for 20X7 rather than the 11.2% when Fatima Co is included. If we break ROCE down into net profit% and asset turnover, we can see that Fatima Co's results have increased the net profit% by almost six times, while having an adverse effect on the asset turnover due to the $100m funding through loan notes. There is some distortion in the 20X7 figures arising from interest charges which are not deducted in calculating ROCE but have been deducted in arriving at net profit.

*Liquidity*

While it has greatly enhanced Harbin Co's profitability, the purchase of Fatima Co has done little for liquidity, an aspect not touched on in the extract from the chief executive's report. Harbin Co borrowed $100m to pay for Fatima Co, so the purchase was not funded from working capital. However, it has paid $8m loan note interest, increased its inventory holding by $10m, invested in additional property, plant and equipment and paid a $10m dividend. In this way it has, despite the increased profit, converted a positive cash balance of $14m to an overdraft of $17m. The ratios show this very clearly. Harbin Co's current ratio has declined from 2.5:1 to 0.86:1 and its quick ratio (not shown above) has declined from 1.47:1 to 0.30:1, casting some doubt upon whether it will be able to continue to meet its commitments as they fall due.

The increase in the inventory holding period is worrying, as it suggests that Harbin Co may have inventory which is slow moving, and the increase in the payables period by ten days suggests problems paying suppliers. Harbin Co has a $4m tax bill outstanding. If this is not paid on time it will incur interest, which will further weaken the cash position.

*Gearing*

The cost of acquiring Fatima Co is directly reflected in the gearing ratio, which has gone from nil in 20X6 to 46.7% in 20X7, with the issue of the loan notes. This will reduce profits available for distribution to shareholders in the future and if Harbin Co's cash position does not improve it may be forced to seek further loans. In the light of this, the increase of 25% in the dividend is hard to justify.

**Appendix – ratios adjusted for purchase of Fatima Co**

|  | With Fatima Co 20X7 | Without Fatima Co 20X7 |
|---|---|---|
| Return on year-end capital employed | 11.2% | |
| 24,000* – 22,000 / 114,000 – (22,000 – 5.500**) | | 2.05% |
| (profit before interest and tax over total assets less current liabilities) | | |
| Net asset (equal to capital employed) turnover | 1.17 | |
| 250,000 – 70,000 / 114,000 – (22,000 – 5,500) | | 1.85 |
| Net profit (before tax) margin | 6.4% | |
| 24,000 – 22,000 / 250,000 – 70,000 | | 1.1% |

* Without the acquisition of Fatima Co the finance costs of $8,000 would not be incurred.

** $5,500 = 25% tax

# 223 Quartile (Dec12 amended)

> **Text references.** Chapters 19 and 20.
>
> **Top tips.** A bit of planning is useful for a question like this and the categories of profitability, liquidity and gearing give you a structure around which to base your analysis. Note that this is a retail business, so this will affect the ratios.
>
> **Easy marks.** Analysis of the ratios is straightforward and some useful points on the limitations on usefulness of a sector average comparison could have earned four marks.

## Marking scheme

|  |  | Marks |
|---|---|---:|
| (a) | Ratios | 6 |
| (b) | 1 mark per valid comment | 10 |
| (c) | 1 mark per issue | 4 |
| Total for question |  | 20 |

(a)

| | |
|---|---|
| Return on year-end capital employed (ROCE) | 12.1% |
| Net asset (total assets less current liabilities) turnover | 1.6 times |
| Gross profit margin | 25% |
| Operating profit margin | 7.5% |
| Current ratio | 1.55:1 |
| Average inventory turnover | 4.5 times |
| Trade payables' payment period | 45 days |
| Debt to equity | 30% |

(b)   **Analysis of financial and operating performance of Quartile Co compared to sector average**

**Profitability**

Quartile Co has a ROCE **significantly lower** at 12.1% than the sector average of 16.8%. This is mainly due to the lower than average gross profit margin and consequent **low operating profit margin**. The operating expenses are actually lower (17.5%) as a percentage of revenue than the sector average of 23% (35% – 12%) so the problem lies between revenue and cost of sales. Inventory turnover is quite brisk (4.5 times compared to a sector average of 3 times) but Quartile Co's mark-up of 33.3% ((25 / 75) × 100) is significantly below the sector average of 54% ((35 / 65) × 100). Quartile Co is maintaining turnover **by keeping prices down**.

The other component of ROCE, net asset turnover, is slightly higher than the sector average. This is due to the buoyant turnover, as the ratio will have been depressed by the property revaluation and the capitalisation of the development expenditure, which have increased the asset base. It is to be hoped that the development expenditure will generate the expected revenue. If it had been necessary to expense it for the year ended 30 September 20X2 Quartile Co would have reported a loss before tax of $1.6m.

**Liquidity**

Quartile Co has a current ratio of 1.55:1 compared to the sector average of 1.25:1. Both appear low, but satisfactory for the retail sector as the cash cycle is fairly rapid. Inventory can be turned into immediate cash and this is particularly true for Quartile Co with its high inventory turnover level. The lower than average payables days (45 compared to 64) and the absence of an overdraft suggest that **Quartile Co is not suffering liquidity problems**.

### Gearing

Quartile Co's debt to equity ratio is 30%, well below the sector average of 38% and the interest rate on the loan notes is below the ROCE of 12.1%, meaning that the **borrowings are earning a good return** for the business. The interest cover of 5.25 times (4,200 / 800) is satisfactory. Quartile Co is not having any problems servicing its loan and is unlikely to give lenders any particular concern.

### Conclusion

There are no going concern worries for Quartile Co but it does have an issue with **low profitability**. It appears to be positioned at the bottom end of the jewellery market selling high volume cheap items rather than more valuable pieces on which there would be significantly higher profit margins. This may or may not be the most advantageous strategy in a period of recession.

(c)     The following factors may limit the usefulness of comparisons based on business sector averages:

(i)     The companies included in the average may have used different accounting policies. Some may be applying the revaluation basis to their assets and some may not. This will affect asset turnover and ROCE.

(ii)    The average may include a wide variety of entities with different trading methods and risk profiles. Very high-end jewellers may even operate on an invoice rather than a cash basis and will have receivables included in their current assets. Very large chains will probably have more access to cheap borrowing.

(iii)   Some ratios, in particular ROCE and gearing, can be calculated in different ways. It is up to the organisation carrying out the comparison to ensure that a standard definition is used, and they may or may not do this.

# Section A

# Consolidated statement of financial position

**224** $193,125

| | $ |
|---|---|
| Fair value at acquisition (200,000 × 30% × $1.75) | 105,000 |
| Share of post-acquisition retained earnings ((750 – 450) × 30%) | 90,000 |
| Depreciation on fair value adjustment ((250 / 40) × 30%) | (1,875) |
| | 193,125 |

**225** $139,370

| | $ | $ |
|---|---|---|
| Consideration transferred: | | |
| Cash | | 250,000 |
| Deferred consideration (400,000 / 1.08) | | 370,370 |
| Shares (30,000 × $2.30) | | 69,000 |
| | | 689,370 |
| Fair value of non-controlling interest | | 400,000 |
| | | 1,089,370 |
| Fair value of net assets: | | |
| Shares | 100,000 | |
| Retained earnings | 850,000 | |
| | | (950,000) |
| | | 139,370 |

**226** Increase $40,000

($1.2 million / 8 × 4/12) × 80% = $40,000

The adjustment will reduce depreciation over the next eight years, so it will **increase** retained earnings.

**227** $105 million

| | $'000 |
|---|---|
| Shares (18m × 2/3 × $5.75) | 69,000 |
| Deferred consideration (18m × $2.42 × 1 / $1.1^2$) | 36,000 |
| | 105,000 |

**228** D This adjustment reduces (debits) the liability and the credit is to retained earnings. The re-measurement relates to the post-acquisition period, so goodwill is not affected.

**229** D

| | $ | $ |
|---|---|---|
| Consideration transferred | | 800,000 |
| Fair value of non-controlling interest | | 220,000 |
| | | 1,020,000 |
| Fair value of net assets: | | |
| Shares | 100,000 | |
| Retained earnings | 570,000 | |
| Revaluation surplus | 150,000 | |
| Intangible assets | 90,000 | |
| | | (910,000) |
| | | 110,000 |

230 C

| | $ | $ |
|---|---|---|
| Consideration | | 200,000 |
| NCI | | 82,800 |
| Net assets: | | |
| Shares | 100,000 | |
| Retained earnings | 156,000 | 256,000 |
| Goodwill | | 26,800 |
| | | |
| Phantom Co | | 275,000 |
| Ghost Co: | | |
| (177 – 156) × 70% | | 14,700 |
| Goodwill impairment (26,800 / 2) × 70% | | (9,380) |
| Group retained earnings | | 280,320 |

231 A    This combination results in a bargain purchase of $1.2 million which should be credited to profit or loss.

# Consolidated statement of profit or loss and other comprehensive income

232 C

| | $m |
|---|---|
| Decrease | 12.0 |
| Increase ($2m × 25% (profit margin)) | 0.5 |
| Net decrease | 11.5 |

233 D    There will be no effect on group retained earnings

| | $'000 |
|---|---|
| Loss of investment income(10m × 8% × 6/12) | (400) |
| Saving of interest payable | 400 |

234 B

| | $ |
|---|---|
| Profit to 30 June 20X8 (1.6m × 6/12) | 800,000 |
| Additional depreciation on FVA ((2m/20) × 6/12) | (50,000) |
| Goodwill impairment | (500,000) |
| | 250,000 |
| NCI share 20% | 50,000 |

235 $717,463

| | $ |
|---|---|
| Basil Co | 547,700 |
| Parsley Co (206,900 × 10/12) | 172,417 |
| PURP ((46,000 × 30 / 130) × 25%) | (2,654) |
| | 717,463 |

236 $80,000    $2m × 25/ 125 × 20% = $80,000

237 $264,000

| | $'000 |
|---|---|
| Profit for the year | 1,300 |
| Intragroup interest (5m × 8%) | (400) |
| Impairment (50,000 – 30,000) | (20)* |
| | 880 |
| × 30% | 264 |

* The revaluation surplus is eliminated first and the remainder charged to profit or loss.

**238** $145,000

|  | $ | $ |
|---|---|---|
| Sales proceeds | | 450,000 |
| Share capital | 100,000 | |
| Retained earnings | 185,000 | |
| Goodwill | 20,000 | |
| | | (305,000) |
| | | 145,000 |

**239** $150,000 (450,000 – 300,000)

**240** $245,000 profit

|  | $ |
|---|---|
| Disposal proceeds | 950,000 |
| Goodwill on disposal (600,000 – (700,000 × 70%)) | (110,000) |
| Share of net assets at disposal (850,000 × 70%) | (595,000) |
| | 245,000 |

# Accounting for associates

**241** A

|  | $m |
|---|---|
| Cost (75m × $1.60) | 120 |
| Share of post-acquisition retained earnings (100 – 20) × 30% | 24 |
| | 144 |

**242** C The group's share of the associate's profit after tax is recorded as a one-line entry. Line by line treatment would be correct for a subsidiary, not an associate. The dividends received from the associate are all that is recorded in the individual entity financial statements of the parent, but in the consolidated financial statements this is replaced by the group share of profit after tax.

**243** D No effect on group inventory.
The transaction will be posted as:

Debit       Share of profit of associate
Credit      Investment in associate.

**244** $5,230,000

|  | $'000 |
|---|---|
| Cost of investment | 5,000 |
| Share of post-acquisition profit (8,500 – 7,400) × 25% | 275 |
| PURP (600 × 30% × 25%) | (45) |
| | 5,230 |

**245** $10,200,000

|  | $'000 |
|---|---|
| Cost of investment | 10,000 |
| Share of post-acquisition profit (6,000 × 8/12) – 1,000) × 30% | 900 |
| Impairment | (700) |
| | 10,200 |

**246** The correct answers are:

The investor owns 330,000 of the 1,500,000 equity voting shares of the investee.
The investor has representation on the board of directors of the investee.

The presence of significant influence is indicated by a shareholding of 20% or more or representation on the board. Regarding the third option, material transactions would need to be between the investor itself and the investee. The final option denotes control, not significant influence.

**247** $3,000      ($160,000 / 4) × 25% × 30% = $3,000

# Presentation of published financial statements

**248 B** The fact that a liability has arisen during the current accounting period does not make it a current liability. The other options would all lead to classification as a current liability.

**249 D** The revaluation gain on the factory will be presented under 'other comprehensive income'. The other items will be recognised in profit or loss. Note that gains on investment properties go through profit or loss.

**250 C** Inventories, provisions and intangible assets are shown separately. There is no such requirement for government grants.

**251 D** The time between acquisition of assets for processing and receipt of cash from customers

**252 A** Equity dividends are presented in the statement of changes in equity.

# Statement of cash flows

**253 A**

|  | $m |
|---|---|
| B/f (500 + 100) | 600 |
| Cash received (β) | 500 |
| C/f (750 + 350) | 1,100 |

**254 B**

|  | $'000 |
|---|---|
| Balance b/f | 1,860 |
| Revaluation | 100 |
| Disposal | (240) |
| Depreciation | (280) |
|  | 1,440 |
| Additions (β) | 1,440 |
| Balance c/f | 2,880 |

**255 A**

|  | $'000 |
|---|---|
| Carrying amount 20X3 | 14,400 |
| Depreciation | (2,500) |
| Sale of plant | (3,000) |
| Revaluation | 2,000 |
| Environmental provision | 4,000 |
|  | 14,900 |
| Purchases (β) | 8,500 |
|  | 23,400 |

**256 $305 million**

|  | $m |
|---|---|
| B/f | 410 |
| Depreciation | (115) |
| Revaluation | 80 |
| Purchases (β) | 305 |
| C/f | 680 |

**257**

|  | $'000 |
|---|---|
| $2,100,000 |  |
| B/f (2,000 + 800) | 2,800 |
| Additions (6,500 – 2,500 + 1,800) | 5,800 |
| Payments made (β) | (2,100) |
| C/f (4,800 + 1,700) | 6,500 |

# Section B

## Root Co and Branch Co OTQ case

258  $268 million

|  | $m |
|---|---|
| Cash | 210 |
| Shares (116m × 100/200) | 58 |
|  | 268 |

259  $5.6 million

|  | Acquisition | Movement (2 years) |
|---|---|---|
|  | $m | $m |
| Property | 20 | (2) |
| Brand | 25 | (5) |
|  |  | (7) |

$7 million × 80% = $5.6 million

260  $16 million

$56m × 40/140

261  The correct answer is:

DR Cost of sales / CR Inventories

The unrealised profit is added to cost of sales and removed from inventories.

262  The correct answer is:

Control of the subsidiary has been lost.

Exclusion from consolidation is only allowed when control has been lost.

## Port Co and Alfred Co OTQ case

263  The correct answer is:

Share capital $235,000 / Share premium $1,115,000

*Issue of shares*

|  | Draft | New issue | Revised |
|---|---|---|---|
|  | $'000 | $'000 | $'000 |
| Share capital | 200 | 35 | 235 |
| Share premium | 500 | 615 | 1,115 |
| Fair value of proceeds |  | 650 |  |

264  $500,000

|  | $'000 |
|---|---|
| Net assets at date of acquisition |  |
| Share capital | 100 |
| Share premium | 85 |
| Retained earnings 331 − (96 × 2/12) | 315 |
|  | 500 |

265  The correct answers are:

The non-controlling interest share of profit is part of the consolidated statement of profit or loss.

If a subsidiary is acquired during the year, its results are apportioned over the year of acquisition.

The statement of financial position shows all non-current assets. Goodwill is not amortised, it is subject to an annual impairment review.

266   $404,000     Port Co $364,000 and Alfred Co ($240,000 × 2/12) = $404,000

267   $2,912,000

|  | Port $'000 | Alfred $'000 |
|---|---|---|
| Port retained earnings | 2,900 | |
| Alfred post-acquisition (96,000 × 2/12) | | 16 |
| Share of Alfred Co: (16 × 75%) | 12 | |
|  | 2,912 | |

# Polestar Co OTQ case

268   $22.3 million

|  | $'000 |
|---|---|
| Share capital | 6,000 |
| Retained earnings at 30.9.X3 | 14,300 |
| Fair value adjustment on property | 2,000 |
|  | 22,300 |

269   $130 million

    (110m + (66m × 6/12) − 13m intragroup)

270   The correct answer is:
    DR Liability / CR Profit or loss

    This fall has taken place since acquisition, so goodwill is not adjusted.

271   $150,000
    Unrealised profit = 9m − 5.4m = 3.6m
    Still in inventory = 3.6m × 1.5/9 = 600,000 × 25% = 150,000

272   The correct answer is:
    The non-controlling interest will be allocated their share of any goodwill impairment.

    The other options are incorrect.

# Plateau Co OTQ case

273   C   $12,750,000 ((3m / 2 × $6) + (3m × $1.25))

274   C   The contract is estimated to have an indefinite life.

275   A

|  | $'000 |
|---|---|
| NCI at acquisition (1m shares @ $3.25) | 3,250 |
| NCI share of post-acquisition retained earnings ((W) 2,600 × 25%) | 650 |
|  | 3,900 |

    *Working*

|  | $'000 |
|---|---|
| Retained earnings per draft | 2,900 |
| Less unrealised profit ($2.7m × 50/150 × 1/3) | (300) |
|  | 2,600 |

276   B   $10,500,000

|  | $'000 |
|---|---|
| Cost (4m × 30% × $7.50) | 9,000 |
| Share of post-acquisition retained earnings (5,000 × 30%) | 1,500 |
|  | 10,500 |

277   B   Axle Co is not a member of the group, so group inventory is unaffected.

# Pinto Co OTQ case

**278** $10,000 received

|  | $ |
|---|---|
| B/f current (asset) | – |
| B/f deferred tax | 30,000 |
| Charge for the year | 160,000 |
| Received (balance) | 10,000 |
| C/f (current + deferred) | 200,000 |

**279** $1,250,000

|  | $'000 |
|---|---|
| Proceeds from sale of plant (240 – 90) | 150 |
| Purchase of plant (W) | (1,440) |
| Investment property income (60 – 20) | 40 |
|  | 1,250 |

*Working*

|  | $'000 |
|---|---|
| B/f | 1,860 |
| Revaluation gain | 100 |
| Disposal | (240) |
| Depreciation | (280) |
| Purchases (β) | 1,440 |
|  | 2,880 |

**280** $150,000

(1,310 (retained earnings) + 280 – 1,440) or (1,000 × 5 × 0.03)

**281** The correct answer is:

Operating activities and financing activities

Dividends paid can be presented under operating activities or financing activities.

**282** The correct answer is:

The proceeds from sale of plant

It is the profit on disposal of the plant that will be adjusted against profit before tax, not the proceeds of disposal.

# Section C

# 283 Pedantic Co (Dec08 amended)

> **Text references**. Chapters 8 and 9.
>
> **Top tips**. The first point to note here is that the subsidiary was acquired mid-year. Remember this when it comes to working out the depreciation on the fair value adjustment. This question had lots to do but no real problems. Get the formats down, note the adjustments on the question paper and then start working through.
>
> **Easy marks**. There were lots of easy marks here. There were lots of marks available in the statement of financial position even if you did not get the goodwill quite right. Correctly calculating the figures from the share exchange would have gained you marks on goodwill, share capital and share premium.

|  |  | | Marks |
|---|---|---|---|
| (a) | Statement of financial position: | | |
| | Property, plant and equipment | 2 | |
| | Goodwill | 5 | |
| | Current assets | 1½ | |
| | Equity shares | 1 | |
| | Share premium | 1 | |
| | Retained earnings | 2 | |
| | Non-controlling interest | 2 | |
| | 10% loan notes | ½ | |
| | Current liabilities | 1 | 16 |
| (b) | 1 mark per valid point to maximum | | 4 |
| | | | 20 |

(a)   PEDANTIC CO – CONSOLIDATED STATEMENT OF FINANCIAL POSITION AT 30 SEPTEMBER 20X8

|  | $'000 |
|---|---|
| *Non-current assets* | |
| Property, plant and equipment (40,600 + 12,600 + 1,800 (W6)) | 55,000 |
| Goodwill (W2) | 4,500 |
| | 59,500 |
| *Current assets* (16,000 + 6,600 – 800 – 600 + 200) (or see (W9)) | 21,400 |
| Total assets | 80,900 |
| *Equity attributable to owners of the parent* | |
| Share capital (10,000 +1,600 (W5)) | 11,600 |
| Share premium (W5) | 8,000 |
| Retained earnings (W3) | 35,700 |
| | 55,300 |
| Non-controlling interests (W4) | 6,100 |
| | 61,400 |
| *Non-current liabilities* | |
| 10% loan notes (3,000 + 4,000) | 7,000 |
| *Current liabilities* (8,200 + 4,700 – 400 (W9)) | 12,500 |
| | 80,900 |

(b)   Pedantic Co cannot take assurance from the Tradhat group financial statements that Trilby Co would be able to meet its liability in respect of the goods. The group financial statements will have aggregated the assets and liabilities of all the group companies and it will not be possible to use them to calculate liquidity ratios for any one company.

This is important, because Pedantic Co's contract would not be with the Tradhat group, it would be with Trilby Co. If Trilby Co defaulted on its obligations, the Tradhat group would be under no legal obligation to step in, so that the fact that the group has a strong financial position is not really relevant. It would only become relevant if Tradhat group were willing to offer a parent company guarantee.

In the absence of a parent company guarantee, Pedantic Co must base its decision on the financial position of Trilby Co as shown in its individual company financial statements. It should also obtain references from other suppliers of Trilby Co, specifically those who supply it with large orders on 90 day credit terms.

*Workings*

1    *Group structure*

Pedantic Co

1.4.X8                    60%              Mid-year acquisition, six months before year end

Sophistic Co

2    *Goodwill*

| | $'000 | $'000 |
|---|---|---|
| Consideration transferred (W5) | | 9,600 |
| Fair value of non-controlling interests | | 5,900 |
| Less: Fair value of net assets at acquisition: | | |
| Share capital | 4,000 | |
| Retained earnings | 5,000 | |
| Fair value adjustment (W6) | 2,000 | |
| | | (11,000) |
| Goodwill | | 4,500 |

3    *Retained earnings*

| | Pedantic Co | Sophistic Co |
|---|---|---|
| | $'000 | $'000 |
| Per question | 35,400 | 6,500 |
| Movement on FV adjustment (W6) | | (200) |
| PUP (W7) | | (800) |
| Pre-acquisition | | (5,000) |
| | | 500 |
| Group share (500 × 60%) | 300 | |
| | 35,700 | |

4    *Non-controlling interests*

| | $'000 |
|---|---|
| NCI at acquisition | 5,900 |
| NCI share of post-acquisition retained earnings ((W3) 500 × 40%) | 200 |
| | 6,100 |

5    *Share exchange*

| | Dr | Cr |
|---|---|---|
| | $'000 | $'000 |
| Consideration transferred (4,000 × 60% × 2/3 = 1,600 × $6) | 9,600 | |
| Share capital of Pedantic Co (1,600 × $1) | | 1,600 |
| Share premium of Pedantic Co (1,600 × $5) | | 8,000 |

6    *Fair value adjustments*

| | $'000 | $'000 | $'000 |
|---|---|---|---|
| | Acq'n | Mov't | Year end |
| | 1.4.X8 | 6/12 | 30.9.X8 |
| Plant (*$2m / 5 × 6/12) | 2,000 | (200)* | 1,800 |

7    *Intragroup trading*

| | $'000 | $'000 |
|---|---|---|
| Eliminate unrealised profit | | |
| Cost of sales/retained earnings ((8,000 – 5,200) × 40 / 140) | 800 | |
| Inventories (SOFP) | | 800 |

8    Current assets (supplementary working)

|                                          | $'000 |
|------------------------------------------|-------:|
| Pedantic Co                              | 16,000 |
| Sophistic Co                             | 6,600 |
| Unrealised profit in inventory (W7)      | (800) |
| Intercompany receivables (per question)  | (600) |
| Cash in transit (W9)                     | 200 |
|                                          | 21,400 |

9    Cash in transit

|             | Dr  | Cr  |
|-------------|----:|----:|
| Receivables |     | 600 |
| Payables    | 400 |     |
| Cash        | 200 |     |

# 284 Highveldt Co

> **Text reference.** Chapter 9.
>
> **Top tips.** Make sure that you read the question before doing anything. You are not asked to prepare a statement of financial position; just the goodwill and reserves. This makes the question easier to manage effectively as you are just doing the workings without having to tie it all together in a set of financial statements.
>
> There are quite a few complications to consider. For each calculation go through each of the six additional pieces of information and make appropriate adjustments when relevant.
>
> **Examining Team's comments.** This question was unusual in asking for extracts from the statement of financial position. Many candidates were confused by this and wasted time preparing a full statement of financial position. Other common errors were: fair value adjustments; consolidated reserves; revaluation and share premium reserves; and the cost of the investment.

|       |                              |                            |     | Marks |
|-------|------------------------------|----------------------------|----:|------:|
| (i)   | *Goodwill*                   |                            |     |       |
|       | –                            | Consideration transferred  | 2   |       |
|       | –                            | Non-controlling interest   | 1   |       |
|       | –                            | Share capital and premium  | 1   |       |
|       | –                            | Retained earnings          | 1   |       |
|       | –                            | Fair value adjustments     | 2   |       |
|       | –                            | Goodwill impairment        | 1   |       |
|       | Maximum                      |                            |     | 8     |
| (ii)  | *Non-controlling interest*   |                            |     |       |
|       | –                            | Share capital and premium  | 1   |       |
|       | –                            | Retained earnings          | 2   |       |
|       | –                            | Fair value adjustment      | 1   |       |
|       | Maximum                      |                            |     | 4     |
| (iii) | *Consolidated reserves*      |                            |     |       |
|       | –                            | Share premium              | 1   |       |
|       | –                            | Revaluation surplus        | 2   |       |
|       | *Retained earnings*          |                            |     |       |
|       | –                            | Post-acquisition profit    | 2   |       |
|       | –                            | Interest receivable        | 1   |       |
|       | –                            | Finance cost               | 1   |       |
|       | –                            | Goodwill impairment        | 1   |       |
|       | Maximum                      |                            |     | 8     |
|       |                              | **Maximum for question**   |     | 20    |

(i) *Goodwill in Samson Co*

|  | $m | $m |
|---|---:|---:|
| Consideration transferred |  |  |
| 80m shares × 75% × $3.50 |  | 210 |
| Deferred consideration: $108m × $^1/_{1.08}$ |  | 100 |
|  |  | 310 |
| Non-controlling interest |  | 83 |
| Fair value of net assets at acquisition: |  |  |
| Carrying amount of net assets at 1.4.20X4: |  |  |
| Ordinary shares | 80 |  |
| Share premium | 40 |  |
| Retained earnings | 134 |  |
| Fair value adjustments (W) | 42 |  |
|  |  | (296) |
|  |  | 97 |
| Impairment charge given in question |  | (20) |
| Carrying amount at 31 March 20X5 |  | 77 |

*Working*

|  | $m |
|---|---:|
| *Fair value adjustment:* |  |
| Revaluation of land | 20 |
| Recognition of fair value of brands | 40 |
| Derecognition of capitalised development expenditure | (18) |
|  | 42 |

(ii) *Non-controlling interest in Samson Co's net assets*

|  | $m |
|---|---:|
| NCI at acquisition (per question) | 83 |
| NCI share of post-acquisition retained earnings ((iii) 48 × 25%) | 12 |
| NCI share of post-acquisition revaluation surplus ((iii) 4 × 25%) | 1 |
| NCI share of goodwill impairment ($20m × 25%) | (5) |
|  | 91 |

(iii) *Consolidated Reserves*

*Share premium*

The share premium of a group, like the share capital, is the share premium of the parent only ($80m)

*Revaluation surplus*

|  | $m |
|---|---:|
| Parent's own revaluation surplus | 45 |
| Group share of Samson Co's post-acquisition revaluation; $4m × 75% | 3 |

*Retained earnings attributable to owners of the parent*

|  | Highveldt $m | Samson $m |
|---|---:|---:|
| Per question | 350 | 76 |
| Accrued interest from Samson Co ($60m × 10%) | 6 | – |
| Unwinding of discount on deferred consideration | (8) | – |
| Amortisation of brand ($40m/10 years) | – | (4) |
| Write off development expenditure as incurred ($50m – $18m) | – | (32) |
| Write back amortisation of development expenditure | – | 10 |
| Unrealised profit | – | (2) |
|  | 348 | 48 |
| Group share (75%) | 36 |  |
| Impairment of goodwill in Samson Co – group share (20 × 75%) | (15) |  |
|  | 369 |  |

# 285 Paradigm Co

## Marking scheme

|  | Marks |
|---|---|
| Statement of financial position | |
| Property, plant and equipment | 1½ |
| Goodwill | 5 |
| Equity investments | 1 |
| Inventories | 1 |
| Trade receivables | 1½ |
| Cash and cash equivalents | 1 |
| Equity shares | 1½ |
| Share premium | ½ |
| Retained earnings | 3 |
| Non-controlling interest | 1½ |
| 10% loan notes | 1 |
| Trade payables | 1 |
| Bank overdraft | ½ |
|  | 20 |

# CONSOLIDATED STATEMENT OF FINANCIAL POSITION AS AT 31 MARCH 20X3

| | $'000 | $'000 |
|---|---|---|
| **ASSETS** | | |
| *Non-current assets* | | |
| Property, plant and equipment (47,400 + 25,500 – 2,500 (W6)) | | 70,400 |
| Goodwill (W1) | | 8,500 |
| Financial asset: equity investments (7,100 + 3,900) | | 11,000 |
| | | 89,900 |
| *Current assets* | | |
| Inventories (17,400 + 8,400 – 600 (W2)) | 25,200 | |
| Trade receivables (14,800 + 9,000 – 900 (W3) – 2,800 interco) | 20,100 | |
| Cash and cash equivalents (5,100 + 900 (W3)) | 6,000 | |
| | | 51,300 |
| *Total assets* | | 141,200 |
| **EQUITY AND LIABILITIES** | | |
| *Equity attributable to owners of Paradigm Co* | | |
| Share capital (40,000 + 6,000 (W1)) | | 46,000 |
| Share premium (W1) | | 6,000 |
| Retained earnings (W4) | | 34,000 |
| | | 86,000 |
| Non-controlling interest (W5) | | 8,800 |
| | | 94,800 |
| *Non-current liabilities* | | |
| 10% loan notes (8,000 + 1,500 (W1)) | | 9,500 |
| *Current liabilities* | | |
| Trade payables (17,600 + 13,000 – 2,800 intercompany) | 27,800 | |
| Overdraft | 9,100 | |
| | | 36,900 |
| *Total equity and liabilities* | | 141,200 |

## Workings

### 1  Goodwill

| | $'000 | $'000 |
|---|---|---|
| Consideration transferred: | | |
| Shares (20m × 2/5 × 75% × $2) | | 12,000 |
| Loan notes (15m × 100 / 1,000) | | 1,500 |
| | | 13,500 |
| Non-controlling interest (5m × $1.2) | | 6,000 |
| | | 19,500 |
| Net assets at acquisition; | | |
| Share capital | 20,000 | |
| Retained earnings ((4,000) + (2,000)) | (6,000) | |
| Fair value adjustment (W5) | (3,000) | |
| | | (11,000) |
| Goodwill | | 8,500 |

### 2  PURP

Intercompany sales in inventory $4.6m
PURP = $4.6m × 15 / 115 = $600,000

### 3  Intercompany cash in transit

| | $'000 | $'000 |
|---|---|---|
| Dr Cash | 900 | |
| Cr Receivables | | 900 |

4    *Retained earnings*

|  | Paradigm $'000 | Strata $'000 |
|---|---|---|
| Per draft | 26,600 | 4,000 |
| Add back pre-acquisition loss |  | 6,000 |
|  |  | 10,000 |
| PURP (W2) | (600) |  |
| Gain (loss) on equity investments* | (400) | 700 |
| Movement on fair value adjustment (W6) |  | 500 |
|  |  | 11,200 |
| Group share of Strata Co – 75% × 11,200 | 8,400 |  |
| Group retained earnings | 34,000 |  |

*Loss on equity investments in Paradigm Co: (7,500 – 7,100)

5    *Non-controlling interest*

|  | $'000 |
|---|---|
| Fair value at acquisition (W1) | 6,000 |
| Share of post-acquisition retained earnings (11,200 (W4) × 25%) | 2,800 |
|  | 8,800 |

6    Movement on fair value adjustment

|  | At acquisition $'000 | Movement $'000 | At year end $'000 |
|---|---|---|---|
| FVA on plant (W1) | (3,000) | 500 | (2,500) |

# Section C

# 286 Boo Co and Goose Co

BOO GROUP – CONSOLIDATED STATEMENT OF PROFIT OR LOSS AND OTHER COMPREHENSIVE INCOME FOR THE YEAR ENDED 31 DECEMBER 20X8

|  | $'000 |
|---|---|
| Revenue (5,000 + 1,000 – 100 (W5)) | 5,900 |
| Cost of sales (2,900 + 600 – 100 + 20 (W5)) | (3,420) |
| Gross profit | 2,480 |
| Other expenses (1,700 + 320) | (2,020) |
| Profit before tax | 460 |
| Tax (130 + 30) | (160) |
| Profit for the year | 300 |
| Other comprehensive income |  |
| Gain on property revaluation | 20 |
| Total comprehensive income for the year | 320 |
| Profit attributable to |  |
|   Owners of the parent | 290 |
|   Non-controlling interest (20% × 50) | 10 |
|  | 300 |
| Total comprehensive income attributable to |  |
|   Owners of the parent (ß) | 310 |
|   Non-controlling interest | 10 |
|  | 320 |

CONSOLIDATED STATEMENT OF FINANCIAL POSITION AS AT 31 DECEMBER 20X8

|  | $'000 | $'000 |
|---|---|---|
| *Assets* |  |  |
| Non-current assets (1,940 + 200) |  | 2,140 |
| Goodwill (W2) |  | 70 |
| Current assets |  |  |
| Inventories (500 + 120 + 80) | 700 |  |
| Trade receivables (650 – 100 (W5) + 40) | 590 |  |
| Cash and cash equivalents (170 + 35) | 205 |  |
|  |  | 1,495 |
| Total assets |  | 3,705 |
| *Equity and liabilities* |  |  |
| Equity attributable to owners of the parent |  |  |
| Share capital (Boo only) |  | 2,000 |
| Retained earnings (W3) |  | 520 |
| Revaluation surplus |  | 20 |
|  |  | 2,540 |
| Non-controlling interest (W4) |  | 70 |
| Total equity |  | 2,610 |
| *Current liabilities* |  |  |
| Trade payables (910 + 30) | 940 |  |
| Tax (130 + 25) | 155 |  |
|  |  | 1,095 |
| Total equity and liabilities |  | 3,705 |

*Workings*

1    *Group structure*

Boo Co

|   80%

↓

Goose Co

2    *Goodwill*

|  | $'000 | $'000 |
|---|---|---|
| Consideration transferred | | 300 |
| Fair value of non-controlling interest | | 60 |
| | | 360 |
| Fair value of net assets: | | |
|   Share capital | 100 | |
|   Retained earnings | 190 | (290) |
| Goodwill | | 70 |

3    *Retained earnings*

|  | Boo Co | Goose Co |
|---|---|---|
|  | $'000 | $'000 |
| Per question | 500 | 240 |
| Unrealised profit (W5) | (20) | |
|  | 480 | |
| Less pre-acquisition | | (190) |
|  | | 50 |
| Goose: 80% × 50 | 40 | |
| Group total | 520 | |

4    *Non-controlling interest*

|  | $'000 |
|---|---|
| NCI at acquisition | 60 |
| NCI share of post-acquisition retained earnings (50 × 20%) | 10 |
| | 70 |

5    *Intragroup issues*

**Step 1: Record Goose Co's purchase**

| DEBIT Cost of sales | $100,000 | |
|---|---|---|
| CREDIT Payables | | $100,000 |
| DEBIT Closing inventory (SFP) | $100,000 | |
| CREDIT Cost of sales | | $100,000 |

These transactions can be simplified to:

| DEBIT Inventory | $100,000 | |
|---|---|---|
| CREDIT Payables | | $100,000 |

**Step 2: Cancel unrealised profit**

| DEBIT COS (and retained earnings) in Boo | $20,000 | |
|---|---|---|
| CREDIT Inventory (SFP) | | $20,000 |

**Step 3: Cancel intragroup transaction**

| DEBIT Revenue | $100,000 | |
|---|---|---|
| CREDIT Cost of sales | | $100,000 |

**Step 4: Cancel intragroup balances**

| DEBIT Payables | $100,000 | |
|---|---|---|
| CREDIT Receivables | | $100,000 |

# 287 Viagem Co (Dec12 amended)

**Text reference.** Chapter 9.

**Top tips.** The goodwill impairment must be deducted from the consolidated profit or loss. The subsidiary has been owned for nine months so revenue and expenses must be apportioned. You have not been told that the parent has accounted for the unwinding of the discount on the deferred consideration, so you should assume that (as is normal for this exam) you have to make this adjustment.

**Easy marks.** There were plenty of marks available here for standard workings.

## Marking scheme

|  | Marks |
|---|---|
| Goodwill | 6 |
| Consolidated statement of profit or loss: |  |
|     Revenue | 2 |
|     Cost of sales | 2 |
|     Distribution costs | 1 |
|     Administrative expenses | 2 |
|     Share of profit of associate | 1½ |
|     Finance costs | 2 |
|     Income tax | 1 |
|     Profit for year – attributable to parent | ½ |
|                   – attributable to NCI | 2 |
|  | 14 |
|  | 20 |

(a)    Consolidated goodwill at acquisition

|  | $'000 | $'000 |
|---|---|---|
| Consideration transferred: |  |  |
| Shares (9m × 2/3 × $6.50) |  | 39,000 |
| Deferred consideration ((9m × $1.76) / 1.1) |  | 14,400 |
|  |  | 53,400 |
| Non-controlling interest ((10m × $2.50) × 10%) |  | 2,500 |
|  |  | 55,900 |
| Fair value of net assets: |  |  |
| Share capital | 10,000 |  |
| Retained earnings: b/f | 35,000 |  |
|              three months to 1 Jan 20X2 (6,200 × 3/12) | 1,550 |  |
| FVA on plant | 1,800 |  |
| Contingent liability | (450) |  |
|  |  | (47,900) |
| Goodwill |  | 8,000 |

(b)  CONSOLIDATED STATEMENT OF PROFIT OR LOSS FOR THE YEAR ENDED 30 SEPTEMBER 20X2

|  | $'000 |
|---|---|
| Revenue (64,600 + (38,000 × 9/12) − 7,200 (W2)) | 85,900 |
| Cost of sales (51,200 + (26,000 × 9/12) − 7,200 + 300 (W2) + 450 (W3)) | (64,250) |
| Gross profit | 21,650 |
| Distribution costs (1,600 + (1,800 × 9/12)) | (2,950) |
| Administrative expenses (3,800 + (2,400 × 9/12) + 2,000 (goodwill impairment)) | (7,600) |
| Finance costs (W4) | (1,500) |
| Share of profit of associate (2,000 × 40%) | 800 |
| Profit before tax | 10,400 |
| Income tax expense (2,800 + (1,600 × 9/12)) | (4,000) |
| Profit for the year | 6,400 |
|  |  |
| Profit attributable to |  |
| Owners of the parent (ß) | 6,180 |
| Non-controlling interest (W5) | 220 |
|  | 6,400 |

*Workings*

1   *Group structure*

Viagem Co

1 Jan 20X2  |  90%   Mid-year acquisition, nine months before year end

↓

Greca Co

2   *Intragroup trading*

|  | $'000 | $'000 |
|---|---|---|
| Intragroup trading (800 × 9 months) |  |  |
| DEBIT  Revenue | 7,200 |  |
| CREDIT  Cost of sales |  | 7,200 |
|  |  |  |
| PURP (1,500 × 25/125) |  |  |
| DEBIT  Cost of sales | 300 |  |
| CREDIT Group inventory (SFP) |  | 300 |

3   *Fair value adjustment*

|  | Acquisition | Movement | Year end |
|---|---|---|---|
|  | $'000 | $'000 | $'000 |
| Plant | 1,800 | (450)* | 1,350 |

*(1,800 / 3) × 9/12

4   *Finance costs*

|  | $'000 |
|---|---|
| Viagem Co per statement of profit or loss | 420 |
| Unwinding of discount on deferred consideration: |  |
| ((14,400 × 10%) × 9/12) | 1,080 |
|  | 1,500 |

5   *Non-controlling interest*

|  | $'000 |
|---|---|
| Profit for the year (6,200 × 9/12) | 4,650 |
| Depreciation on fair value adjustment (W3) | (450) |
| Goodwill impairment | (2,000) |
|  | 2,200 |
|  |  |
| Non-controlling share 10% | 220 |

# 288 Prodigal Co (Jun11 amended)

**Text reference**. Chapter 9.

**Top tips**. The first point to note is that Sentinel Co was acquired mid-year. Always pay close attention to dates.

**Easy marks**. Revenue is relatively straightforward for two marks and for all of the expense categories apart from cost of sales it was only necessary to take Prodigal Co's balance plus 6/12 Sentinel Co. The other comprehensive income was also easy.

**Examining Team's comments**. There were many good scores here. Two problem areas were dealing with the elimination of intragroup sales and the additional depreciation on the asset transfer. Some candidates failed to calculate NCI in the total comprehensive income.

## Marking scheme

|     |                                                               | Marks |    |
|-----|---------------------------------------------------------------|-------|----|
| (a) | Goodwill on acquisition                                       |       |    |
|     | Consideration transferred                                     | 2     |    |
|     | Fair value of NCI                                             | ½     |    |
|     | Fair value of net assets                                      | 1½    | 4  |
| (b) | Statement of profit or loss and other comprehensive income    |       |    |
|     | Revenue                                                       | 2     |    |
|     | Cost of sales                                                 | 4     |    |
|     | Distribution costs and administrative expenses                | 2     |    |
|     | Finance costs                                                 | 1½    |    |
|     | Income tax expense                                            | 1     |    |
|     | Non-controlling interest in profit for the year               | 1½    |    |
|     | Other comprehensive income                                    | 2½    |    |
|     | Non-controlling interest in other comprehensive income        | 1½    | 16 |
|     |                                                               |       | 20 |

---

(a) Goodwill on acquisition of Sentinel Co

|                                                      | $'000   | $'000     |
|------------------------------------------------------|---------|-----------|
| Consideration (((160,000 × 75%) × 2/3) × $4)         |         | 320,000   |
| Fair value of non-controlling interest               |         | 100,000   |
|                                                      |         | 420,000   |
| Fair value of net assets:                            |         |           |
| Shares                                               | 160,000 |           |
| Other equity reserve (2,200-(400 × 6/12)*)           | 2,000   |           |
| Retained earnings (125,000 + (66,000 × 6/12))        | 191,000 |           |
|                                                      |         | (353,000) |
| Goodwill                                             |         | 67,000    |

*__Note.__ Of the $400,000 loss on the investment in equity instruments, half (6/12) is pre-acquisition and goes to the goodwill calculation. The remainder is post-acquisition and goes to the consolidated statement of profit or loss.

(b) CONSOLIDATED STATEMENT OF PROFIT OR LOSS AND OTHER COMPREHENSIVE INCOME
FOR THE YEAR ENDED 31 MARCH 20X1

| | $'000 |
|---|---:|
| Revenue (450,00 + (240,000 × 6/12) – (W4) 40,000) | 530,000 |
| Cost of sales (260,000 + (110,000 × 6/12) + (W3) 800 – (W4) 40,000 + 3,000) | (278,800) |
| Gross profit | 251,200 |
| Distribution costs (23,600 + (12,000 × 6/12)) | (29,600) |
| Administrative expenses (27,000 + (23,000 × 6/12)) | (38,500) |
| Finance costs (1,500 + (1,200 × 6/12)) | (2,100) |
| Profit before tax | 181,000 |
| Income tax expense (48,000 + (27,800 × 6/12)) | (61,900) |
| Profit for the year | 119,100 |
| Other comprehensive income: | |
| Gain on land revaluation (2,500 + 1,000)* | 3,500 |
| Investments in equity instruments** (700 + (400 × 6/12)) | (900) |
| Other comprehensive income, net of tax | 2,600 |
| Total comprehensive income for the year | 121,700 |
| Profit attributable to: | |
| Owners of the parent (bal) | 111,550 |
| Non-controlling interests (W2) | 7,550 |
| | 119,100 |
| Total comprehensive income attributable to: | |
| Owners of the parent (bal) | 113,950 |
| Non-controlling interests (W2) | 7,750 |
| | 121,700 |

*All post-acquisition
**Could also be described as equity financial asset investments

*Workings*

1 *Group structure and timeline*

Prodigal Co

⬇

Sentinel Co 1.10.20X0 75%

1.4.20X0    1.10.20X0    31.3.20X1

Prodigal Co                    >

Sentinel Co× 6/12

2 *Non-controlling interests*

| | Profit for year $'000 | Total comprehensive income $'000 |
|---|---:|---:|
| Per question (66,000 × 6/12) ((66,000 – 400) × 6/12 + 1,000)) | 33,000 | 33,800 |
| Non-current asset PURP (W3) excess depreciation | 200 | 200 |
| PUP (W4) | (3,000) | (3,000) |
| | 30,200 | 31,000 |
| × | 25% | 25% |
| | 7,550 | 7,750 |

3    *Transfer of plant*

|                                                    | $'000  |
|----------------------------------------------------|--------|
| 1.10.20X0 Profit on transfer (5,000 – 4,000)       | 1,000  |
| Proportion depreciated (½ / 2½)                    | (200)  |
| Adjustment to plant                                | 800    |

Required adjustment:

| Dr Cost of sales (and retained earnings) | 850 |
| Cr Plant                                 | 800 |
| Cr NCI (200 × 25%)                       | 50  |

Note that the excess depreciation is credited to the subsidiary. This is netted off against the unrealised profit in group cost of sales, but 25% must be credited to the NCI.

4    *Intragroup trading*

Cancel intragroup sales/purchases:

|                                                      | $'000  | $'000  |
|------------------------------------------------------|--------|--------|
| Dr Group revenue                                     | 40,000 |        |
| Cr Group cost of sales                               |        | 40,000 |
| ((40,000 – 30,000) × 12,000 / 40,000) = 3,000        |        |        |
| DR Cost of sales (Sentinel Co) (NCI)                 | 3,000  |        |
| CR Group inventories                                 |        | 3,000  |

# 289 Plastik Co (Dec14 amended)

**Text references.** Chapters 3, 4 and 14.

**Top tips.** This is quite a time-pressured question so you need to work fast. Get the proforma down for the statement of profit or loss and then go methodically through the workings, filling in the proforma as you go.

**Easy marks.** There are some marks available for figures that can be lifted straight from the question and good, clear workings will help you to fill in several gaps.

**Marking scheme**

|       |                                                               |      | Marks |
|-------|---------------------------------------------------------------|------|-------|
| (a)   | Goodwill                                                      |      | 4     |
| (b)   | Group retained earnings                                       | 4    |       |
|       | Non-controlling interest                                      | 2    |       |
|       |                                                               |      | 6     |
| (c)   | Consolidated statement of profit or loss and other comprehensive income |      |       |
|       | Revenue                                                       | 1½   |       |
|       | Cost of sales                                                 | 2½   |       |
|       | Distribution costs                                            | ½    |       |
|       | Administrative expenses (including goodwill impairment)       | 1    |       |
|       | Finance costs                                                 | 1    |       |
|       | Income tax expense                                            | ½    |       |
|       | Gain on revaluation of properties                             | 1    |       |
|       | Non-controlling interest  – profit for the year              | 1    |       |
|       |                 – total comprehensive income                  | 1    |       |
|       |                                                               |      | 10    |
|       | Total for question                                            |      | 20    |

(a) *Goodwill*

|  | $'000 | $'000 |
|---|---|---|
| Consideration transferred – 4.8m shares @ $3 |  | 14,400 |
| Deferred consideration (7.2m × $0.275 × 1/1.1) |  | 1,800 |
|  |  | 16,200 |
| Fair value of NCI (1.8m shares @ $2.50) |  | 4,500 |
|  |  | 20,700 |
| Fair value of net assets: |  |  |
| Shares | 9,000 |  |
| Retained earnings (3,500 – (2,000 × 9/12)) | 2,000 |  |
| Fair value adjustment – property | 4,000 |  |
|  |  | (15,000) |
| Goodwill at acquisition |  | 5,700 |

(b) *Retained earnings*

|  | Plastik $'000 | Subtrak $'000 |
|---|---|---|
| Per question | 6,300 | 3,500 |
| Less pre-acquisition (1,500 + (2,000 × 3/12)) |  | (2,000) |
| Goodwill impairment |  | (500) |
| Unwinding of discount on deferred consideration (1,800 (a) × 10% × 9/12) | (135) |  |
| Depreciation on FVA |  | (100) |
| PURP (600,000 × 25/125) | (120) |  |
|  | 6,045 | 900 |
| Share of Subtrak Co (900 × 80%) | 720 |  |
|  | 6,765 |  |

*Non-controlling interest*

|  | $'000 |
|---|---|
| NCI at acquisition (see goodwill) | 4,500 |
| Share of post-acquisition retained earnings (900 × 20%) | 180 |
| Share of property revaluation gain (600 × 20%) | 120 |
|  | 4,800 |

(c) CONSOLIDATED STATEMENT OF PROFIT OR LOSS AND OTHER COMPREHENSIVE INCOME FOR THE YEAR ENDED 30 SEPTEMBER 20X4

|  | $'000 |
|---|---|
| Revenue (62,600 + (30,000 × 9/12) – 2,700 (W2)) | 82,400 |
| Cost of sales (45,800 + (24,000 × 9/12) – 2,580 (W2) + 100 (b)) | 61,320 |
| Gross profit | 21,080 |
| Distribution costs (2,000 + (1,200 × 9/12)) | (2,900) |
| Administrative expenses (3,500 + (1,800 × 9/12) + 500 (goodwill)) | (5,350) |
| Finance costs (200 + 135 (see retained earnings)) | (335) |
| Profit before tax | 12,495 |
| Income tax (3,100 + (1,000 × 9/12)) | (3,850) |
|  | 8,645 |
| Other comprehensive income |  |
| Gain on revaluation of property (1,500 + 600) | 2,100 |
| Total comprehensive income | 10,745 |
| Profit for the year attributable to: |  |
| Owners of the parent (β) | 8,465 |
| Non-controlling interest (W1) | 180 |
|  | 8,645 |
| Total comprehensive income attributable to: |  |
| Owners of the parent (β) | 10,445 |
| Non-controlling interest (W1) | 300 |
|  | 10,745 |

1     *Non-controlling interests*

|  | Profit for year<br>$'000 | Total comprehensive income<br>$'000 |
|---|---|---|
| Per (b) above | 900 | 900 |
| Gain on property revaluation |  | 600 |
|  | 900 | 1,500 |
| NCI 20% | 180 | 300 |

2     *Intragroup trading*

|  |  | $'000 | $'000 |
|---|---|---|---|
| (1) | *Cancel intragroup sales/purchases* |  |  |
|  | DEBIT Group revenue (300,000 × 9) | 2,700 |  |
|  | CREDIT Group cost of sales |  | 2,700 |
| (2) | *Eliminate unrealised profit* |  |  |
|  | DEBIT Cost of sales (600,000 × 25/125) | 120 |  |
|  | CREDIT Group inventories |  | 120 |

# 290 Laurel Co

STATEMENT OF FINANCIAL POSITION AS AT 31 DECEMBER 20X9

|  | $m |
|---|---|
| *Non-current assets* |  |
| Property, plant and equipment (220 + 160 + (W7) 3) | 383 |
| Goodwill (W2) | 9 |
| Investment in associate (W3) | 96.8 |
|  | 488.8 |
| *Current assets* |  |
| Inventories (384 + 234 – (W6) 10) | 608 |
| Trade receivables (275 + 166) | 441 |
| Cash and cash equivalents (42 + 10) | 52 |
|  | 1,101 |
|  | 1,589.8 |
| *Equity attributable to owners of the parent* |  |
| Share capital – $1 ordinary shares | 400 |
| Share premium | 16 |
| Retained earnings (W4) | 326.8 |
|  | 742.8 |
| Non-controlling interests (W5) | 47 |
|  | 789.8 |
| *Current liabilities* |  |
| Trade payables (457 + 343) | 800.0 |
|  | 1,589.8 |

*Workings*

1     *Group structure*

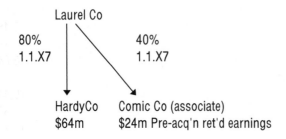

2   *Goodwill*

|  | $m | $m |
|---|---|---|
| Consideration transferred | | 160 |
| Non-controlling interests (at fair value) | | 39 |
| Fair value of net assets at acq'n: | | |
| Share capital | 96 | |
| Share premium | 3 | |
| Retained earnings | 64 | |
| Fair value adjustment (W7) | 12 | |
| | | (175) |
| | | 24 |
| Impairment losses | | (15) |
| | | 9 |

3   *Investment in associate*

|  | $m |
|---|---|
| Cost of associate | 70 |
| Share of post-acquisition retained reserves (W4) | 29.2 |
| Unrealised profit (W6) | (2.4) |
| Impairment losses | (0) |
| | 96.8 |

4   *Consolidated retained earnings*

|  | *Laurel* $m | *Hardy* $m | *Comic* $m |
|---|---|---|---|
| Per question | 278 | 128 | 97 |
| Less: PUP re Hardy Co (W6) | (10) | | |
| PUP re Comic Co (W6) | (2.4) | | |
| Fair value adjustment movement (W7) | | (9) | |
| Less pre-acquisition retained earnings | | (64) | (24) |
| | | 55 | 73 |
| Group share of post-acquisition retained earnings: | | | |
| Hardy Co (55 × 80%) | 44 | | |
| Comic Co (73 × 40%) | 29.2 | | |
| Less group share of impairment losses (15 × 80%) | (12.0) | | |
| | 326.8 | | |

5   *Non-controlling interests*

|  | $m |
|---|---|
| Non-controlling interests at acquisition (W2) | 39 |
| NCI share of post-acquisition retained earnings: | |
| Hardy Co (55 × 20%) | 11 |
| Less NCI share of impairment losses (15 × 20%) | (3) |
| | 47 |

6   *Unrealised profit*

Laurel Co's sales to Hardy Co: $32m − $22m =   $10m

| DR Retained earnings (Laurel Co) | $10m |
|---|---|
| CR Group inventories | $10m |

Laurel Co's sales to Comic Co (associate) ($22m − $10m) × ½ × 40% share = $2.4m.

| DR Retained earnings (Laurel Co) | $2.4m |
|---|---|
| CR Investment in associate | $2.4m |

7   *Fair value adjustments*

|  | At acquisition date $m | Movement $m | At year end $m |
|---|---|---|---|
| PPE (57 – 45) | +12 | (9)* | +3 |
|  | ↓ | ↓ | ↓ |
|  | Goodwill | Ret'd earnings | PPE |

*Extra depreciation $12m × ¾

# 291 Tyson Co

STATEMENT OF PROFIT OR LOSS AND OTHER COMPREHENSIVE INCOME FOR THE YEAR ENDED 31 DECEMBER 20X8

|  | $m |
|---|---|
| Revenue (500 + 150 – 66) | 584 |
| Cost of sales (270 + 80 – 66 + (W3) 18) | (302) |
| Gross profit | 282 |
| Other expenses (150 + 20 + 15) | (185) |
| Finance income (15 + 10) | 25 |
| Finance costs | (20) |
| Share of profit of associate ((10 × 40%) – 2.4*) | 1.6 |
| Profit before tax | 103.6 |
| Income tax expense (25 + 15) | (40) |
| Profit for the year | 63.6 |
| Other comprehensive income: |  |
| Gains on property revaluation, net of tax (20 + 10) | 30 |
| Share of other comprehensive income of associate (5 × 40%) | 2 |
| Other comprehensive income for the year, net of tax | 32.0 |
| Total comprehensive income for the year | 95.6 |
|  |  |
| Profit attributable to: |  |
| Owners of the parent (63.6 – 2.4) | 61.2 |
| Non-controlling interests (W2) | 2.4 |
|  | 63.6 |
|  |  |
| Total comprehensive income attributable to: |  |
| Owners of the parent (95.6 – 4.4) | 91.2 |
| Non-controlling interests (W2) | 4.4 |
|  | 95.6 |

*Impairment losses could either be included in expenses or deducted from the share of profit of associates figure. IAS 28 is not prescriptive.

*Workings*

1 *Group structure*

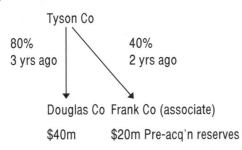

Tyson Co

80%
3 yrs ago

40%
2 yrs ago

Douglas Co  Frank Co (associate)

$40m        $20m Pre-acq'n reserves

2 *Non-controlling interests*

|  | PFY $m | TCI $m |
|---|---|---|
| PFY/TCI per question | 45 | 55 |
| Unrealised profit (W3) | (18) | (18) |
| Impairment loss | (15) | (15) |
|  | 12 | 22 |
| × NCI share (20%) | 2.4 | 4.4 |

3 *Unrealised profit*

|  | $m |
|---|---|
| Selling price | 66 |
| Cost | (48) |
| PUP | 18 |

# 292 Paladin Co (Dec11 amended)

**Text references**. Chapters 4 and 8.

**Top tips**. This is a pretty straightforward consolidated statement of financial position. Set out the proformas and then work methodically through the numbers. There are quite a few adjustments to retained earnings, so make sure your retained earnings working is very clear.

**Easy marks**. There are a lot of easy marks in this question. The complications are dealing with the deferred payment and the unwinding of the discount, capitalising and amortising the intangible asset and remembering to deduct the intercompany balance from receivables and payables. Most of the rest of it is quite easy, the PURP is only in the parent and two marks are available for investment in associate, which is not a complicated working. Part (b) is easy marks for correctly assessing the situation.

**Examining Team's comments**. The parts of this question that related to basic consolidation adjustments were well dealt with by most candidates. Errors occurred in the more complex aspects. Some candidates failed to discount the deferred consideration and some did not treat the customer relationship as an intangible asset. Others deducted the post-acquisition additional depreciation from the goodwill. Some students only deducted 25% of the impairment loss on the investment in associate, when the loss applied to the whole of the investment. A common error was to offset the subsidiary's overdraft against the parent's bank balance. No such right of offset exists.

| | Marks |
|---|---|
| Consolidated statement of financial position | |
| Property, plant and equipment | 2 |
| Goodwill | 4 |
| Other intangibles | 2 |
| Investment in associate | 2 |
| Inventories | 1 |
| Trade receivables | 1 |
| Cash and cash equivalents | ½ |
| Equity shares | ½ |
| Retained earnings | 4 |
| Non-controlling interest | 2 |
| Deferred tax | ½ |
| Bank overdraft | ½ |
| Deferred consideration | 1 |
| Trade payables | 1 |
| | 22 |
| Maximum | 20 |

CONSOLIDATED STATEMENT OF FINANCIAL POSITION AS AT 30 SEPTEMBER 20X1

| | $'000 |
|---|---|
| ASSETS | |
| *Non-current assets* | |
| Property, plant and equipment (40,000 + 31,000 + 3,000 (W6)) | 74,000 |
| Goodwill (W2) | 15,000 |
| Intangible assets (7,500 + 2,500 (W6)) | 10,000 |
| Investment in associate (W3) | 7,700 |
| | 106,700 |
| *Current assets* | |
| Inventories (11,200 + 8,400 – 600 (W7)) | 19,000 |
| Trade receivables (7,400 + 5,300 – 1,300 (W7)) | 11,400 |
| Cash and cash equivalents | 3,400 |
| | 33,800 |
| Total assets | 140,500 |
| EQUITY AND LIABILITIES | |
| *Equity attributable to owners of Paladin* | |
| Share capital | 50,000 |
| Retained earnings (W4) | 35,200 |
| | 85,200 |
| Non-controlling interests (W5) | 7,900 |
| | 93,100 |
| *Non-current liabilities* | |
| Deferred tax (15,000 + 8,000) | 23,000 |
| *Current liabilities* | |
| Overdraft | 2,500 |
| Trade payables (11,600 + 6,200 – 1,300 (W7)) | 16,500 |
| Deferred consideration (5,000 + 400 (W2)) | 5,400 |
| | 24,400 |
| Total equity and liabilities | 140,500 |

*Workings*

1    *Group structure*

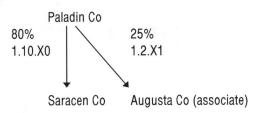

2    *Goodwill*

|  | $'000 | $'000 |
|---|---|---|
| Consideration transferred: |  |  |
| Cash |  | 32,000 |
| Deferred consideration |  | 5,000 |
|  |  | 37,000 |
| Non-controlling interest |  | 7,000 |
|  |  | 44,000 |
| Fair value of net assets: |  |  |
| Share capital | 10,000 |  |
| Retained earnings | 12,000 |  |
| Fair value adjustment on plant | 4,000 |  |
| Intangible asset | 3,000 |  |
|  |  | (29,000) |
| Goodwill |  | 15,000 |

3    *Investment in associate*

|  | $'000 |
|---|---|
| Cost of investment | 10,000 |
| Share of post-acquisition retained earnings (800 (W4) × 25%) | 200 |
| Impairment | (2,500) |
|  | 7,700 |

4    *Retained earnings*

|  | Paladin Co | Saracen Co | Augusta Co |
|---|---|---|---|
|  | $'000 | $'000 | $'000 |
| Per question – 1.10.20X0 | 25,700 | 12,000 | 31,800 |
|         – year to 30.9.20X1 | 9,200 | 6,000 | 1,200 |
|  |  | 18,000 | 33,000 |
| PURP (W7) | (600) |  |  |
| Depreciation on fair value adjustments (W6) |  | (1,500) |  |
| Unwinding of discount (5,400 – 5,000 (W2)) | (400) |  |  |
| Less pre-acquisition retained earnings to |  |  |  |
| 1.10.20X0 |  | (12,000) | (31,800) |
| Less pre-acquisition to 1.2.X1 (1,200 × 4/12) |  | – | (400) |
|  |  | 4,500 | 800 |
| Saracen Co (4,500 × 80%) | 3,600 |  |  |
| Augusta Co (800 × 25%) | 200 |  |  |
| Impairment of investment in associate (W3) | (2,500) |  |  |
|  | 35,200 |  |  |

5    *Non-controlling interests*

|  | $'000 |
|---|---|
| NCI at acquisition (W2) | 7,000 |
| Share of post-acquisition retained earnings (4,500 (W4) × 20%) | 900 |
|  | 7,900 |

6    *Fair value adjustments*

|  | Acquisition $'000 | | Movement $'000 | Year end $'000 |
|---|---|---|---|---|
| Plant | 4,000 | 1/4 | (1,000) | 3,000 |
| Intangible asset (customer relationships) | 3,000 | 1/6 | (500) | 2,500 |
|  | 7,000 | | (1,500) | 5,500 |

7    *Intragroup trading*

Unrealised profit:

|  | $'000 | $'000 |
|---|---|---|
| Dr Cost of sales/retained earnings (2,600 × 30/130) | 600 | |
| Cr Inventories | | 600 |
| Current account: | | |
| Dr Group trade payables | 1,300 | |
| Cr Group trade receivables | | 1,300 |

at the year end, so this is the only option which would require adjustment. The others have all taken place after the year end.

# 293 Dargent Co

**Text references.** Chapters 7, 8 and 10

**Top tips.** This question required good knowledge of accounting for groups including correctly accounting for intragroup trading, dividends and accounting for new acquisitions (including goodwill).

**Easy marks.** Calculating the plant and machinery and goodwill (including consideration) carried the most marks in this question. Lay out the consolidation workings clearly, ensuring accurate time apportionment of earnings, goods in transit, intra-group balances and dealing with the investment in the associate. Don't forget the easy marks regarding the loan and the interest. Trickier points were the calculation of the fair value adjustment for the decommissioning of the mine. Remember to only time apportion SPL and not SOFP balances!

**Examining Team's comments.** Most candidates prepared good consolidation workings, including the time-apportioned retained earnings at the date of acquisition, and few made any errors with the calculation of the purchase consideration of the acquisition of the subsidiary. The intra-group balances, goods in transit and the principles behind the investment in the associate were generally dealt with to allow candidates to earn high or maximum marks.

**Marking scheme**

|  | Marks |
|---|---|
| Property, plant and equipment | 2 |
| Goodwill: consideration | 2.5 |
| Goodwill: fair value net assets | 2 |
| Investments in associate | 1 |
| Inventory | 1.5 |
| Receivables | 1 |
| Bank | 0.5 |
| Equity shares and share premium | 1 |
| Retained earnings: post-acquisition sub | 2 |
| Retained earnings: other | 2 |
| Non-controlling interests | 1.5 |
| 8% loan notes | 0.5 |
| Environmental provision | 1.5 |
| Current liabilities | 1 |
|  | 20 |

DARGENT CO – CONSOLIDATED STATEMENT OF FINANCIAL POSITION AS AT 31 MARCH 20X6

|  | $'000 | $'000 |
|---|---|---|
| **ASSETS** | | |
| *Non-current assets* | | |
| Property, plant and equipment (75,200+31,500+4,000 re mine – 200 depreciation) | | 110,500 |
| Goodwill (W1)) | | 11,000 |
| Investment in associate (4,500+1,200 (W3) | | 5,700 |
| | | 127,200 |
| *Current assets* | | |
| Inventories (19,400+18,800+700 GIT – 800 URP (W2) | 38,100 | |
| Trade receivables (28,500 – 4,000 (W4)) | 24,100 | |
| Cash and cash equivalents (1,200+600) | 1,800 | |
| | | 64,100 |
| Total assets | | 191,300 |
| **EQUITY AND LIABILITIES** | | |
| Equity attributable to owners of the parent | | |
| Equity shares of $1 each ( 50,000 _ 10,000 (W1)) | | 60,000 |
| Other equity reserves (share premium) (W1) | 22,000 | |
| Retained earnings (W3) | 37,390 | 59,390 |
| | | 119,390 |
| Non-controlling interest (W4) | | 9,430 |
| Total equity | | 128,820 |
| *Non-current liabilities* | | |
| 8% loan notes (5,000 +15,000 consideration) | 20,000 | |
| Accrued loan interest (W3) | 300 | |
| Environmental provision (4,000 + 80 interest (W3)) | 4,080 | 24,380 |
| Current liabilities (24,000+16,400-(3,000-700 GIT) intra-group W2)) | | 38,100 |
| Total equity and liabilities | | 191,300 |

*Workings (figures in brackets are in $'000)*

1   *Goodwill in Latree Co*

|  | $'000 | $'000 |
|---|---|---|
| Controlling interest | | |
| Share exchange (20,000 × 75% × 2/3 = 10,000 × $3.20) | | 32,000 |
| 8% loan notes (20,000 × 75% × $1,000/1,000) | | 15,000 |
| Non-controlling interest (20,000 × 25% × $1.80) | | 9,000 |
| | | 56,000 |
| Equity shares | 20,000 | |
| Retained earnings at 1 April 20X5 | 19,000 | |
| Earnings 1 April 20X5 to acquisition (8,000 × 9/12) | 6,000 | |
| Fair value adjustments – asset re mine | 4,000 | |
| – Provision re mine | (4,000) | (45,000) |
| Goodwill arising on acquisition | | 11,000 |

The share exchange of $32 million would be recorded as share capital of $10 million (10,000 × $1) and share premium of $22 million (10,000 × ($3.20 – $1.00)).

Applying the group policy to the environmental provision would mean adding $4 million to the carrying amount of the mine and the amount recorded as a provision at the date of acquisition. This has no overall effect on goodwill, but it does affect the consolidated statement of financial position and post-acquisition profit.

2   *Inventory*

The inventory of Latree Co includes unrealised profit (URP) of $600,000 (2,100 × 40/140). Similarly, the goods in transit sale of $700,000 includes URP of $200,000 (700 × 40/140).

3     *Consolidated retained earnings*

|  | $'000 |
|---|---|
| Dargent Co's retained earnings | 36,000 |
| Latree Co's post-acquisition profit (1,720 x 75% see below) | 1,290 |
| Unrecorded share of Amery's retained profit ((6,000 – 2,000) × 30%) | 1,200 |
| Outstanding loan interest at 31 March 20X6 (15,000 × 8% × 3/12) | (300) |
| URP in inventory (W2) | (800) |
|  | 37,390 |

| The adjusted post-acquisition profits of Latree Co are: |  |
|---|---|
| As reported and time apportioned (8,000 × 3/12) | 2,000 |
| Interest on environmental provision (4,000 × 8% × 3/12) | (80) |
| Additional depreciation re.mine (4,000/5 years × 3/12) | (200) |
|  | 1,720 |

4     *Non-controlling interest*

|  | $'000 |
|---|---|
| Fair value on acquisition (W1) | 9,000 |
| Post-acquisition profit (1,720 × 25% (W4) | 430 |
|  | 9,430 |

# 294 Fresco Co (Jun12 amended)

**Text references.** Chapters 4 and 16.

**Top tips.** There was a lot to get through in this question. Get the formats down quickly and then go through the question and transfer any figures that can go straight from the trial balance to the financial statements. You needed to do workings for PPE and for the leased plant but these were not complicated.

**Easy marks.** The statement of changes in equity was all straightforward. If you had remembered the transfer to retained earnings it was possible to score full marks on this. The PPE working made it possible to score marks on both the statement of profit or loss and other comprehensive income and the statement of financial position, so it was worth spending a bit of time on this. The lease working, on the other hand, carried very few marks.

**Examining Team's comments.** Most candidates showed a sound knowledge of preparing financial statements. Most of the errors arose in the adjustments:

Some candidates deducted the loss on the fraud from revenue for the year rather adding it to expenses and treating it as a prior year adjustment, with the other entry being a deduction from receivables.

There were some difficulties with the lease, mainly involving the timing of the lease payments and the initial deposit. Many candidates were confused with the tax, especially failing to realise that the tax for the year was a refund.

| | Marks | |
|---|---|---|
| Statement of profit or loss and other comprehensive income: | | |
| Revenue | ½ | |
| Cost of sales | 3 | |
| Distribution costs | ½ | |
| Administrative expenses | ½ | |
| Finance costs | 1½ | |
| Income tax | 1 | |
| Other comprehensive income | 1 | 8 |
| Statement of financial position: | | |
| Property, plant and equipment | 2½ | |
| Inventory | ½ | |
| Trade receivables | ½ | |
| Share capital | 1 | |
| Share premium | 1 | |
| Revaluation surplus | 1 | |
| Retained earnings | 2 | |
| Current tax | ½ | |
| Non-current lease obligation | ½ | |
| Deferred tax | 1 | |
| Trade payables | ½ | |
| Current lease obligation | ½ | |
| Bank overdraft | ½ | 12 |
| | | 20 |

(a)  STATEMENT OF PROFIT OR LOSS AND OTHER COMPREHENSIVE INCOME
FOR THE YEAR ENDED 31 MARCH 20X2

| | $'000 |
|---|---|
| Revenue | 350,000 |
| Cost of sales (W1) | (311,000) |
| Gross profit | 39,000 |
| Distribution costs (W1) | (16,100) |
| Administrative expenses (W1) | (29,900) |
| Finance costs (300 + 2,300 (W3)) | (2,600) |
| Loss before tax | (9,600) |
| Income tax (W5) | 1,800 |
| Loss for the year | (7,800) |
| Other comprehensive income: | |
| Gain on revaluation of property (W2) | 4,000 |
| Total comprehensive loss for the year | (3,800) |

(b)    STATEMENT OF FINANCIAL POSITION AS AT 31 MARCH 20X2

|  | $'000 |
|---|---:|
| ASSETS | |
| *Non-current assets* | |
| Property, plant and equipment (W2) | 62,700 |
| *Current assets* | |
| Inventories | 25,200 |
| Trade receivables (28,500 – 4,000 (W4)) | 24,500 |
| Tax asset (W5) | 2,400 |
| Total assets | 114,800 |
| EQUITY AND LIABILITIES | |
| *Equity* | |
| Share capital 50c shares(45,000 + 9,000(W6)) | 54,000 |
| Share premium (5,000 + 4,500(W6)) | 9,500 |
| Revaluation surplus (4,000 – 500 (W2)) | 3,500 |
| Retained earnings (5,100 – 1,000(W4) – 7,800 + 500(W2)) | (3,200) |
|  | 63,800 |
| *Non-current liabilities* | |
| Deferred tax (W5) | 3,000 |
| Lease payable (W3) | 15,230 |
| *Current liabilities* | |
| Trade and other payables | 27,300 |
| Lease payable (19,300 – 15,230 (W3)) | 4,070 |
| Bank overdraft | 1,400 |
| Total equity and liabilities | 114,800 |

*Workings*

1    *Expenses*

|  | Cost of sales $'000 | Distribution costs $'000 | Administrative expenses $'000 |
|---|---:|---:|---:|
| Per trial balance | 298,700 | 16,100 | 26,900 |
| Depreciation (W2) | 7,800 | – | – |
| Amortisation (W2) | 4,500 | – | – |
| Fraud – current year cost (W4) | – | – | 3,000 |
|  | 311,000 | 16,100 | 29,900 |

2    *Property, plant and equipment*

|  | Leased property $'000 | Plant and equipment $'000 | Leased plant $'000 | Total $'000 |
|---|---:|---:|---:|---:|
| Cost | 48,000 | 47,500 | | |
| Acc. amortisation/depreciation | (16,000) | (33,500) | | |
| Balance 1 April 20X1 | 32,000 | 14,000 | 25,000 | |
| Revaluation surplus | 4,000 | | | |
| Revised carrying amount | 36,000 | | | |
| Depreciation / amortisation: | | | | |
| 36,000 / 8 | (4,500) | | | |
| 14,000 × 20% | | (2,800) | | |
| 25,000 / 5 | | | (5,000) | |
|  | 31,500 | 11,200 | 20,000 | 62,700 |

The transfer to retained earnings = 4,000/8 = 500

3    *Lease liability*

|  | $'000 |
|---|---|
| Initial measurement | 25,000 |
| Deposit | (2,000) |
| Balance 1.4.X1 | 23,000 |
| Interest 10% | 2,300 |
| Instalment 31.3.X2 | (6,000) |
| Balance 31.3.X2 | 19,300 |
| Interest 10% | 1,930 |
| Instalment 31.3.X3 | (6,000) |
| Balance 31.3.X3 | 15,230 |

4    *Fraud*

|  | DEBIT | CREDIT |
|---|---|---|
|  | $'000 | $'000 |
| Retained earnings – prior year | 1,000 | |
| Current year profit | 3,000 | |
| Receivables | | 4,000 |

5    *Tax credit*

|  | $'000 |
|---|---|
| Underprovided in prior year | 800 |
| Tax refund due (asset in SFP) | (2,400) |
| Reduction in deferred tax provision (3,200 – (12,000 × 25%)) | (200) |
| Current tax (credit to profit or loss) | (1,800) |

6    *Share issue*

Shares issued = 13.5m / 0.75 = 18m

| | | $'000 |
|---|---|---|
| Share capital | 18m × 50c | 9,000 |
| Share premium | 18m × 25c | 4,500 |
| | | 13,500 |

# 295 Dexon Co

(a)

| | $'000 | $'000 |
|---|---|---|
| Draft retained profit | | 96,700 |
| Dividends paid | | 15,500 |
| Draft profit for the year | | 112,200 |
| Depreciation: | | |
| Buildings (165,000 / 15) | 11,000 | |
| Plant (180,500 × 20%) | 36,100 | |
| | | (47,100) |
| Gain on investment (W2) | | 1,000 |
| Current year fraud loss | | (2,500) |
| Increase in deferred tax provision (W4) | | (800) |
| Current year tax | | (11,400) |
| | | 51,400 |

(b)    DEXON CO – STATEMENT OF FINANCIAL POSITION AS AT 31 MARCH 20X8

|  | $'000 | $'000 |
|---|---|---|
| *Non-current assets* | | |
| Property (W1) | | 180,000 |
| Plant (W1) | | 144,400 |
| Investments (W2) | | 13,500 |
| | | 337,900 |
| *Current assets* | | |
| Inventories | 84,000 | |
| Trade receivables (W5) | 48,200 | |
| Cash and cash equivalents | 3,800 | |
| | | 136,000 |
| *Total assets* | | 473,900 |
| | | |
| *Equity and liabilities* | | |
| Share capital | | 250,000 |
| Share premium | | 40,000 |
| Revaluation surplus (W6) | | 22,800 |
| Retained earnings (12,300 – 1,500(W3) + 51,400 – 15,500) | | 46,700 |
| *Total equity* | | 359,500 |
| *Non-current liabilities* | | |
| Deferred tax (19,200 + 2,000 (W4)) | | 21,200 |
| *Current liabilities* | | |
| As per draft SFP | 81,800 | |
| Tax payable | 11,400 | |
| | | 93,200 |
| *Total equity and liabilities* | | 473,900 |

*Workings*

1    Property, plant and equipment

|  | Property | Plant | Total |
|---|---|---|---|
| | $'000 | $'000 | $'000 |
| Per question | 185,000 | 180,500 | 365,500 |
| Depreciation (165,000 / 15) | (11,000) | (36,100) | (47,100) |
| | 174,000 | 144,400 | 318,400 |
| Revaluation | 6,000 | – | 6,000 |
| Balance c/d | 180,000 | 144,400 | 324,400 |

2    Financial assets at FV through profit or loss

|  | $'000 |
|---|---|
| FV at year end (12,500 × 1,296 / 1,200) | 13,500 |
| Per draft SOFP | (12,500) |
| Gain – to profit or loss | 1,000 |

3    Fraud

|  | $'000 | $'000 |
|---|---|---|
| DR Retained earnings re prior year | 1,500 | |
| DR Current year profit | 2,500 | |
| CR Receivables | | 4,000 |

4    Deferred tax

|  | $'000 | $'000 |
|---|---|---|
| DR Revaluation surplus (6,000 × 20%) | 1,200 | |
| DR Profit or loss (tax charge) (4,000 × 20%) | 800 | |
| CR Deferred tax liability (10,000 × 20%) | | 2,000 |

| 5 | *Trade receivables* | $'000 |
|---|---|---|
| | Per draft SFP | 52,200 |
| | Adjustment re fraud | (4,000) |
| | | 48,200 |

| 6 | *Revaluation surplus* | $'000 |
|---|---|---|
| | B/f | 18,000 |
| | Surplus re land and buildings | 6,000 |
| | | 24,000 |
| | Deferred tax provision (6,000 × 20%) | (1,200) |
| | Net surplus | 4,800 |

# 296 Xtol Co (Jun14 amended)

**Text references.** Chapters 16, 17 and 18.

**Top tips.** You have two financial statements to produce here, so be very organised. Note that you will have to work out the effects of the rights issue to get the dividend payments.

**Examining Team's comments**. This question was generally well answered. Most of the errors that occurred involved the agency sale, the rights issue (such as failing to notice that the shares were 25c, not $1), the convertible loan note and the tax.

| | | | **Marks** |
|---|---|---|---|
| (a) | Statement of profit or loss | | |
| | Revenue | 1 | |
| | Cost of sales | 2 | |
| | Distribution costs | ½ | |
| | Administrative expenses | ½ | |
| | Agency sales | 1 | |
| | Finance costs | 1½ | |
| | Income tax | 1½ | |
| | | | 8 |
| (b) | Statement of financial position | | |
| | Property, plant and equipment | 1½ | |
| | Inventory | ½ | |
| | Trade receivables | ½ | |
| | Share capital | ½ | |
| | Share premium | ½ | |
| | Equity option | 1 | |
| | Retained earnings | 2 | |
| | Deferred tax | 1 | |
| | Loan note | 1½ | |
| | Trade payables | 1½ | |
| | Bank overdraft | ½ | |
| | Current tax payable | 1 | |
| | | | 12 |
| | Total for question | | 20 |

(a)   STATEMENT OF PROFIT OR LOSS FOR THE YEAR ENDED 31 MARCH 20X4

|  | $'000 |
|---|---|
| Revenue (490,000 – 20,000 (W3)) | 470,000 |
| Cost of sales (W1) | (294,600) |
| Gross profit | 175,400 |
| Distribution costs (W1) | (33,500) |
| Administrative expenses (W1) | (36,800) |
| Other operating income – agency sales (W3) | 2,000 |
| Finance costs (13,380 + 900 + 1,176 (W4) – 10,880 (W5)) | (4,576) |
| Profit before tax | 102,524 |
| Income tax expense (28,000 + 3,200 + 3,700 (W6)) | (34,900) |
| Profit for the year | 67,624 |

(b)   STATEMENT OF FINANCIAL POSITION AS AT 31 MARCH 20X4

|  | $'000 | $'000 |
|---|---|---|
| ASSETS | | |
| *Non-current assets* | | |
| Property, plant and equipment (W2) | | 168,000 |
| *Current assets* | | |
| Inventories | 61,000 | |
| Trade receivables | 63,000 | |
| | | 124,000 |
| Total assets | | 292,000 |
| | | |
| EQUITY AND LIABILITIES | | |
| *Equity* | | |
| Equity shares 25c | | 56,000 |
| Share premium | | 25,000 |
| Other component of equity – equity option (W4) | | 4,050 |
| Retained earnings (26,080 – 10,880 (W5) + 67,624) | | 82,824 |
| | | 167,874 |
| *Non-current liabilities* | | |
| Deferred tax (4,600 + 3,700 (W6)) | 8,300 | |
| 5% convertible loan note (50,000 – 4,050 (W4) + 1,176) | 47,126 | |
| | | 55,426 |
| *Current liabilities* | | |
| Trade payables (32,200 + 3,000 (W3)) | 35,200 | |
| Bank overdraft | 5,500 | |
| Current tax payable | 28,000 | |
| | | 68,700 |
| Total equity and liabilities | | 292,000 |

*Workings*

1   *Expenses*

|  | Cost of sales $'000 | Distribution costs $'000 | Administrative expenses $'000 |
|---|---|---|---|
| Per question | 290,600 | 33,500 | 36,800 |
| Agent not principal | (15,000) | | |
| Depreciation – property (W2) | 5,000 | | |
| Depreciation – plant and equipment (W2) | 14,000 | | |
| | 294,600 | 33,500 | 36,800 |

## 2 Property, plant and equipment

| | Property | Plant and equipment | Total |
|---|---|---|---|
| | $'000 | $'000 | $'000 |
| Cost per TB | 100,000 | 155,500 | 255,500 |
| Acc depreciation b/d per TB | (25,000) | (43,500) | (68,500) |
| | 75,000 | 112,000 | 187,000 |
| Depreciation property (100,000/20 years) | (5,000) | | (5,000) |
| Depreciation P&E (112,000 × 12.5%) | | (14,000) | (14,000) |
| | 70,000 | 98,000 | 168,000 |

## 3 Agency transaction

| Should have been: | | Did: | | Correction: | |
|---|---|---|---|---|---|
| | $'000 | | $'000 | | $'000 |
| DR Cash | 20,000 | DR Cash | 20,000 | DR Revenue | 20,000 |
| CR Other income (10%) | 2,000 | CR Revenue | 20,000 | CR Cost of sales | 15,000 |
| CR Trade payables | 18,000 | DR Cost of sales | 15,000 | CR Other income | 2,000 |
| | | CR Cash | 15,000 | CR Trade payables | 3,000 |
| DR Trade payables | 15,000 | | | | |
| CR Cash | 15,000 | | | | |

## 4 Loan notes

| | | $'000 | $'000 |
|---|---|---|---|
| PV of principal | (50,000 × 0.79) | | 39,500 |
| PV interest flows: | | | |
| 20X4 | 50,000 × 5% = 2,500 × 0.93 = | 2,325 | |
| 20X5 | 50,000 × 5% = 2,500 × 0.86 = | 2,150 | |
| 20X6 | 50,000 × 5% = 2,500 × 0.79 = | 1,975 | |
| | | | 6,450 |
| Debt component | | | 45,950 |
| Equity component (β) | | | 4,050 |
| Cash received | | | 50,000 |
| Liability component b/d | 1.4.20X3 | 45,950 | |
| Effective interest | (45,950 × 8%) | 3,676 | |
| Cash coupon paid | | (2,500) | |
| Liability component c/d | 31.3.20X4 | 47,126 | |

Adjustment required:

| | | | |
|---|---|---|---|
| DR Loan notes | | 4,050 | |
| CR Other components of equity | | | 4,050 |
| DR Finance costs (3,676 – 2,500) | | 1,176 | |
| CR Loan notes | | | 1,176 |

## 5 Dividend paid

| | $'000 | $'000 |
|---|---|---|
| Before rights issue (56,000 × $1/25c × 5/7 = 160m × 4c) | | 6,400 |
| After rights issue (56,000 × $1/25c × 2c) | | 4,480 |
| | | 10,880 |
| DR Retained earnings | 10,880 | |
| CR Loan note interest and dividends paid | | 10,880 |

## 6 Tax

| | $'000 | $'000 |
|---|---|---|
| Current tax: DR Current tax (P/L) | 28,000 | |
| CR Current tax payable | | 28,000 |
| Deferred tax: | | |
| B/d (per TB) | | 4,600 |
| To P/L | | 3,700 |
| C/d | | 8,300 |

# 297 Atlas Co

## Marking scheme

|  |  |  | Marks |
|---|---|---|---|
| (a) | Statement of profit or loss and OCI | | |
| | Revenue | 1 | |
| | Cost of sales | 2 | |
| | Distribution costs | ½ | |
| | Administrative expenses | ½ | |
| | Finance costs | ½ | |
| | Income tax | 2½ | |
| | Other comprehensive income | 1 | |
| | | | 8 |
| (b) | Statement of financial position | | |
| | Property, plant and equipment | 3½ | |
| | Inventory | ½ | |
| | Trade receivables | ½ | |
| | Retained earnings | 2½ | |
| | Deferred tax | 1½ | |
| | Trade payables | ½ | |
| | Current tax | ½ | |
| | Bank overdraft | ½ | |
| | | | 10 |
| (c) | Earnings per share | | 2 |
| | | | 20 |

(a)  STATEMENT OF PROFIT OR LOSS AND OTHER COMPREHENSIVE INCOME FOR THE YEAR ENDED 31 MARCH 20X3

|  | $'000 |
|---|---|
| Revenue | 550,000 |
| Cost of sales (W1) | (428,000) |
| Gross profit | 122,000 |
| Distribution costs | (21,500) |
| Administrative expenses | (30,900) |
| Finance costs | (700) |
| Profit before tax | 68,900 |
| Income tax expense ((27,200 – 1,200) + (9,400 – 6,200)) | (29,200) |
| Profit for the year | 39,700 |
| Other comprehensive income: | |
| Gain on revaluation of property (W3) | 7,000 |
| Total comprehensive income for the year | 46,700 |

(b) STATEMENT OF FINANCIAL POSITION AS AT 31 MARCH 20X3

|  | $'000 | $'000 |
|---|---|---|
| **ASSETS** | | |
| *Non-current assets* | | |
| Property, plant and equipment (W2) | | 100,500 |
| | | |
| *Current assets* | | |
| Inventories | 43,700 | |
| Trade receivables | 42,200 | |
| | | 85,900 |
| *Total assets* | | 186,400 |
| | | |
| **EQUITY AND LIABILITIES** | | |
| *Equity* | | |
| Share capital | | 50,000 |
| Share premium | | 20,000 |
| Revaluation surplus | | 7,000 |
| Retained earnings (11,200 + 39,700 – dividend 20,000) | | 30,900 |
| | | 107,900 |
| | | |
| *Non-current liabilities* | | |
| Deferred tax | | 9,400 |
| | | |
| *Current liabilities* | | |
| Trade and other payables | 35,100 | |
| Tax payable | 27,200 | |
| Overdraft | 6,800 | |
| | | 69,100 |
| | | 186,400 |

*Workings*

1 *Expenses*

|  | Cost of sales $'000 | Distribution costs $'000 | Administrative expenses $'000 |
|---|---|---|---|
| Per TB | 411,500 | 21,500 | 30,900 |
| Depreciation (W2) | 16,500 | – | – |
| | 428,000 | 21,500 | 30,900 |

2 *Property, plant and equipment*

|  | Land $'000 | Buildings $'000 | Plant $'000 | Total $'000 |
|---|---|---|---|---|
| Cost | 10,000 | 50,000 | 94,500 | |
| Accumulated depreciation | – | (20,000) | (24,500) | |
| Balance 1 April 20X3 | 10,000 | 30,000 | 70,000 | 110,000 |
| Revaluation surplus | 2,000 | 5,000 | | 7,000 |
| Revalued amount | 12,000 | 35,000 | | |
| Depreciation (35/14) (70 × 20%) | – | (2,500) | (14,000) | (16,500) |
| | 12,000 | 32,500 | 56,000 | 100,500 |

(c) EPS = 39,700/100,000 = $0.40

# 298 Moby Co (Dec13 amended)

## Marking scheme

|  |  |  | Marks |
|---|---|---|---|
| (a) | Statement of profit or loss and other comprehensive income | | |
|  | Revenue | 2 | |
|  | Cost of sales | 3½ | |
|  | Distribution costs | ½ | |
|  | Administrative expenses | 1 | |
|  | Finance costs | 2 | |
|  | Income tax expense | 2 | |
|  | Gain on revaluation | 1 | |
|  | Deferred tax on gain | 1 | |
|  | | | 13 |
| (b) | Statement of changes in equity | | |
|  | Opening balances | 1 | |
|  | Share issue | 2 | |
|  | Dividend | 1 | |
|  | Total comprehensive income | 2 | |
|  | Closing balances | 1 | |
|  | | | 7 |
|  | | | 20 |

(a) STATEMENT OF PROFIT OR LOSS AND OTHER COMPREHENSIVE INCOME FOR THE YEAR ENDED 30 SEPTEMBER 20X3

|  | $'000 |
|---|---|
| Revenue (227,800 + 10,000 (W3)) | 237,800 |
| Cost of sales (W1) | (187,900) |
| Gross profit | 49,900 |
| Distribution costs | (13,500) |
| Administrative expenses (W1) | (16,350) |
| Finance costs (900 + 4,000 (W5) + 2,930 (W6)) | (7,830) |
| Profit before tax | 12,220 |
| Income tax expense (W4) | (350) |
| Profit for the year | 11,870 |
| Other comprehensive income: | |
| Gain on revaluation of land and buildings (W2) | 4,400 |
| Deferred tax on gain (W4) | (1,100) |
| Total other comprehensive income | 3,300 |
| Total comprehensive income for the year | 15,170 |

(b) STATEMENT OF CHANGES IN EQUITY FOR THE YEAR ENDED 30 SEPTEMBER 20X3

| | Share capital $'000 | Share premium $'000 | Retained earnings $'000 | Revaluation surplus $'000 | Total $'000 |
|---|---|---|---|---|---|
| Balance at 1 October 20X2 | 45,000 | – | 19,800 | – | 64,800 |
| Share issue | 800 | 3,200 | | | 4,000 |
| Dividend paid | | | (2,000) | | (2,000) |
| Total comprehensive income | – | – | 11,870 | 3,300 | 15,170 |
| Balance at 30 September 20X3 | 45,800 | 3,200 | 29,670 | 3,300 | 81,970 |

*Workings*

1  *Expenses*

| | Cost of sales $'000 | Distribution costs $'000 | Administrative expenses $'000 |
|---|---|---|---|
| Per question | 164,500 | 13,500 | 16,500 |
| Contract (W3) | 8,000 | | |
| Depreciation (W2) – building | 2,400 | | |
| – owned plant | 6,000 | | |
| – leased plant | 7,000 | | |
| Insurance provision reversal | | | (150) |
| | 187,900 | 13,500 | 16,350 |

2  *Property, plant and equipment*

| | Land $'000 | Building $'000 | Plant $'000 | Leased plant $'000 |
|---|---|---|---|---|
| Cost 1.10.X2 | 12,000 | 48,000 | 65,700 | 35,000 |
| Depreciation b/f | | (10,000) | (17,700) | (7,000) |
| | 12,000 | 38,000 | 48,000 | 28,000 |
| Revaluation | 4,000 | 400 | | |
| | 16,000 | 38,400 | 48,000 | 28,000 |
| Depreciation: | | | | |
| Building (38,400 / 16) | | (2,400) | | |
| Plant (48,000 × 12.5%) | | | (6,000) | |
| Leased (35,000 / 5) | | | | (7,000) |

3  *Contract with performance obligations satisfied over time*

This contract is currently expected to make a profit of $5m.

| | $'000 |
|---|---|
| Revenue (work certified) (10 / 25 = 40%) | 10,000 |
| Cost of sales ((14 + 6) × 40%) | (8,000) |
| Profit to date | 2,000 |

4  *Income tax*

| | $'000 |
|---|---|
| Deferred tax balance: | |
| On taxable temporary difference ($24m × 25%) | 6,000 |
| On revaluation (4,400 × 25%) | 1,100 |
| Liability at 30 September 20X3 | 7,100 |
| Balance b/f at 1 October 20X2 | 8,000 |
| Reduce balance by | 900 |
| Income tax charge: | |
| Provision for year | 3,400 |
| Prior year over-provision | (1,050) |
| Reduction in deferred tax balance | (900) |
| Deferred tax on revaluation debited to revaluation surplus | (1,100) |
| Charge for year | 350 |

5    *Loan note*

| | $'000 |
|---|---|
| Proceeds | 40,000 |
| Interest 10% | 4,000 |
| Balance | 44,000 |

6    *Leased plant*

| | $'000 |
|---|---|
| Cost 1.10.X1 | 35,000 |
| Interest 10% | 3,500 |
| Instalment paid | (9,200) |
| Balance 30.9.X2 | 29,300 |
| Interest 10% | 2,930 |

# 299 Dickson Co

(a)    STATEMENT OF CASH FLOWS FOR YEAR ENDED 31 MARCH 20X8

| *Cash flows from operating activities* | $'000 | $'000 |
|---|---|---|
| Profit before taxation | 342 | |
| Adjustments for: | | |
|   Depreciation | 57 | |
|   Amortisation (W1) | 60 | |
|   Interest expense | 15 | |
|   Profit on disposal of assets (110 – 103) | (7) | |
| | 467 | |
|   Increase in inventories (W4) | (133) | |
|   Decrease in trade receivables (W4) | 50 | |
|   Decrease in trade payables (W4) | (78) | |
| Cash generated from operations | 306 | |
| Interest paid (W3) | (10) | |
| Income taxes paid (W3) | (256) | |
| *Net cash from operating activities* | | 40 |
| *Cash flows from investing activities* | | |
| Development expenditure | (190) | |
| Purchase of property, plant & equipment (W1) | (192) | |
| Proceeds from sale of property, plant & equipment | 110 | |
| *Net cash used in investing activities* | | (272) |
| *Cash flows from financing activities* | | |
| Proceeds from issue of shares (W2) | 300 | |
| Proceeds from issue of debentures | 50 | |
| Payment of lease liabilities (W3) | (31) | |
| Dividends paid (W2) | (156) | |
| *Net cash from financing activities* | | 163 |
| *Net decrease in cash and cash equivalents* | | (69) |
| *Cash and cash equivalents at beginning of period* | | 109 |
| *Cash and cash equivalents at end of period* | | 40 |

*Workings*

1    *Assets*

| | Property, plant and equipment | Development expenditure |
|---|---|---|
| | $'000 | $'000 |
| B/d | 737 | 160 |
| Disposals | (103) | |
| P/L | (57) | |
| OCI | 100 | |
| Purchase under lease | 56 | |
| Additions (β) | | 190 |
| Amortisation | | (60) |
| Cash additions (β) | 192 | – |
| C/d | 925 | 290 |

2    *Equity*

| | Share capital and premium | Revaluation surplus | Retained earnings |
|---|---|---|---|
| | $'000 | $'000 | $'000 |
| B/d | 500 | 60 | 255 |
| P/L | | | 180 |
| OCI | | 100 | |
| Bonus issue | 50 | | (50) |
| Rights issue (β) | 300 | | |
| Dividend paid (β) | – | – | (156) |
| C/d | 850 | 160 | 229 |

3    *Liabilities*

| | Debentures | Leases | Taxation | Interest |
|---|---|---|---|---|
| | $'000 | $'000 | $'000 | $'000 |
| B/d | 100 | 92* | 198** | – |
| SPLOCI | | | 162 | 15 |
| New lease | | 56 | | |
| Cash received (paid) (β) | 50 | (31) | (256) | (10) |
| C/d | 150 | 117 | 104 | 5 |

*Non-current + current

**Deferred + current

4    *Working capital*

| | Inventories | Receivables | Payables |
|---|---|---|---|
| | $'000 | $'000 | $'000 |
| B/d | 227 | 324 | 352 |
| Movement (β) | 133 | (50) | (78) |
| C/d | 360 | 274 | 274 |

(b) CASH FLOWS FROM OPERATING ACTIVITIES (direct method)

|  | $'000 |
|---|---|
| Cash received from customers (W2) | 1,526 |
| Cash paid to suppliers and employees (W1) | (1,220) |
| Cash generated from operations | 306 |
| Interest paid | (10) |
| Income taxes paid | (256) |
| Net cash from operating activities | 40 |

*Workings*

1 *Payables*

|  | $'000 |
|---|---|
| Payables balance b/d | 352 |
| Purchases (W3) | 1,095 |
| Other expenses (W4) | 47 |
| Payments (β) | 1,220 |
| Payables balance c/d | 274 |

2 *Receivables*

|  | $'000 |
|---|---|
| Receivables balance b/d | 324 |
| Sales revenue | 1,476 |
| Cash received (β) | (1,526) |
|  | 274 |

3 *Purchases*

|  | $'000 |
|---|---|
| Inventory balance b/d | 227 |
| Transfer to cost of sales | (962) |
| Purchases (β) | 1,095 |
| Inventory balance c/d | 360 |

4 *Other expenses*

|  | $'000 |
|---|---|
| Balance per statement of profit or loss | 157 |
| Depreciation | (57) |
| Amortisation | (60) |
| Profit on disposal | 7 |
|  | 47 |

# 300 Mocha Co (Dec11 amended)

**Marking scheme**

|  | Marks |
|---|---|
| Profit before tax | ½ |
| Depreciation | 1 |
| Profit on disposal of property | 1 |
| Investment income deducted | ½ |
| Interest expense added back | ½ |
| Working capital items | 1½ |
| Decrease in product warranty | 1½ |
| Interest paid | 1 |
| Income tax paid | 2 |
| Purchase of PPE | 1½ |
| Disposal of PPE | 1 |
| Disposal of investment | 1 |
| Dividends received | 1 |
| Share issue | 2½ |
| Payments under lease | 2½ |
| Cash b/f / c/f | 1 |
|  | 20 |

(a)     STATEMENT OF CASH FLOWS FOR THE YEAR ENDED 30 SEPTEMBER 20X1

|  | $'000 | $'000 |
|---|---|---|
| *Cash flows from operating activities* |  |  |
| Profit before tax | 3,900 |  |
| Adjustments for: |  |  |
| Depreciation | 2,500 |  |
| Profit on sale of property | (4,100) |  |
| Investment income | (1,100) |  |
| Interest expense | 500 |  |
|  | 1,700 |  |
| Increase in inventories (W4) | (3,000) |  |
| Decrease in receivables (W4) | 200 |  |
| Decrease in payables (W4) | (1,400) |  |
| Decrease in warranty provision (4,000 – 1,600) | (2,400) |  |
| Cash used in operations | (4,900) |  |
| Interest paid | (500) |  |
| Income tax paid (W3) | (800) |  |
| *Net cash used in operating activities* |  | (6,200) |

|  | $'000 | $'000 |
|---|---|---|
| *Cash flows from investing activities* | | |
| Sale of property | 8,100 | |
| Purchase of plant | (8,300) | |
| Sale of investment | 3,400 | |
| Dividends received | 200 | |
| Net cash from investing activities | | 3,400 |
| *Cash flows from financing activities* | | |
| Issue of share capital (W2) | 2,400 | |
| Payments under leases (W3) | (3,900) | |
| Net cash from financing activities | | (1,500) |
| Decrease in cash and cash equivalents | | (4,300) |
| Cash and cash equivalents b/f | | 1,400 |
| Cash and cash equivalents c/f | | (2,900) |

*Workings*

### 1 Assets

|  | PPE | Financial asset |
|---|---|---|
|  | $'000 | $'000 |
| B/d | 24,100 | 7,000 |
| Right-of-use asset additions | 6,700 | |
| Purchase of new plant | 8,300 | |
| Disposal | (4,000) | (3,000) |
| Depreciation | (2,500) | |
| Increase in fair value | | 500 |
|  | 32,600 | 4,500 |

### 2 Equity

|  | Share capital | Share premium | Revaluation surplus | Retained earnings |
|---|---|---|---|---|
|  | $'000 | $'000 | $'000 | $'000 |
| B/d | 8,000 | 2,000 | 3,600 | 10,100 |
| Bonus issue: | 3,600 | (2,000) | (1,600) | |
| SPLOCI | | | | 2,900 |
| Issued for cash (β) | 2,400 | – | – | – |
| C/d | 14,000 | – | 2,000 | 13,000 |

### 3 Liabilities

|  | Leases | Income tax |
|---|---|---|
|  | $'000 | $'000 |
| B/d | 9,000* | 2,100** |
| Additions | 6,700 | |
| SPLOCI | | 1,000 |
| Paid (β) | (3,900) | (800) |
|  | 11,800* | 2,300** |

*Non-current + current
**Deferred + current

### 4 Working capital

|  | Inventories | Receivables | Payables |
|---|---|---|---|
|  | $'000 | $'000 | $'000 |
| B/d | 7,200 | 3,700 | 4,600 |
| Movement | 3,000 | (200) | (1,400) |
| C/d | 10,200 | 3,500 | 3,200 |

# 301 Hassle Co

(a)

| | | |
|---|---|---|
| ROCE | $(2,500 - 500 - 10)/(2,800 + 3,200 + 3,000 + 500)\%$ | = 20.9% |
| Pre-tax ROE | $(1,400/2,800)\%$ | = 50% |
| Net asset turnover | $20,500/(14,800 - 5,700)$ | = 2.3 times |
| Gross profit margin | $(2,500/20,500)\%$ | = 12.2% |
| Operating profit margin | $(2,000/20,500)\%$ | = 9.8% |
| Current ratio | $7,300/5,700$ | = 1.3 : 1 |
| Closing inventory holding period | $(3,600/18,000) \times 365$ | = 73 days |
| Trade receivables collection period | $(3,700/20,500) \times 365$ | = 66 days |
| Trade payables payment period | $(3,800/18,000) \times 365$ | = 77 days |
| Gearing | $(3,200 + 500 + 3,000)/9,500\%$ | = 71% |
| Interest cover | $2,000/600$ | = 3.3 times |
| Dividend cover | $1,000/700$ | = 1.4 times |

(b) **Assessment of relative position and performance of Astral Co and Breakout Co**

**Profitability**

At first sight it appears that Hassle Co would see a much greater return on its investment if it acquired Breakout Co rather than Astral Co. A closer analysis of the figures suggests that this may not be the case.

Breakout Co has a ROCE over 40% higher than Astral Co's and a ROE more than double Astral Co's ROE. However, the difference is due more to the lower level of equity in Breakout Co than to the superiority of its profit. Breakout Co's equity ($2.8m) is only half that of Astral Co ($5.5m). This reduces the denominator for ROCE and doubles the ROE. A closer look at the profits of both companies shows that the operating profit margin of Astral Co is 10.5% and that of Breakout Co is 9.75%.

The net asset turnover of Breakout Co (2.3 times) suggests that it is running the more efficient operation. Breakout Co has certainly achieved a much greater turnover than Astral Co and with a lower level of net assets. The problem is that, on a much higher level of turnover, its net profit is not much higher than Astral Co's.

Further analysis of net assets shows that Astral Co owns its factory, while Breakout Co's factory must be rented, partly accounting for the higher level of operating expenses. Astral Co's factory is carried at current value, as shown by the property revaluation reserve, which increases the negative impact on Astral Co's ROCE.

**Gearing**

Breakout Co has double the gearing of Astral Co, due to its lease obligations. At 7.5% Breakout Co is paying less on the lease than on its loan notes, but this still amounts to a doubling of its interest payments. Its interest cover is 3.4 times compared to 6 times for Astral Co, making its level of risk higher. In a bad year Breakout Co could have trouble servicing its debts and have nothing left to pay to shareholders. However, the fact that Breakout Co has chosen to operate with a higher level of gearing rather than raise funds from a share issue also increases the potential return to shareholders.

BPP
LEARNING MEDIA

**Liquidity**

Astral Co and Breakout Co have broadly similar current ratios, but showing a slightly higher level of risk in the case of Breakout Co. Breakout Co is also running an overdraft while Astral Co has $1.2m in the bank. Astral Co is pursuing its receivables slightly less aggressively than Breakout Co, but taking significantly longer to pay its suppliers. As this does not appear to be due to shortage of cash, it must be due to Astral Co being able to negotiate more favourable terms than Breakout Co.

**Summary**

Breakout Co has a higher turnover than Astral Co and a policy of paying out most of its earnings to shareholders. This makes it an attractive proposition from a shareholder viewpoint. However, if its turnover were to fall, there would be little left to distribute. This is the risk and return of a highly geared company. Breakout Co is already running an overdraft and so has no cash to invest in any more plant and equipment. In the light of this, its dividend policy is not particularly wise. Astral Co has a lower turnover and a much more conservative dividend policy but may be a better long-term investment. Hassle Co's decision will probably depend upon its attitude to risk and the relative purchase prices of Astral Co and Breakout Co.

# Mock Exams

# ACCA

# Financial Reporting (FR)

# Mock Examination 1 (Specimen Exam)

**Time allowed:** 3 hours 15 minutes

This mock exam is divided into three sections:

Section A – ALL 15 questions are compulsory and MUST be attempted

Section B – ALL 15 questions are compulsory and MUST be attempted

Section C – BOTH questions are compulsory and MUST be attempted

**Do NOT open this question paper until instructed by the supervisor.**

**Do NOT record any of your answers on the question paper.**

**This question paper must not be removed from the examination hall.**

# Section A – ALL 15 questions are compulsory and MUST be attempted

Each question is worth 2 marks.

1   Which of the following should be capitalised in the initial carrying amount of an item of plant?

(1)   Cost of transporting the plant to the factory
(2)   Cost of installing a new power supply required to operate the plant
(3)   Cost of a three-year plant maintenance agreement
(4)   Cost of a three-week training course for staff to operate the plant

A   (1) and (3)
B   (1) and (2)
C   (2) and (4)
D   (3) and (4)

2   When a parent is evaluating the assets of a potential subsidiary, certain intangible assets can be recognised separately from goodwill, even though they have not been recognised in the subsidiary's own statement of financial position.

Which of the following is an example of an intangible asset of the subsidiary which may be recognised separately from goodwill when preparing consolidated financial statements?

A   A new research project which the subsidiary has correctly expensed to profit or loss but the directors of the parent have reliably assessed to have a substantial fair value

B   A global advertising campaign which was concluded in the previous financial year and from which benefits are expected to flow in the future

C   A contingent asset of the subsidiary from which the parent believes a flow of future economic benefits is possible

D   A customer list which the directors are unable to value reliably

3   On 1 October 20X4, Flash Co acquired an item of plant under a five-year lease agreement. The present value of the lease payments was $25m. The agreement had an implicit finance cost of 10% per annum and required an immediate deposit of $2m and annual rentals of $6m paid on 30 September each year for five years.

What is the current liability for the leased plant in Flash Co's statement of financial position as at 30 September 20X5?

$ _____

4   Financial statements represent transactions in words and numbers. To be useful, financial information must represent faithfully these transactions in terms of how they are reported.

Identify, by selecting the relevant box in the table below, whether the statement regarding faithful representation is true or false?

| | | |
|---|---|---|
| Charging the rental payments for an item of plant to the statement of profit or loss where the rental agreement meets the criteria for a lease | True | False |
| Including a convertible loan note in equity on the basis that the holders are likely to choose the equity option on conversion | True | False |
| Treating redeemable preference shares as part of equity in the statement of financial position | True | False |
| Derecognising factored trade receivables sold without recourse to the seller | True | False |

5   On 1 October 20X4, Kalatra Co commenced drilling for oil from an undersea oilfield. Kalatra Co is required to dismantle the drilling equipment at the end of its five-year licence. This has an estimated cost of $30m on 30 September 20X9. Kalatra Co's cost of capital is 8% per annum and $1 in five years' time has a present value of 68 cents.

Selecting your answer from the drop down box, identify the provision which Kalatra Co would report in its statement of financial position as at 30 September 20X5 in respect of its oil operations?

**Picklist**

$32,400,000
$22,032,000
$20,400,000
$1,632,000

---

6   When a single entity makes purchases or sales in a foreign currency, it will be necessary to translate the transactions into its functional currency before the transactions can be included in its financial records.

In accordance with IAS 21 *The Effect of Changes in Foreign Currency Exchange Rates*, which of the following foreign currency exchange rates may be used to translate the foreign currency purchases and sales?

(1)     The rate which existed on the day that the purchase or sale took place
(2)     The rate which existed at the beginning of the accounting period
(3)     An average rate for the year, provided there have been no significant fluctuations throughout the year
(4)     The rate which existed at the end of the accounting period

A       (2) and (4)
B       (1) only
C       (3) only
D       (1) and (3)

---

7   On 1 October 20X4, Hoy Co had $2.5 million of equity Share capital (shares of 50 cents each) in issue.

No new shares were issued during the year ended 30 September 20X5, but on that date there were outstanding share options which had a dilutive effect equivalent to issuing 1.2 million shares for no consideration.

Hoy's profit after tax for the year ended 30 September 20X5 was $1,550,000.

In accordance with IAS 33 *Earnings per Share*, what is Hoy's diluted earnings per share for the year ended 30 September 20X5?

A       $0.25
B       $0.41
C       $0.31
D       $0.42

8    Fork Co owns an 80% investment in Spoon Co which it purchased several years ago. The goodwill on acquisition was valued at $1,674,000 and there has been no impairment of that goodwill since the date of acquisition.

On 30 September 20X4, Fork Co disposed of its entire investment in Spoon Co, details of which are as follows:

|  | $'000 |
|---|---|
| Sales proceeds of Fork Co's entire investment in Spoon Co | 5,580 |
| Cost of Fork Co's entire investment in Spoon Co | 3,720 |

Immediately before the disposal, the consolidated financial statements of Fork Co included the following amounts in respect of Spoon Co:

|  | $'000 |
|---|---|
| Carrying amount of the net assets (excluding goodwill) | 4,464 |
| Carrying amount of the non-controlling interests | 900 |

What is the profit/loss on disposal (before tax) which will be recorded in Fork Co's **CONSOLIDATED** statement of profit or loss for the year ended 30 September 20X4?

A    $1,860,000 profit
B    $2,016,000 profit
C    $342,000 profit
D    $558,000 loss

9    Consolidated financial statements are presented on the basis that the companies within the group are treated as if they are a single economic entity.

Which **TWO** of the following are requirements of preparing consolidated financial statements?

☐    All subsidiaries must adopt the accounting policies of the parent in their individual financial statements

☐    Subsidiaries with activities which are substantially different to the activities of other members of the group should not be consolidated

☐    All entity financial statements within a group should normally be prepared to the same accounting year end prior to consolidation

☐    Unrealised profits within the group must be eliminated from the consolidated financial statements

10   Dashing Group sells goods to its 80% owned subsidiary, Dancer Co, during the financial year, some of which remains in inventory at the year end.

Using the drag and drop options below, select the correct adjustment required in the consolidated statement of financial position to eliminate any unrealised profit in inventory?

| Debit | | | Group retained earnings |
|---|---|---|---|
| Credit | | | Inventory |
| | | | Non-controlling interest |

11   Caddy Co acquired 240,000 of Ambel Co's 800,000 equity shares for $6 per share on 1 October 20X4. Ambel Co's profit after tax for the year ended 30 September 20X5 was $400,000 and it paid an equity dividend on 20 September 20X5 of $150,000.

On the assumption that Ambel Co is an associate of Caddy Co, what would be the carrying amount of the investment in Ambel Co in the consolidated statement of financial position of Caddy Co as at 30 September 20X5?

A   $1,560,000
B   $1,395,000
C   $1,515,000
D   $1,690,000

---

12   Quartile Co is in the jewellery retail business which can be assumed to be highly seasonal. For the year ended 30 September 20X5, Quartile Co assessed its operating performance by comparing selected accounting ratios with those of its business sector average as provided by an agency. Assume that the business sector used by the agency is a meaningful representation of Quartile Co's business.

Which TWO of the following circumstances may invalidate the comparison of Quartile Co's ratios with those of the sector average?

☐   In the current year, Quartile Co has experienced significant rising costs for its purchases

☐   The sector average figures are compiled from companies whose year ends are between 1 July 20X5 and 30 September 20X5

☐   Quartile Co does not revalue its properties, but is aware that other entities in this sector do

☐   During the year, Quartile Co discovered an error relating to the inventory count at 30 September 20X4. This error was correctly accounted for in the financial statements for the current year ended 30 September 20X5

---

13   Which of the following criticisms does **NOT** apply to historical cost financial statements during a period of rising prices?

A   They are difficult to verify because transactions could have happened many years ago
B   They contain mixed values; some items are at current values and some are at out of date values
C   They understate assets and overstate profit
D   They overstate gearing in the statement of financial position

---

14   The following information has been taken or calculated from Fowler's financial statements for the year ended 30 September 20X5:

| | |
|---|---|
| Cash cycle at 30 September 20X5 | 70 days |
| Inventory turnover | six times |
| Year-end trade payables at 30 September 20X5 | $230,000 |
| Credit purchases for the year ended 30 September 20X5 | $2 million |
| Cost of sales for the year ended 30 September 20X5 | $1.8 million |

What is Fowler's trade receivables collection period as at 30 September 20X5?

A   106 days
B   89 days
C   56 days
D   51 days

15     On 1 October 20X4, Pyramid Co acquired 80% of Square Co's 9 million equity shares. At the date of acquisition, Square Co had an item of plant which had a fair value of $3m in excess of its carrying amount. At the date of acquisition it had a useful life of five years. Pyramid Co's policy is to value non-controlling interests at fair value at the date of acquisition. For this purpose, Square Co's shares had a value of $3.50 each at that date. In the year ended 30 September 20X5, Square Co reported a profit of $8m.

At what amount should the non-controlling interests in Square Co be valued in the consolidated statement of financial position of the Pyramid group as at 30 September 20X5?

A     $26,680,000
B     $7,900,000
C     $7,780,000
D     $12,220,000

**(30 marks)**

# Section B – ALL 15 questions are compulsory and MUST be attempted

Each question is worth 2 marks.

The following scenario relates to questions 16–20.

Telepath Co has a year end of 30 September and owns an item of plant which it uses to produce and package pharmaceuticals. The plant cost $750,000 on 1 October 20X0, and at that date, had an estimated useful life of five years. A review of the plant on 1 April 20X3 concluded that the plant would last for a further three and a half years and that its fair value was $560,000.

Telepath Co adopts the policy of revaluing its non-current assets to their fair value but does not make an annual transfer from the revaluation surplus to retained earnings to represent the additional depreciation charged due to the revaluation.

On 30 September 20X3, Telepath Co was informed by a major customer that it would no longer be placing orders with Telepath Co. As a result, Telepath revised its estimates that net cash inflows earned from the plant for the next three years would be:

| Year ended 30 September: | $ |
|---|---|
| 20X4 | 220,000 |
| 20X5 | 180,000 |
| 20X6 | 200,000 |

Telepath Co's cost of capital is 10% which results in the following discount factors:
Value of $1 at 30 September:

| | |
|---|---|
| 20X4 | 0.91 |
| 20X5 | 0.83 |
| 20X6 | 0.75 |

Telepath Co also owns Rilda Co, a 100% subsidiary, which is treated as a cash-generating unit. On 30 September 20X3, there was an impairment to Rilda's assets of $3,500,000. The carrying amount of the assets of Rilda Co immediately before the impairment were:

| | $ |
|---|---|
| Goodwill | 2,000,000 |
| Factory building | 4,000,000 |
| Plant | 3,500,000 |
| Receivables and cash (at recoverable amount) | 2,500,000 |
| | 12,000,000 |

16   In accordance with IAS 36 *Impairment of Assets*, which of the following explains the impairment of an asset and how to calculate its recoverable amount?

   A   An asset is impaired when the carrying amount exceeds its recoverable amount and the recoverable amount is the higher of its fair value less costs of disposal and its value in use

   B   An asset is impaired when the recoverable amount exceeds its carrying amount and the recoverable amount is the lower of its fair value less costs of disposal and its value in use

   C   An asset is impaired when the recoverable amount exceeds its carrying amount and the recoverable amount is the higher of its fair value less costs of disposal and its value in use

   D   An asset is impaired when the carrying amount exceeds its recoverable amount and the recoverable amount is the lower of its fair value less costs of disposal and its value in use

17    Prior to considering any impairment, what is the carrying amount of Telepath Co's plant and the balance on the revaluation surplus at 30 September 20X3?

|   | Plant carrying amount | Revaluation surplus |
|---|---|---|
|   | $000 | $000 |
| A | 480 | nil |
| B | 300 | 185 |
| C | 480 | 185 |
| D | 300 | nil |

18    What is the value in use of Telepath Co's plant as at 30 September 20X3?

A    $600,000
B    $450,000
C    $499,600
D    $nil

19    Which of the following are **TRUE** in accordance with IAS 36 *Impairment of Assets*?

(1)    A cash-generating unit is the smallest identifiable group of assets for which individual cash flows can be identified and measured

(2)    When considering the impairment of a cash-generating unit, the calculation of the carrying amount and the recoverable amount does not need to be based on exactly the same group of net assets

(3)    When it is not possible to calculate the recoverable amount of a single asset, then that of its cash-generating unit should be measured instead

A    (1) only
B    (2) and (3)
C    (3) only
D    (1) and (3)

20    What is the carrying amount of Rilda Co's plant at 30 September 20X3 after the impairment loss has been correctly allocated to its assets? Select your answer from the picklist provided.

**Picklist**

$2,479,000
$2,800,000
$2,211,000
$3,500,000

The following scenario relates to questions 21–25.

At a board meeting in June 20X3, Neutron Co's directors made the decision to close down one of its factories by 30 September 20X3 and market both the building and the plant for sale. The decision had been made public, was communicated to all affected parties and was fully implemented by 30 September 20X3.

The directors of Neutron Co have provided the following information relating to the closure:

Of the factory's 250 employees, 50 will be retrained and deployed to other subsidiaries within the Neutron group during the year ended 30 September 20X4 at a cost of $125,000. The remainder accepted redundancy at an average cost of $5,000 each.

The factory's plant had a carrying amount of $2.2 million, but is only expected to sell for $500,000, incurring $50,000 of selling costs. The factory itself is expected to sell for a profit of $1.2 million.

The company also rented a number of machines in the factory under short-term leases which have an average of three months to run after 30 September 20X3. The present value of these future lease payments at 30 September 20X3 was $1 million, however, the lessor has stated that they will accept $850,000 if paid on 30 October 20X3 as a full settlement.

Penalty payments, due to the non-completion of supply contracts, are estimated to be $200,000, 50% of which is expected to be recovered from Neutron Co's insurers.

21    Identify, by selecting the relevant box in the table below, whether the statement regarding for an operation to be classified as a discontinued operation in accordance with IFRS 5 *Non-current Assets Held for Sale and Discontinued Operations*?

| The operation represents a separate major line of business or geographical area | True | False |
|---|---|---|
| The operation is a subsidiary | True | False |
| The operation has been sold or is held for sale | True | False |
| The operation is considered not to be capable of making a future profit following a period of losses | True | False |

22    IFRS 5 *Non-current Assets Held for Sale and Discontinued Operations* prescribes the recognition criteria for non-current assets held for sale. For an asset or a disposal group to be classified as held for sale, the sale must be highly probable.

Which of the following must apply for the sale to be considered highly probable?

(1)    A buyer must have been located
(2)    The asset must be marketed at a reasonable price
(3)    Management must be committed to a plan to sell the asset
(4)    The sale must be expected to take place within the next six months

A    (2) and (3)
B    (3) and (4)
C    (1) and (4)
D    (1) and (2)

23    What is the employee cost associated with the closure and sale of Neutron Co's factory which should be charged to profit or loss for the year ended 30 September 20X3?

A    $125,000
B    $1,250,000
C    $1,125,000
D    $1,000,000

24    What is the profit or loss on discontinued operations relating to property, plant and equipment for the year ended 30 September 20X3?

A    $1.75 million loss
B    $1.75 million profit
C    $550,000 loss
D    $550,000 profit

25    In respect of the leases and penalty payments, what provision is required in the statement of financial position of Neutron Co as at 30 September 20X3?

A    $950,000
B    $1,200,000
C    $1,050,000
D    $1,100,000

The following scenario relates to questions 26–30.

Speculate Co is preparing its financial statements for the year ended 30 September 20X3. The following issues are relevant:

(i)  **Financial assets**

Shareholding A – a long-term investment in 10,000 of the equity shares of another company. These shares were acquired on 1 October 20X2 at a cost of $3.50 each. Transaction costs of 1% of the purchase price were incurred. On 30 September 20X3 the fair value of these shares is $4.50 each.

Shareholding B – a short-term speculative investment in 2,000 of the equity shares of another company. These shares were acquired on 1 December 20X2 at a cost of $2.50 each. Transaction costs of 1% of the purchase price were incurred. On 30 September 20X3 the fair value of these shares is $3.00 each.

Where possible, Speculate Co makes an irrevocable election for the fair value movements on financial assets to be reported in other comprehensive income.

(ii)  **Taxation**

The existing debit balance on the current tax account of $2.4m represents the over/under provision of the tax liability for the year ended 30 September 20X2. A provision of $28m is required for income tax for the year ended 30 September 20X3. The existing credit balance on the deferred tax account is $2.5m and the provision required at 30 September 20X3 is $4.4m.

(iii)  **Revenue**

On 1 October 20X2, Speculate Co sold one of its products for $10 million. As part of the sale agreement, Speculate Co is committed to the ongoing servicing of the product until 30 September 20X5 (ie three years after the sale). The sale value of this service has been included in the selling price of $10 million. The estimated cost to Speculate Co of the servicing is $600,000 per annum and Speculate Co's gross profit margin on this type of servicing is 25%. Ignore discounting.

26  Which of the following meet the definition of a financial asset in accordance with IFRS 9 *Financial Instruments*?

(1)  An equity instrument of another entity

(2)  A contract to exchange financial instruments with another entity under conditions which are potentially favourable

(3)  A contract to exchange financial instruments with another entity under conditions which are potentially unfavourable

(4)  Cash

A  (1) and (2) only
B  (1), (2) and (4)
C  (1), (3) and (4)
D  (4) only

27  Using the drop down box below, select the correct amount will be included in other comprehensive income for the year ended 30 September 20X3, in respect of the financial assets of Speculate Co.

[ ▼ ]

**Picklist**

Nil
$9,650
$10,000
$10,650

28    What is the total amount which will be charged to the statement of profit or loss for the year ended
      30 September 20X3 in respect of taxation?

      A    $28,000,000
      B    $30,400,000
      C    $32,300,000
      D    $29,900,000

29    What is the amount of deferred income which Speculate Co should recognise in its statement of financial
      position as at 30 September 20X3 relating to the contract for the supply and servicing of products?

      A    $1.2 million
      B    $1.6 million
      C    $600,000
      D    $1.5 million

30    Which TWO of the following are **TRUE** in respect of the income which Speculate Co has deferred at
      30 September 20X3?

      ☐    The deferred income will be split evenly between the current and non-current liabilities in
           Speculate Co's statement of financial position as at 30 September 20X3

      ☐    The costs associated with the deferred income of Speculate Co should be recognised in the statement
           of profit or loss at the same time as the revenue is recognised

      ☐    The deferred income can only be recognised as revenue by Speculate Co when there is a signed
           written contract of service with its customer

      ☐    When recognising the revenue associated with the service contract of Speculate Co, the stage of its
           completion is irrelevant

                                                                                              **(30 marks)**

# Section C – Both questions are compulsory and MUST be attempted

31   After preparing a draft statement of profit or loss for the year ended 30 September 20X5 and adding the current year's draft profit (before any adjustments required by notes (i) to (iii) below) to retained earnings, the summarised trial balance of Kandy Co as at 30 September 20X5 is:

|  | $'000 | $'000 |
|---|---|---|
| Equity shares of $1 each |  | 20,000 |
| Retained earnings as at 30 September 20X5 |  | 15,500 |
| Proceeds of 6% loan note (note (i)) |  | 30,000 |
| Investment properties at fair value (note (ii)) | 20,000 |  |
| Land ($5 million) and buildings – at cost (note (ii)) | 35,000 |  |
| Plant and equipment – at cost (note (ii)) | 58,500 |  |
| Accumulated depreciation at 1 October 20X4: buildings |  | 20,000 |
| plant and equipment |  | 34,500 |
| Current assets | 68,700 |  |
| Current liabilities |  | 43,400 |
| Deferred tax (notes (ii) and (iii)) |  | 2,500 |
| Interest paid (note (i)) | 1,800 |  |
| Current tax (note (iii)) |  | 1,100 |
| Suspense account (note (ii)) |  | 17,000 |
|  | 184,000 | 184,000 |

The following notes are relevant:

(i)    The loan note was issued on 1 October 20X4 and incurred issue costs of $1 million which were charged to profit or loss. Interest of $1.8 million ($30 million at 6%) was paid on 30 September 20X5. The loan is redeemable on 30 September 20X9 at a substantial premium which gives an effective interest rate of 9% per annum. No other repayments are due until 30 September 20X9.

(ii)   Non-current assets:

On 1 October 20X4, Kandy owned two investment properties. The first property had a carrying amount of $15 million and was sold on 1 December 20X4 for $17 million. The disposal proceeds have been credited to a suspense account in the trial balance above. On 31 December 20X4, the second property became owner occupied and so was transferred to land and buildings at its fair value of $6 million. Its remaining useful life on 31 December 20X4 was considered to be 20 years. Ignore any deferred tax implications of this fair value.

The price of property has increased significantly in recent years and so the directors decided to revalue the land and buildings. The directors accepted the report of an independent surveyor who, on 1 October 20X4, valued the land at $8 million and the buildings at $39 million on that date. This revaluation specifically excludes the transferred investment property described above. The remaining life of these buildings at 1 October 20X4 was 15 years. Kandy does not make an annual transfer to retained profits to reflect the realisation of the revaluation gain; however, the revaluation will give rise to a deferred tax liability. The income tax rate applicable to Kandy is 20%.

Plant and equipment is depreciated at 12.5% per annum using the reducing balance method.

No depreciation has yet been charged on any non-current asset for the year ended 30 September 20X5.

(iii)  A provision of $2.4 million is required for income tax on the profit for the year to 30 September 20X5. The balance on current tax in the trial balance is the under/over provision of tax for the previous year. In addition to the temporary differences relating to the information in note (ii), Kandy has further taxable temporary differences of $10 million as at 30 September 20X5.

*Required*

(a)     Prepare a schedule of adjustments required to the retained earnings of Kandy Co as at 30 September 20X5 as a result of the information in notes (i) to (iii) above.

(b)     Prepare the statement of financial position of Kandy Co as at 30 September 20X5.

**Note.** The notes to the statement of financial position are not required.

(c)     Prepare the extracts from Kandy Co's statement of cash flows for operating and investing activities for the year ended 30 September 20X5 which relate to property, plant and equipment.

The following mark allocation is provided as guidance for this question:

(a)     8 marks
(b)     9 marks
(c)     3 marks

**(20 marks)**

32     The summarised consolidated financial statements for the year ended 30 September 20X5 (and the comparative figures) for the Tangier group are shown below.

Consolidated statements of profit or loss for the year ended 30 September:

|  | 20X5 | 20X4 |
|---|---|---|
|  | $m | $m |
| Revenue | 2,700 | 1,820 |
| Cost of sales | (1,890) | (1,092) |
| Gross profit | 810 | 728 |
| Administrative expense | (345) | (200) |
| Distribution costs | (230) | (130) |
| Finance costs | (40) | (5) |
| Profit before taxation | 195 | 393 |
| Income tax expense | (60) | (113) |
| Profit for the year | 135 | 280 |

Consolidated statements of financial position as at 30 September:

|  | 20X5 $m | 20X5 $m | 20X4 $m | 20X4 $m |
|---|---|---|---|---|
| Non-current assets |  |  |  |  |
| Property, plant and equipment |  | 680 |  | 310 |
| Intangible asset: manufacturing licences |  | 300 |  | 100 |
| Goodwill |  | 230 |  | 200 |
|  |  | 1,210 |  | 610 |
| Current assets |  |  |  |  |
| Inventory | 200 |  | 110 |  |
| Trade receivables | 195 |  | 75 |  |
| Bank | nil |  | 120 |  |
|  |  | 395 |  | 305 |
| Total assets |  | 1,605 |  | 915 |
| Equity and liabilities |  |  |  |  |
| Equity shares of $1 each |  | 330 |  | 250 |
| Other components of equity |  | 100 |  | nil |
| Retained earnings |  | 375 |  | 295 |
|  |  | 805 |  | 545 |
| Non-current liabilities |  |  |  |  |
| 5% secured loan notes | 100 |  | 100 |  |
| 10% secured loan notes | 300 | 400 | nil | 100 |
| Current liabilities |  |  |  |  |
| Bank overdraft | 110 |  | nil |  |
| Trade payables | 210 |  | 160 |  |
| Current tax payable | 80 | 400 | 110 | 270 |
| Total equity and liabilities |  | 1,605 |  | 915 |

At 1 October 20X4, the Tangier group consisted of the parent, Tangier Co, and two wholly owned subsidiaries which had been owned for many years. On 1 January 20X5, Tangier Co purchased a third 100% owned investment in a subsidiary called Raremetal Co. The consideration paid for Raremetal Co was a combination of cash and shares. The cash payment was partly funded by the issue of 10% loan notes. On 1 January 20X5, Tangier Co also won a tender for a new contract to supply aircraft engines which Tangier Co manufactures under a recently acquired long-term licence. Raremetal Co was purchased with a view to securing the supply of specialised materials used in the manufacture of these engines. The bidding process had been very competitive and Tangier Co had to increase its manufacturing capacity to fulfil the contract.

*Required*

(a)     Comment on how the new contract and the purchase of Raremetal Co may have affected the comparability of the consolidated financial statements of Tangier Co for the years ended 30 September 20X4 and 20X5.

(b)     Calculate appropriate ratios and comment on Tangier Co's profitability and gearing. Your analysis should identify instances where the new contract and the purchase of Raremetal Co have limited the usefulness of the ratios and your analysis.

   **Note.** Your ratios should be based on the consolidated financial statements provided and you should not attempt to adjust for the effects of the new contract or the consolidation. Working capital and liquidity ratios are not required.

(c)     Explain what further information you might require to make your analysis more meaningful.

The following mark allocation is provided as guidance for this question:

(a)     5 marks
(b)     12 marks (up to 5 marks for the ratio calculations)
(c)     3 marks

**(20 marks)**

# Answers

DO NOT TURN THIS PAGE UNTIL YOU HAVE
COMPLETED THE MOCK EXAM

# A plan of attack

What's the worst thing you could be doing right now if this was the actual exam? Wondering how to celebrate the end of the exam in just over three hours' time? Panicking, flapping and generally getting in a right old state?

Well, they're all pretty bad, so turn back to the exam and let's sort out a **plan of attack**!

## First things first

You have three hours and fifteen minutes for this exam. This exam is the examining team's specimen exam, so it is the best indication of what you will see in your exam. Read it carefully.

The Financial Reporting paper has 15 2-mark questions in Section A, 15 2-mark questions in Section B and two long-form questions in Section C. All questions are compulsory. Therefore, you do not have to spend time working out which questions to answer.

It's a good idea to just start with the Section A questions. Once you have them done, you will feel more relaxed. Leave any that you are unsure of and come back to them later but don't leave any unanswered.

Section B: Questions 16–20 are on non-current assets. Questions 21–25 are on discontinued operations. Questions 26–30 cover three issues – financial assets, taxation and revenue. For each of these Section B questions make sure you read the scenario carefully.

Question 31 requires you to adjust retained earnings and prepare a statement of financial position and some cash flow extracts. There is nothing difficult here but you need to work methodically.

Question 32 is an interpretation question. Remember you do not get marks for simply saying that a ratio went up or down. It is your job to look at why this happened.

## You've got spare time at the end of the exam...?

If you have allocated your time properly then you **shouldn't have time on your hands** at the end of the exam and you should start by checking the Section A questions to make sure you have left none unanswered. But if you find yourself with five or ten minutes to spare, check over your work to make sure that there are no silly arithmetical errors.

## Forget about it!

And don't worry if you found the exam difficult. More than likely other candidates will too. If this were the real thing you would need to **forget** the exam the minute you leave the exam hall and **think about the next one**. Or, if it's the last one, **celebrate**!

# Section A

1   B   Only the transportation and the power supply can be included. The maintenance agreement and the training course are profit or loss items.

2   A   The research project only as the customer list cannot be reliably valued. The advertising campaign cannot be capitalised and contingent assets are not recognised.

3   $4,070,000

25,000 – 2,000 = 23,000 + 2,300 (10% int) – 6,000 (pmt) = 19,300
19,300 + 1,930 (10% int) – 6,000 (pmt) = 15,230
Current liability = 19,300 – 15,230 = $4,070

4

| | | |
|---|---|---|
| Charging the rental payments for an item of plant to the statement of profit or loss where the rental agreement meets the criteria for a lease | True | False |
| Including a convertible loan note in equity on the basis that the holders are likely to choose the equity option on conversion | True | False |
| Treating redeemable preference shares as part of equity in the statement of financial position | True | False |
| Derecognising factored trade receivables sold without recourse to the seller | True | False |

Trade receivables factored without recourse are no longer an asset of the seller. The other options are incorrect.

5   $22,032,000

Dismantling provision at 1 October 20X4 is $20.4 million (30,000 × 0.68) discounted
This will increase by an 8% finance cost by 30 September 20X5 = $22,032,000

6   D   The rate at the transaction date or the average rate

7   A

$(1,550/(2,500 \times 2 + 1,200)) = \$0.25$

8   C

| | | $'000 |
|---|---|---|
| Sales proceeds | | 5,580 |
| Net assets at disposal | 4,464 | |
| Goodwill at disposal | 1,674 | |
| Less: carrying value of NCI | (900) | (5,238) |
| | | 342 |

9   All entity financial statements within a group should normally be prepared to the same accounting year end prior to consolidation

Unrealised profits within the group must be eliminated from the consolidated financial statements

Adjustments will be made on consolidation for different accounting policies. Subsidiaries with dissimilar activities are still consolidated.

10

| Debit | Group retained earnings |
|---|---|

| Credit | Inventory |
|---|---|

As the sale is made by the parent there is no charge against non-controlling interest.

11  C

|  | $'000 |
|---|---|
| Cost (240,000 × $6) | 1,440 |
| Share of associate's profit (400 × 240/800) | 120 |
| Less dividend received (150 × 240/800) | (45) |
|  | 1,515 |

12  The sector average figures are compiled from companies whose year ends are between 1 July 20X5 and 30 September 20X5

Quartile Co does not revalue its properties, but is aware that other entities in this sector do

Rising costs will have affected all of the business sector and the inventory adjustment will have been corrected in the prior year, so no actual effect in 20X5.

13  A  They are easy to verify because there will be a record of the transaction.

14  D

Inventory turnover is 61 days (365/6).
Trade payables period is 42 days (230,000 × 365/2 million).
Therefore, receivables collection period is 51 days (70 – 61 + 42).

15  C

|  | $000 |
|---|---|
| FV NCI at 1 October 14 (9000 × 20% × $3.50) | 6,300 |
| Post-acquisition profit (8000 – (3000/5)) = 7,400 at 20% | 1,480 |
|  | 7,780 |

# Section B

16    A

17    C

> Annual depreciation prior to the revaluation is $150,000 (750/5). At the date of revaluation (1 April 20X3), the carrying amount is $375,000 (750–(150 × 2.5 yrs)). Revalued to $560,000 with a remaining life of 3.5 years results in a depreciation charge of $160,000 per annum which means $80,000 for six months. The carrying amount at 30 September 20X3 is therefore $480,000 (560 – 80).
>
> Alternative calculation: $560,000 – ($560,000/3.5 × 6/12) = $480,000.
>
> The revaluation surplus has a balance of $185,000 (560,000 – 375,000).

18    C

|  | Cash flow<br>$'000 | Discount factor at 10% | Present value<br>$'000 |
|---|---|---|---|
| Year ended: 30 September 20X4 | 220 | 0.91 | 200.2 |
| 30 September 20X5 | 180 | 0.83 | 149.4 |
| 30 September 20X6 | 200 | 0.75 | 150.0 |
|  |  |  | 499.6 |

19    D    The assets of the CGU must remain the same when calculating impairment.

20    $2,800,000

|  | Carrying amount before<br>$'000 | Impairment loss<br>$'000 | Carrying amount after<br>$'000 |
|---|---|---|---|
| Goodwill | 2,000 | 2,000 | Nil |
| Property | 4,000 | 800 | 3,200 |
| Plant | 3,500 | 700 | 2,800 |
| Cash and receivables | 2,500 | Nil | 2,500 |
|  | 12,000 | 3,500 | 8,500 |

21

| The operation represents a separate major line of business or geographical area | True | False |
|---|---|---|
| The operation is a subsidiary | True | False |
| The operation has been sold or is held for sale | True | False |
| The operation is considered not to be capable of making a future profit following a period of losses | True | False |

The operation does not have to be a subsidiary. Future profit forecasts are not relevant.

22    A    A buyer does not need to have been specifically located and the sale must be expected to take place within the next 12 months.

23    D    200 employees at $5,000 = $1,000,000 redundancy costs. The retraining costs are a future cost.

24    A    Impairment loss on plant is $1,750,000 (2,200,000 – (500,000 – 50,000)).

25    C    Onerous contract $850,000 + penalty payments $200,000 = $1,050,000. The possible insurance receipt should be ignored as there is no certainty that it would be received and it would not be netted off against the provision anyway.

26    B    A contract to exchange financial instruments under potentially unfavourable conditions would be a financial liability.

27 $9,650

Shareholding A is not held for trading as an election made – FVTOCI.

Shareholding B is held for trading and so FVTPL (transaction costs are not included in carrying amount).

Cost of shareholding A is 10,000 × $3.50 × 1.01 = $35,350.

FV at 30 September 20X3 10,000 × $4.50 = $45,000.

Gain = 45,000 – 35,350 = $9,650.

28 C

|  | $'000 |
|---|---|
| DT provision required at 30 September 20X3 | 4,400 |
| DT Provision at 1 October 20X2 | (2,500) |
|  | 1,900 |
| Write off of the underprovision for the year ended 30 September 20X2 | 2,400 |
| Income tax for the year ended 30 September 20X3 | 28,000 |
| Charge for the year ended 30 September 20X3 | 32,300 |

29 B At 30 September 20X3 there are two more years of servicing work, thus $1.6 million ((600,000 × 2) × 100/75) must be treated as deferred income.

30 The deferred income will be split evenly between the current and non-current liabilities in Speculate Co's statement of financial position as at 30 September 20X3

The costs associated with the deferred income of Speculate Co should be recognised in the statement of profit or loss at the same time as the revenue is recognised

A written service contract is not needed, but the stage of completion is important in recognising revenue.

# Section C

## 31

|  |  | Marks |
|---|---|---|
| (a) | Schedule of retained earnings as at 30 September 20X4 | |
| | Retained earnings per trial balance | ½ |
| | Issue costs | 1 |
| | Loan finance costs | 1 |
| | Gains on investment properties | 1 |
| | Depreciation charges | 3 |
| | Income tax expense | 1½ |
| | | **8** |
| (b) | Statement of financial position | |
| | Property, plant and equipment | 2 |
| | Current assets | ½ |
| | Equity shares | ½ |
| | Revaluation surplus | 2 |
| | Deferred tax | 1 |
| | 6% loan note | 1½ |
| | Current liabilities (per trial balance) | ½ |
| | Current tax payable | 1 |
| | | **9** |
| (c) | Extracts from the statement of cash flows | |
| | Cash flows from operating activities: | |
| |     Add back depreciation | 1 |
| |     Less gain on revaluation of investment property | ½ |
| |     Less gain on disposal of investment property | ½ |
| | Cash flows from investing activities: | |
| |     Investment property disposal proceeds | 1 |
| | | **3** |
| | | **20** |

(a) Schedule of retained earnings of Kandy as at 30 September 20X5

|  | $'000 |
|---|---|
| Retained earnings per trial balance | 15,500 |
| Adjustments re: | |
| Note (i) | |
| Add back issue costs of loan note (W1) | 1,000 |
| Loan finance costs (29,000 × 9%) (W1) | (2,610) |
| Note (ii) | |
| Gain on disposal of investment property (17,000 – 15,000) | 2,000 |
| Gain on revaluation of investment property prior to transfer (6,000 – 5,000) | 1,000 |
| Depreciation of buildings (W2) | (2,825) |
| Depreciation of plant and equipment (W2) | (3,000) |
| Note (iii) | |
| Income tax expense (W3) | (800) |
| Adjusted retained earnings | 10,265 |

(b)    STATEMENT OF FINANCIAL POSITION AS AT 30 SEPTEMBER 20X5

|  | $'000 | $'000 |
|---|---|---|
| *Assets* | | |
| Non-current assets | | |
| Property, plant and equipment (50,175 + 21,000 (W2)) | | 71,175 |
| Current assets (per trial balance) | | 68,700 |
| Total assets | | 139,875 |
| *Equity and liabilities* | | |
| *Equity* | | |
| Equity shares of $1 each | | 20,000 |
| Revaluation surplus (32,000 – 6,400 (W2) and (W3)) | 25,600 | |
| Retained earnings (from (a)) | 10,265 | 35,865 |
| | | 55,865 |
| *Non-current liabilities* | | |
| Deferred tax (W3) | 8,400 | |
| 6% loan note (W1) | 29,810 | 38,210 |
| *Current liabilities* | | |
| Per trial balance | 43,400 | |
| Current tax payable | 2,400 | 45,800 |
| Total equity and liabilities | | 139,875 |

*Workings* (monetary figures in brackets in $'000)

1    *Loan note*

The issue costs should be deducted from the proceeds of the loan note and not charged as an expense. The finance cost of the loan note, at the effective rate of 9% applied to the carrying amount of the loan note of $29 million (30,000 – 1,000), is $2,610,000. The interest actually paid is $1.8 million. The difference between these amounts of $810,000 (2,610 – 1,800) is added to the carrying amount of the loan note to give $29,810,000 (29,000 + 810) for inclusion as a non-current liability in the statement of financial position.

2    *Non-current assets*

Land and buildings

The gain on revaluation and carrying amount of the land and buildings will be:

|  | $'000 |
|---|---|
| Carrying amount at 1 October 20X4 (35,000 – 20,000) | 15,000 |
| Revaluation at that date (8,000 + 39,000) | 47,000 |
| Gain on revaluation | 32,000 |
| | |
| Buildings depreciation for the year ended 30 September 20X5: | |
| Land and buildings existing at 1 October 20X4 (39,000/15 years) | 2,600 |
| Transferred investment property (6,000/20 × 9/12) | 225 |
| | 2,825 |
| Carrying amount at 30 September 20X5 (47,000 + 6,000 – 2,825) | 50,175 |
| | |
| Plant and equipment | |
| Carrying amount at 1 October 20X4 (58,500 – 34,500) | 24,000 |
| Depreciation for year ended 30 September 20X5 (12.5% reducing balance) | (3,000) |
| Carrying amount at 30 September 20X5 | 21,000 |

3    *Taxation*

|  | $'000 |
|---|---|
| Income tax expense: | |
| Provision for year ended 30 September 20X5 | 2,400 |
| Less over provision in previous year | (1,100) |
| Deferred tax (see below) | (500) |
| | 800 |

|  | $'000 |
|---|---|
| Deferred tax | |
| Provision required at 30 September 20X5 ((10,000 + 32,000) × 20%) | 8,400 |
| Provision at 1 October 20X4 | (2,500) |
| Movement in provision | 5,900 |
| Charge to revaluation of land and buildings (32,000 × 20%) | (6,400) |
| Balance – credit to profit or loss | (500) |

(c)

|  | $'000 |
|---|---|
| *Cash flows from operating activities:* | |
| Add back depreciation | 5,825 |
| Deduct gain on revaluation of investment property | (1,000) |
| Deduct gain on disposal of investment property | (2,000) |
| *Cash flows from investing activities:* | |
| Investment property disposal proceeds | 17,000 |

32

## Marking scheme

|  |  |  | **Marks** |
|---|---|---|---|
| (a) | Analysis of results | | |
| | A like for like comparison taking account of the consolidation and the contract | 5 | |
| (b) | Up to 5 marks for ratio calculations | 5 | |
| | Profitability | 4½ | |
| | Gearing and interest cover | 2½ | |
| | | 12 | |
| (c) | Additional information | | |
| | Any three of the six suggestions provided | 3 | |
| | | | 20 |

(a) **Note.** References to '20X5' are in respect of the year ended 30 September 20X5 and '20X4' refers to the year ended 30 September 20X4.

The key matter to note is that the ratios for 20X4 and 20X5 will not be directly comparable because two significant events, the acquisition of Raremetal Co and securing the new contract, have occurred between these dates. This means that the underlying financial statements are not directly comparable. For example, the 20X4 statement of profit or loss (SOPL) will not include the results of Raremetal Co or the effect of the new contract. However, the 20X5 SOPL will contain nine months of the results of Raremetal Co (although intragroup transactions will have been eliminated) and nine months of the effects of the new contract (which may have resulted in either a net profit or loss). Likewise, the 20X4 statement of financial position does not contain any of Raremetal Co's assets and liabilities, whereas that of 20X5 contains all of the net assets of Raremetal Co and the cost of the new licence. This does not mean that comparisons between the two years are not worthwhile, just that they need to be treated with caution. For some ratios, it may be necessary to exclude all of the subsidiaries from the analysis and use the single entity financial statements of Tangier Co as a basis for comparison with the performance of previous years. Similarly, it may still be possible to compare some of the ratios of the Tangier group with those of other groups in the same sector although not all groups will have experienced similar acquisitions.

Assuming there has been no impairment of goodwill, the investment in Raremetal Co has resulted in additional goodwill of $30 million which means that the investment has cost more than the carrying amount of Raremetal Co's net assets. Although there is no indication of the precise cost, it is known to have been achieved by a combination of a share exchange (hence the $180 million new issue of shares) and a cash element (funded from the proceeds of the loan issue and the decrease in the bank balance). Any intragroup sales have been eliminated on consolidation and it is not possible to determine in which individual company any profit on these intragroup sales will be reported; it is therefore difficult to measure any benefits of the investment. Indeed, the benefit of the investment might not be a financial one but merely to secure the supply of raw materials. It would be useful to establish the cost of the investment and the profit (if any) contributed by Raremetal Co so that an assessment of the benefit of the investment might be made.

(b)

| Relevant ratios: | 20X5 | 20X4 |
|---|---|---|
| Gross profit margin % (810/2,700 × 100) | 30.0% | 40.0% |
| Operating profit margin (235/2,700 × 100) | 8.7% | 21.9% |
| ROCE (235/(805 + 400)) | 19.5% | 61.7% |
| Non-current asset turnover (2,700/1,210) | 2.23 times | 2.98 times |
| Debt/equity (400/805) | 49.7% | 18.3% |
| Interest cover (235/40) | 5.9 times | 79.6 times |

All of the issues identified in part (a) make a comparison of ratios difficult and, if more information was available, then some adjustments may be required. For example, if it is established that the investment is not generating any benefits, then it might be argued that the inclusion of the goodwill in the ROCE and non-current asset turnover is unjustified (it may be impaired and should be written off). Goodwill has not been excluded from any of the following ratios.

The increase in revenues of 48.4% (880/1,820 × 100) in 20X5 will be partly due to the consolidation of Raremetal Co and the revenues associated with the new contract. Yet, despite these increased revenues, the company has suffered a dramatic fall in its profitability. This has been caused by a combination of a falling gross profit margin (from 40% in 20X4 to only 30% in 20X5) and markedly higher operating overheads (operating profit margin has fallen from 21·9% in 20X4 to 8.7% in 20X5). Again, it is important to note that some of these costs will be attributable to the consolidation of Raremetal Co and some to the new contract. It could be speculated that the 73% increase in administrative expenses may be due to one-off costs associated with the tendering process (consultancy fees, etc) and the acquisition of Raremetal Co and the 77% increase in higher distribution costs could be due to additional freight, packing and insurance cost of the engines, delivery distances may also be longer – even to foreign countries (although some of the increase in distribution costs may also be due to consolidation).

This is all reflected in the ROCE falling from an impressive 61.7% in 20X4 to only 19.5% in 20X5 (though even this figure is respectable). The fall in the ROCE is attributable to a dramatic fall in profit margin at operating level (from 21.9% in 20X4 to only 8.7% in 20X5) which has been compounded by a reduction in the non-current asset turnover, with only $2·23 being generated from every $1 invested in non-current assets in 20X5 (from $2.98 in 20X4).

The information in the question points strongly to the possibility (even probability) that the new contract may be responsible for much of the deterioration in Tangier Co's operating performance. For example, it is likely that the new contract may account for some of the increased revenue; however, the bidding process was 'very competitive' which may imply that Tangier Co had to cut its prices (and therefore its profit margin) in order to win the contract.

The costs of fulfilling the contract have also been heavy: investment in property, plant and equipment has increased by $370 million (at carrying amount), representing an increase of 61% (no doubt some of this increase will be due to the acquisition of Raremetal Co). The increase in licence costs to manufacture the new engines has cost $200 million plus any amortisation and there is also the additional goodwill of $30 million.

An eight-fold increase in finance cost caused by the increased borrowing at double the interest rate of the borrowing in 20X4 and (presumably) some overdraft interest has led to the dramatic fall in the company's interest cover (from 79.6 in 20X4 to only 5.9 in 20X5). The finance cost of the new $300 million 10% loan notes to partly fund the investment in Raremetal Co and other non-current assets has also increased debt/equity (one form of gearing measure) from 18.3% in 20X4 to 49.7% in 20X5 despite also issuing $180 million in new equity shares. At this level, particularly in view of its large increase from 20X4, it may give debt holders (and others) cause for concern as there is increased risk for all Tangier Co's lenders. If it could be demonstrated that the overdraft could not be cleared for some time, this would be an argument for including it in the calculation of debt/equity, making the 20X5 gearing level even worse. It is also apparent from the movement in the retained earnings that Tangier Co paid a dividend during 20X5 of $55 million (295,000 + 135,000 – 375,000) which may be a questionable policy when the company is raising additional finance through borrowings and contributes substantially to Tangier Co's overdraft.

Overall, the acquisition of Raremetal Co to secure supplies appears to have been an expensive strategy, perhaps a less expensive one might have been to enter into a long-term supply contract with Raremetal Co.

(c)    Further information which would be useful to obtain would therefore include:

(i)    The cost of the investment in Raremetal Co, the carrying amount of the assets acquired and whether Tangier Co has carried out a goodwill impairment test as required under IFRS.

(ii)   The benefits generated from the investment; for example, Raremetal Co's individual financial statements and details of sales to external customers (not all of these benefits will be measurable in financial terms).

(iii)  The above two pieces of information would demonstrate whether the investment in Raremetal Co had been worthwhile.

(iv)   The amount of intragroup sales made during the year and those expected to be made in the short to medium term.

(v)    The pricing strategy agreed with Raremetal Co so that the effects on the profits reported in the individual financial statements of Raremetal Co and Tangier Co can be more readily determined.

(vi)   More information is needed to establish if the new contract has been detrimental to Tangier Co's performance. The contract was won sometime between 1 October 20X4 and 1 January 20X5 and there is no information of when production and sales started, but clearly there has not been a full year's revenue from the contract. Also there is no information on the length or total value of the contract.

# ACCA

# Financial Reporting (FR)

# Mock Examination 2

# September 2016 CBE

---

**Time allowed:** 3 hours 15 minutes

This mock exam is divided into three sections:

Section A – ALL 15 questions are compulsory and MUST be attempted

Section B – ALL 15 questions are compulsory and MUST be attempted

Section C – BOTH questions are compulsory and MUST be attempted

**Do NOT open this question paper until instructed by the supervisor.**

**Do NOT record any of your answers on the question paper.**

**This question paper must not be removed from the examination hall.**

---

# Section A – ALL 15 questions are compulsory and MUST be attempted

Each question is worth 2 marks.

1    Identify, by selecting the relevant box in the table below which of the following are true or false statements regarding the duties of the IFRS Interpretations Committee?

| | | |
|---|---|---|
| To interpret the application of International Financial Reporting Standards | True | False |
| To work directly with national standard setters to bring about convergence with IFRS | True | False |
| To provide guidance on financial reporting issues not specifically addressed in IFRSs | True | False |
| To publish draft interpretations for public comment | True | False |

2    Which of the following will be treated as a subsidiary of Poulgo Co as at 31 December 20X7?

(1)   The acquisition of 60% of Zakron Co's equity share capital on 1 March 20X7. Zakron Co's activities are significantly different from the rest of the Poulgo group of companies.

(2)   The offer to acquire 70% of Unto Co's equity share capital on 1 November 20X7. The negotiations were finally signed off during January 20X8.

(3)   The acquisition of 45% of Speeth Co's equity share capital on 31 December 20X7. Poulgo Co is able to appoint three of the ten members of Speeth Co's board.

A    1 only
B    2 and 3
C    3 only
D    1 and 2

3    On 1 January 20X6, Gardenbugs Co received a $30,000 government grant relating to equipment which cost $90,000 and had a useful life of six years. The grant was netted off against the cost of the equipment. On 1 January 20X7, when the equipment had a carrying amount of $50,000, its use was changed so that it was no longer being used in accordance with the grant. This meant that the grant needed to be repaid in full but by 31 December 20X7, this had not yet been done.

Using the drag and drop options in the table below, state the journal entry required to reflect the correct accounting treatment of the government grant and the equipment in the financial statements of Gardenbugs Co for the year ended 31 December 20X7?

|                              | Debit | Credit |
|------------------------------|-------|--------|
| Depreciation expense         |       |        |
| Liability                    |       |        |
| Property, plant and equipment |       |        |

$10,000

$15,000

$20,000

$30,000

---

4    The following two issues relate to Spiko Co's mining activities:

Issue 1: Spiko Co began operating a new mine in January 20X3 under a five-year government licence which required Spiko Co to landscape the area after mining ceased at an estimated cost of $100,000.

Issue 2: During 20X4, Spiko Co's mining activities caused environmental pollution on an adjoining piece of government land. There is no legislation which requires Spiko Co to rectify this damage, however, Spiko Co does have a published environmental policy which includes assurances that it will do so. The estimated cost of the rectification is $1,000,000.

In accordance with IAS 37 *Provisions, Contingent Liabilities and Contingent Assets*, which of the following statements is correct in respect of Spiko Co's financial statements for the year ended 31 December 20X4?

A    A provision is required for the cost of both issues 1 and 2
B    Both issues 1 and 2 require disclosure only
C    A provision is required for the cost of issue 1 but issue 2 requires disclosure only
D    Issue 1 requires disclosure only and issue 2 should be ignored

---

5 Parket Co acquired 60% of Suket Co on 1 January 20X7. The following extract has been taken from the individual statements of profit or loss for the year ended 31 March 20X7:

|  | Parket Co | Suket Co |
|---|---|---|
|  | $'000 | $'000 |
| Cost of sales | 710 | 480 |

Parket Co consistently made sales of $20,000 per month to Suket Co throughout the year. At the year end, Suket Co held $20,000 of this in inventory. Parket Co made a mark-up on cost of 25% on all sales to Suket Co.

Using the drop down box select the correct figure for Parket Co's consolidated cost of sales for the year ended 31 March 20X7?

**Picklist**

$954,000
$950,000
$774,000
$766,000

---

6 Quilo Co has decided to change its depreciation method to better reflect the pattern of use of its equipment.

Which of the following correctly reflects what this change represents and how it should be applied?

A   It is a change of accounting policy and must be applied prospectively
B   It is a change of accounting policy and must be applied retrospectively
C   It is a change of accounting estimate and must be applied retrospectively
D   It is a change of accounting estimate and must be applied prospectively

---

7 Included within the financial assets of Zinet Co at 31 March 20X9 are the following two recently purchased investments in publicly traded equity shares:

Investment 1 – 10% of the issued share capital of Haruka Co. This shareholding was acquired as a long-term investment as Zinet Co wishes to participate as an active shareholder of Haruka Co.

Investment 2 – 10% of the issued share capital of Lukas Co. This shareholding was acquired for speculative purposes and Zinet Co expects to sell these shares in the near future.

Neither of these shareholdings gives Zinet Co significant influence over the investee companies.

Wherever possible, the directors of Zinet Co wish to avoid taking any fair value movements to profit or loss, so as to minimise volatility in reported earnings.

How should the fair value movements in these investments be reported in Zinet Co's financial statements for the year ended 31 March 20X9?

A   In profit or loss for both investments
B   In other comprehensive income for both investments
C   In profit or loss for investment 1 and in other comprehensive income for investment 2
D   In other comprehensive income for investment 1 and in profit or loss for investment 2

8    Shiba Co entered into a non-cancellable four-month lease to hire an office on 1 December 20X7. The terms of the lease agreement were as follows:

Lease rental                                                    $5,000 per month
Cash back incentive received at the start of the lease          $1,000
Useful life of the property                                     Eight years

What is the charge in the statement of profit or loss of Shiba Co for the year ended 31 December 20X7 in respect of this lease?

A     $2,375
B     $4,000
C     $4,750
D     $5,250

---

9    Trasten Co operates in an emerging market with a fast-growing economy where prices increase frequently.

Which **TWO** of the following statements are true when using historical cost accounting compared to current value accounting in this type of market?

☐    Capital employed which is calculated using historical costs is understated compared to current value capital employed

☐    Historical cost profits are overstated in comparison to current value profits

☐    Capital employed which is calculated using historical costs is overstated compared to current value capital employed

☐    Historical cost profits are understated in comparison to current value profits

---

10    Patula Co acquired 80% of Sanka Co on 1 October 20X5. At this date, some of Sanka Co's inventory had a carrying amount of $600,000 but a fair value of $800,000. By 31 December 20X5, 70% of this inventory had been sold by Sanka Co.

The individual statements of financial position at 31 December 20X5 for both companies show the following:

|               | Patula Co | Sanka Co |
|---------------|-----------|----------|
|               | $'000     | $'000    |
| Inventories   | 3,250     | 1,940    |

What will be the total inventories figure in the consolidated statement of financial position of Patula Co as at 31 December 20X5?

$ [          ]

---

11    Top Trades Co has been trading for a number of years and is currently going through a period of expansion.

An extract from the statement of cash flows for the year ended 31 December 20X7 for Top Trades Co is presented as follows:

|                                                    | $'000  |
|----------------------------------------------------|--------|
| Net cash from operating activities                 | 995    |
| Net cash used in investing activities              | (540)  |
| Net cash used in financing activities              | (200)  |
| Net increase in cash and cash equivalents          | 255    |
| Cash and cash equivalents at the beginning of the period | 200 |
| Cash and cash equivalents at the end of the period | 455    |

Which of the following statements is correct according to the extract of Top Trades Co's statement of cash flows?

A     The company has good working capital management
B     Net cash generated from financing activities has been used to fund the additions to non-current assets
C     Net cash generated from operating activities has been used to fund the additions to non-current assets
D     Existing non-current assets have been sold to cover the cost of the additions to non-current assets

12   Rooney Co acquired 70% of the equity share capital of Marek Co, its only subsidiary, on 1 January 20X6. The fair value of the non-controlling interest in Marek Co at acquisition was $1.1m. At that date the fair values of Marek Co's net assets were equal to their carrying amounts, except for a building which had a fair value of $1.5m above its carrying amount and 30 years remaining useful life.

During the year to 31 December 20X6, Marek Co sold goods to Rooney Co, giving rise to an unrealised profit in inventory of $550,000 at the year end. Marek Co's profit after tax for the year ended 31 December 20X6 was $3.2m.

Using the drop down box provided, state the amount to be presented as the non-controlling interest in the consolidated statement of financial position of Rooney Co as at 31 December 20X6?

**Picklist**

$1,895,000
$1,495,000
$1,910,000
$1,880,000

---

13   When a gain on a bargain purchase (negative goodwill) arises, IFRS 3 *Business Combinations* requires an entity to first of all review the measurement of the assets, liabilities and consideration transferred in respect of the combination.

When a bargain purchase is confirmed, how is it then recognised?

A      It is credited directly to retained earnings
B      It is credited to profit or loss
C      It is debited to profit or loss
D      It is deducted from positive goodwill

---

14   On 1 October 20X5, Anita Co purchased 75,000 of Binita Co's 100,000 equity shares when Binita Co's retained earnings amounted to $90,000.

On 30 September 20X7, extracts from the statements of financial position of the two companies were:

|  | Anita Co | Binita Co |
| --- | --- | --- |
|  | $'000 | $'000 |
| Equity shares of $1 each | 125 | 100 |
| Retained earnings | 300 | 150 |
| Total | 425 | 250 |

What is the total equity which should appear in Anita Co's consolidated statement of financial position as at 30 September 20X7?

$ [          ]

---

15   On 1 October 20X1, Bash Co borrowed $6m for a term of one year, exclusively to finance the construction of a new piece of production equipment. The interest rate on the loan is 6% and is payable on maturity of the loan. The construction commenced on 1 November 20X1 but no construction took place between 1 December 20X1 and 31 January 20X2 due to employees taking industrial action. The asset was available for use on 30 September 20X2 having a construction cost of $6m.

Using the drop down box provided, select the correct figure for the carrying amount of the production equipment in Bash Co's statement of financial position as at 30 September 20X2?

**Picklist**

$5,016,000
$6,270,000
$6,330,000
$6,360,000

(30 marks)

This is a blank page.
Section B begins on page 233.

# Section B – ALL 15 questions are compulsory and MUST be attempted

Please use the grid provided on page two of the Candidate Answer Booklet to record your answers to each multiple choice question. Do not write out the answers to the MCQs on the lined pages of the answer booklet.

Each question is worth 2 marks.

The following scenario relates to questions 16–20.

Aphrodite Co has a year end of 31 December and operates a factory which makes computer chips for mobile phones. It purchased a machine on 1 July 20X3 for $80,000 which had a useful life of ten years and is depreciated on the straight line basis, time apportioned in the years of acquisition and disposal. The machine was revalued to $81,000 on 1 July 20X4. There was no change to its useful life at that date.

A fire at the factory on 1 October 20X6 damaged the machine leaving it with a lower operating capacity. The accountant considers that Aphrodite Co will need to recognise an impairment loss in relation to this damage. The accountant has ascertained the following information at 1 October 20X6:

(1)     The carrying amount of the machine is $60,750.

(2)     An equivalent new machine would cost $90,000.

(3)     The machine could be sold in its current condition for a gross amount of $45,000. Dismantling costs would amount to $2,000.

(4)     In its current condition, the machine could operate for three more years which gives it a value in use figure of $38,685.

16      In accordance with IAS 16 *Property, Plant and Equipment*, what is the depreciation charged to Aphrodite Co's profit or loss in respect of the machine for the year ended 31 December 20X4?

> A      $9,000
> B      $8,000
> C      $8,263
> D      $8,500

17      IAS 36 *Impairment of Assets* contains a number of examples of internal and external events which may indicate the impairment of an asset.

In accordance with IAS 36, which of the following would definitely **NOT** be an indicator of the potential impairment of an asset (or group of assets)?

> A      An unexpected fall in the market value of one or more assets
>
> B      Adverse changes in the economic performance of one or more assets
>
> C      A significant change in the technological environment in which an asset is employed making its software effectively obsolete
>
> D      The carrying amount of an entity's net assets being below the entity's market capitalisation

18      Using the drop down box, select the total impairment loss associated with Aphrodite Co's machine at 1 October 20X6?

**Picklist**

$nil
$17,750
$22,065
$15,750

19    The accountant has decided that it is too difficult to reliably attribute cash flows to this one machine and that it would be more accurate to calculate the impairment on the basis of the factory as a cash generating unit.

In accordance with IAS 36, which of the following is **TRUE** regarding cash generating units?

A    A cash generating unit to which goodwill has been allocated should be tested for impairment every five years

B    A cash generating unit must be a subsidiary of the parent

C    There is no need to consistently identify cash generating units based on the same types of asset from period to period

D    A cash generating unit is the smallest identifiable group of assets for which independent cash flows can be identified

20    On 1 July 20X7, it is discovered that the damage to the machine is worse than originally thought. The machine is now considered to be worthless and the recoverable amount of the factory as a cash generating unit is estimated to be $950,000.

At 1 July 20X7, the cash generating unit comprises the following assets:

|  | $'000 |
|---|---|
| Building | 500 |
| Plant and equipment (including the damaged machine at a carrying amount of $35,000) | 335 |
| Goodwill | 85 |
| Net current assets (at recoverable amount) | 250 |
|  | 1,170 |

In accordance with IAS 36, what will be the carrying amount of Aphrodite Co's plant and equipment when the impairment loss has been allocated to the cash generating unit?

A    $262,500
B    $300,000
C    $237,288
D    $280,838

The following scenario relates to questions 21–25.

On 1 January 20X5, Blocks Co entered into new lease agreements as follows:

Agreement one    This lease relates to a new piece of machinery. The initial measurement of the liability (prior to payment of the deposit) is $220,000. The agreement requires Blocks Co to pay a deposit of $20,000 on 1 January 20X5 followed by five equal annual instalments of $55,000, starting on 31 December 20X5. The implicit rate of interest is 11.65%.

Agreement two    This nine-month lease relates to a van. The fair value of the van is $120,000 and it has an estimated useful life of five years. The agreement requires Blocks Co to make no payment in month one and $4,800 per month in months 2–9.

Agreement three    This sale and leaseback relates to a cutting machine purchased by Blocks Co on 1 January 20X4 for $300,000. The carrying amount of the machine as at 31 December 20X4 was $250,000. On 1 January 20X5, it was sold to Cogs Co for $370,000 (being its fair value) and Blocks Co will lease the machine back for five years, the remainder of its useful life, at $80,000 per annum. The present value of the annual payments is $350,000 and the transaction satisfies the IFRS 15 criteria to be recognised as a sale.

21    According to IFRS 16 *Leases*, which of the following is characteristic of a lease?

A    Ownership of the asset is passed to the lessee by the end of the lease term
B    The lessor is responsible for the general maintenance and repair of the asset
C    The lessee obtains control over the use of the asset
D    The lease term is for a major part of the useful life of the asset

22    For agreement one, what is the finance cost charged to profit or loss for the year ended 31 December 20X6?

A    $23,300
B    $12,451
C    $19,607
D    $16,891

23    The following calculations have been prepared for agreement one:

| Year | Interest | Annual payment | Balance |
| --- | --- | --- | --- |
| | $ | $ | $ |
| 31 December 20X7 | 15,484 | (55,000) | 93,391 |
| 31 December 20X8 | 10,880 | (55,000) | 49,271 |
| 31 December 20X9 | 5,729 | (55,000) | 0 |

How will the lease obligation be shown in the statement of financial position as at 31 December 20X7?

A    $44,120 as a non-current liability and $49,271 as a current liability
B    $49,271 as a non-current liability and $44,120 as a current liability
C    $93,391 as a non-current liability
D    $93,391 as a current liability

24    For agreement two, what would be charged to profit or loss for the quarter ended 31 March 20X5?

$

25    For agreement three, what profit should be recognised for the year ended 31 December 20X5 as a result of the sale and leaseback? Select your answer from the drop down box provided.

**Picklist**

$6,486
$120,000
$113,514
$107,028

The following scenario relates to questions 26–30.

Mighty IT Co provides hardware, software and IT services to small business customers.

Mighty IT Co has developed an accounting software package. The company offers a supply and installation service for $1,000 and a separate two-year technical support service for $500. Alternatively, it also offers a combined goods and services contract which includes both of these elements for $1,200. Payment for the combined contract is due one month after the date of installation.

In December 20X5, Mighty IT Co revalued its corporate headquarters. Prior to the revaluation, the carrying amount of the building was $2m and it was revalued to $2.5m.

Mighty IT Co also revalued a sales office on the same date. The office had been purchased for $500,000 earlier in the year, but subsequent discovery of defects reduced its value to $400,000. No depreciation had been charged on the sales office and any impairment loss is allowable for tax purposes.

Mighty IT Co's income tax rate is 30%.

26    In accordance with IFRS 15 *Revenue from Contracts with Customers*, when should Mighty IT Co recognise revenue from the combined goods and services contract?

   A     Supply and install: on installation
         Technical support: over two years

   B     Supply and install: when payment is made
         Technical support: over two years

   C     Supply and install: on installation
         Technical support: on installation

   D     Supply and install: when payment is made
         Technical support: when payment is made

27    For each combined contract sold, what is the amount of revenue which Mighty IT Co should recognise in respect of the supply and installation service in accordance with IFRS 15?

   $

28    Mighty IT Co sells a combined contract on 1 January 20X6, the first day of its financial year. Mighty IT Co financial statements are prepared in accordance with IFRS 15,

   Using the drop down box, select what is the total amount for deferred income which will be reported in Mighty IT Co's statement of financial position as at 31 December 20X6?

   **Picklist**

   $400
   $250
   $313
   $200

29    In accordance with IAS 12 *Income Taxes*, what is the impact of the property revaluations on the income tax expense of Mighty IT Co for the year ended 31 December 20X5?

   A     Income tax expense increases by $180,000
   B     Income tax expense increases by $120,000
   C     Income tax expense decreases by $30,000
   D     No impact on income tax expense

30  In January 20X6, the accountant at Mighty IT Co produced the company's draft financial statements for the year ended 31 December 20X5. He then realised that he had omitted to consider deferred tax on development costs. In 20X5, development costs of $200,000 had been incurred and capitalised. Development costs are deductible in full for tax purposes in the year they are incurred. The development is still in process at 31 December 20X5.

What adjustment is required to the income tax expense in Mighty IT Co's statement of profit or loss for the year ended 31 December 20X5 to account for deferred tax on the development costs?

A    Increase of $200,000
B    Increase of $60,000
C    Decrease of $60,000
D    Decrease of $200,000

(30 marks)

# Section C – BOTH questions are compulsory and MUST be attempted

Please write your answers to all parts of these questions on the lined pages within the Candidate Answer Booklet.

31    After preparing a draft statement of profit or loss (before interest and tax) for the year ended 31 March 20X6 (before any adjustments which may be required by notes (i) to (iv) below), the summarised trial balance of Triage Co as at 31 March 20X6 is:

|  | $'000 | $'000 |
|---|---|---|
| Equity shares of $1 each | | 50,000 |
| Retained earnings as at 1 April 20X5 | | 3,500 |
| Draft profit before interest and tax for year ended 31 March 20X6 | | 30,000 |
| 6% convertible loan notes (note (i)) | | 40,000 |
| Leased property (original life 25 years) – at cost (note (ii)) | 75,000 | |
| Plant and equipment – at cost (note (ii)) | 72,100 | |
| Accumulated amortisation/depreciation at 1 April 20X5:  leased property | | 15,000 |
| plant and equipment | | 28,100 |
| Trade receivables (note (iii)) | 28,000 | |
| Other current assets | 9,300 | |
| Current liabilities | | 17,700 |
| Deferred tax (note (iv)) | | 3,200 |
| Interest payment (note (i)) | 2,400 | |
| Current tax (note (iv)) | 700 | |
|  | 187,500 | 187,500 |

The following notes are relevant:

(i)    Triage Co issued 400,000 $100 6% convertible loan notes on 1 April 20X5. Interest is payable annually in arrears on 31 March each year. The loans can be converted to equity shares on the basis of 20 shares for each $100 loan note on 31 March 20X8 or redeemed at par for cash on the same date. An equivalent loan without the conversion rights would have required an interest rate of 8%.

The present value of $1 receivable at the end of each year, based on discount rates of 6% and 8%, are:

| | | 6% | 8% |
|---|---|---|---|
| End of year: | 1 | 0.94 | 0.93 |
| | 2 | 0.89 | 0.86 |
| | 3 | 0.84 | 0.79 |

(ii)   Non-current assets:

The directors decided to revalue the leased property at $66.3m on 1 October 20X5. Triage Co does not make an annual transfer from the revaluation surplus to retained earnings to reflect the realisation of the revaluation gain; however, the revaluation will give rise to a deferred tax liability at the company's tax rate of 20%.

The leased property is depreciated on a straight line basis and plant and equipment at 15% per annum using the reducing balance method.

No depreciation has yet been charged on any non-current assets for the year ended 31 March 20X6.

(iii)  In September 20X5, the directors of Triage Co discovered a fraud. In total, $700,000 which had been included as receivables in the above trial balance had been stolen by an employee. $450,000 of this related to the year ended 31 March 20X5, the rest to the current year. The directors are hopeful that 50% of the losses can be recovered from the company's insurers.

(iv)   A provision of $2.7m is required for current income tax on the profit of the year to 31 March 20X6. The balance on current tax in the trial balance is the under/over provision of tax for the previous year. In addition to the temporary differences relating to the information in note (ii), at 31 March 20X6, the carrying amounts of Triage Co's net assets are $12m more than their tax base.

*Required*

(a)    Prepare a schedule of adjustments required to the draft profit before interest and tax (in the above trial balance) to give the profit or loss of Triage Co for the year ended 31 March 20X6 as a result of the information in notes (i) to (iv) above.

(b)    Prepare the statement of financial position of Triage Co as at 31 March 20X6.

(c)    The issue of convertible loan notes can potentially dilute the basic earnings per share (EPS).

       Calculate the diluted earnings per share for Triage Co for the year ended 31 March 20X6 (there is no need to calculate the basic EPS).

**Note.** A statement of changes in equity and the notes to the statement of financial position are not required.

The following mark allocation is provided as guidance for this question:

(a)    5 marks
(b)    12 marks
(c)    3 marks

**(20 marks)**

32    Gregory Co is a listed company and, until 1 October 20X5, it had no subsidiaries. On that date, it acquired 75% of Tamsin Co's equity shares by means of a share exchange of two new shares in Gregory Co for every five acquired shares in Tamsin Co. These shares were recorded at the market price on the day of the acquisition and were the only shares issued by Gregory Co during the year ended 31 March 20X6.

The summarised financial statements of Gregory Co as a single entity at 31 March 20X5 and as a group at 31 March 20X6 are:

|  | Gregory group | Gregory Co single entity |
|---|---|---|
| STATEMENTS OF PROFIT OR LOSS FOR THE YEAR ENDED | 31 March 20X6 | 31 March 20X5 |
|  | $'000 | $'000 |
| Revenue | 46,500 | 28,000 |
| Cost of sales | (37,200) | (20,800) |
| Gross profit | 9,300 | 7,200 |
| Operating expenses | (1,800) | (1,200) |
| Profit before tax (operating profit) | 7,500 | 6,000 |
| Income tax expense | (1,500) | (1,000) |
| Profit for the year | 6,000 | 5,000 |
| Profit for year attributable to: |  |  |
| Equity holders of the parent | 5,700 |  |
| Non-controlling interest | 300 |  |
|  | 6,000 |  |

| STATEMENTS OF FINANCIAL POSITION AS AT | 31 March 20X6 | 31 March 20X5 |
|---|---|---|
| | $'000 | $'000 |
| **Assets** | | |
| Non-current assets | | |
| Property, plant and equipment | 54,600 | 41,500 |
| Goodwill | 3,000 | nil |
| | 57,600 | 41,500 |
| Current assets | 44,000 | 36,000 |
| **Total assets** | 101,600 | 77,500 |
| | | |
| **Equity and liabilities** | | |
| Equity | | |
| Equity shares of $1 each | 46,000 | 40,000 |
| Other component of equity (share premium) | 6,000 | nil |
| Retained earnings | 18,700 | 13,000 |
| Equity attributable to owners of the parent | 70,700 | 53,000 |
| Non-controlling interest | 3,600 | nil |
| | 74,300 | 53,000 |
| Current liabilities | 27,300 | 24,500 |
| Total equity and liabilities | 101,600 | 77,500 |

Other information:

(i)     Each month since the acquisition, Gregory Co's sales to Tamsin Co were consistently $2m. Gregory Co had chosen to only make a gross profit margin of 10% on these sales as Tamsin Co is part of the group.

(ii)    The values of property, plant and equipment held by both companies have been rising for several years.

(iii)   On reviewing the above financial statements, Gregory Co's chief executive officer (CEO) made the following observations:

   (1)    I see the profit for the year has increased by $1m which is up 20% on last year, but I thought it would be more as Tamsin Co was supposed to be a very profitable company.

   (2)    I have calculated the earnings per share (EPS) for 20X6 at 13 cents (6,000/46,000 × 100) and for 20X5 at 12.5 cents (5,000/40,000 × 100) and, although the profit has increased 20%, our EPS has barely changed.

   (3)    I am worried that the low price at which we are selling goods to Tamsin Co is undermining our group's overall profitability.

   (4)    I note that our share price is now $2.30, how does this compare with our share price immediately before we bought Tamsin Co?

*Required*

(a)    Reply to the four observations of the CEO.                                    **(8 marks)**

(b)    Using the above financial statements, calculate the following ratios for Gregory Co for the years ended 31 March 20X6 and 20X5 and comment on the comparative performance:

   (i)     Return on capital employed (ROCE)
   (ii)    Net asset turnover
   (iii)   Gross profit margin
   (iv)    Operating profit margin

   **Note.** Four marks are available for the ratio calculations.                   **(12 marks)**

**Note.** Your answers to (a) and (b) should reflect the impact of the consolidation of Tamsin Co during the year ended 31 March 20X6.

                                                                                     **(20 marks)**

# Answers

**DO NOT TURN THIS PAGE UNTIL YOU HAVE COMPLETED THE MOCK EXAM**

# A plan of attack

## Managing your nerves

As you start this mock exam a number of thoughts are likely to cross your mind. At best, examinations cause anxiety so it is important to stay focused on your task for the exam period! Developing an awareness of what is going on emotionally within you may help you manage your nerves. Remember, you are unlikely to banish the flow of adrenaline, but the key is to harness it to help you work steadily and quickly through your answers.

Working through this mock exam will help you develop the exam stamina you will need to keep going for three hours.

## Managing your time

Planning and time management are two of the key skills which complement the technical knowledge you need to succeed. To keep yourself on time, do not be afraid to jot down your target completion times for each question, perhaps next to the title of the question on the exam. As all the questions are **compulsory**, you do not have to spend time wondering which question to answer!

## Doing the exam

Actually doing the exam is a personal experience. There is not a single **right way**. As long as you submit complete answers to all questions after the three hours are up, then your approach obviously works.

### Looking through the exam

Section A has 15 OTQs. This is the section of the paper where the examining team can test knowledge across the breadth of the syllabus. Make sure you read these questions carefully. The distractors are designed to present plausible, but incorrect, answers. Don't let them mislead you. If you really have no idea – guess. You may even be right.

Section B has 15 OTQs in total – questions 16–30. These are arranged as three scenarios with five questions each.
Scenario 1 is on impairment of assets.
Scenario 2 is on leasing.
Scenario 3 is on revenue recognition.

Section C has two 20-mark questions.
Question 31 is on accounting adjustments and preparation of a statement of financial position.
Question 32 is on interpretation of financial statements.

### Allocating your time

BPP's advice is to always allocate your time **according to the marks for the question**. However, **use common sense**. If you're doing a question but haven't a clue how to do part (b), you might be better off reallocating your time and getting more marks on another question, where you can add something you didn't have time for earlier on. Make sure you leave time to recheck the OTQs and make sure you have answered them all.

# SECTION A

**1**

| | | |
|---|---|---|
| To interpret the application of International Financial Reporting Standards | True | False |
| To work directly with national standard setters to bring about convergence with IFRS | True | False |
| To provide guidance on financial reporting issues not specifically addressed in IFRSs | True | False |
| To publish draft interpretations for public comment | True | False |

**2    A    1 only**

The acquisition of 60% of Zakron Co's equity share capital on 1 March 20X7. Zakron Co's activities are significantly different from the rest of the Poulgo group of companies.

**3**

| | Debit | Credit |
|---|---|---|
| Depreciation expense | $20,000 | |
| Liability | | $30,000 |
| Property, plant and equipment | $10,000 | |

The repayment of the grant must be treated as a change in accounting estimate. The carrying amount of the asset must be increased as the netting off method has been used. The resulting extra depreciation must be charged immediately to profit or loss.

| | Original | As if no grant | Adjustment |
|---|---|---|---|
| | $ | $ | $ |
| Cost | 90,000 | 90,000 | |
| Grant | (30,000) | | |
| | 60,000 | | |
| Depreciation | (10,000) [1 yr] | (30,000) [2 yr] | Dr Dep'n exp 20,000 |
| Carrying amount | 50,000 [1/1/X7] | 60,000 [31/12/X7] | Dr PPE 10,000 |
| | | | Cr Liability 30,000 |

**4    A    A provision is required for the cost of both issues 1 and 2.**

**5    $774,000**

710,000 + (480,000 × 3/12) − (20,000 × 3) + (20,000 × 25/125) = $774,000

**6    D    It is a change of accounting estimate and must be applied prospectively.**

**7    D    In other comprehensive income for investment 1 and in profit or loss for investment 2**

**Note.** Investment 2 is held for trading.

**8    C    $4,750**

Net total being paid over four months (($5,000 × 4 months) − $1,000)  = 19,000
Annual charge spread evenly over the lease term ($19,000/4 months) = 4,750

9    Capital employed which is calculated using historical costs is understated compared to current value capital employed

Historical cost profits are overstated in comparison to current value profits

This is the case in a period of inflation.

10    $5,250,000
$3,250 + 1,940 + (800 - 600 \times 30\%) = 5,250,000$

11    C    Net cash generated from operating activities has been used to fund the additions to non-current assets.

12    $1,880,000

| | | |
|---|---|---|
| FV of NCI at acquisition | | 1,100 |
| Profit for year × 30% | 3,200 | |
| Dep'n on FVA (1.5m/30) | (50) | |
| Unrealised profit | (550) | |
| | 2,600 × 30% | 780 |
| | | 1,880 |

13    B    It is credited to profit or loss

14    $470,000

Retained earnings = $300 + ((150 - 90) \times 75\%) = 345$
Total equity = $125 + 345 = 470$

15    $6,270,000

| | $'000 |
|---|---|
| Production cost of PPE | 6,000 |
| Capitalisation of borrowing costs: | |
| $6m × 6% × 9/12 = | 270 |
| Total cost capitalised (and carrying amount) at 30 September 20X2 | 6,270 |

# Section B

16    D    $8,500

        Depreciation 1 January to 30 June 20X4 (80,000/10 × 6/12) = 4,000
        Depreciation 1 July to 31 December 20X4 (81,000/9 × 6/12) = 4,500
        Total depreciation = 8,500

17    D    The carrying amount of an entity's net assets being below the entity's market capitalisation
        **This means that the share price is high, so the market has positive expectations of the entity.**

18    $17,750

        VIU is lower than FV (less costs to sell), so impairment is 60,750 – 43,000 = $17,750

19    D    A cash-generating unit is the smallest identifiable group of assets for which independent cash flows
        can be identified.

20    A    $262,500

        The impairment loss of $220m (1,170 – 950) is allocated: $35m to damaged plant and $85m to
        goodwill, the remaining $100m allocated proportionally to the building and the undamaged plant. The
        carrying amount of the plant will then be $262,500.

21    C    The lessee obtains control over the use of the asset.
        **The other options are not part of the definition of a lease.**

22    C    $19,607

        Yr 1 200,000 × 11.65% = 23,300
        Yr 2 (200,000 + 23,300 – 55,000) × 11.65% = $19,607

23    B    $49,271 as a non-current liability and $44,120 as a current liability

24    $12,800

        4,800 × 8 = 38,400/3 = 12,800

25    $6,486

        Profit on sale = 120,000
        Amount relating to rights retained = 120,000 × 350,000/370,000 = 113,514
        Amount relating to rights transferred = 120,000 – 113,514 = 6,486

26    A    Supply and install: on installation

        Technical support: over two years

        The performance obligation for the goods is satisfied when the package is supplied. The technical
        support obligation is satisfied over time.

27    $800

        1,000/1,500 × 1,200 = $800

28    $200

        500/1,500 × 1,200 = 400/2 = $200

29    C    Income tax expense decreases by $30,000

        $30,000 (400 – 500 × 30%).
        Revaluation and deferred tax of headquarters goes through OCI.

30    B    Increase of $60,000

        $60,000 (200 × 30%)
        Dr Income tax expense Cr Deferred tax liability

BPP
LEARNING MEDIA

# Section C

31

## Marking scheme

|  |  |  | Marks |
|---|---|---|---|
| (a) | Schedule of adjustments | | |
|  | Profit before interest and tax | ½ | |
|  | Loan finance costs | 1 | |
|  | Depreciation charges | 1½ | |
|  | Fraud loss | ½ | |
|  | Income tax | 1½ | |
|  |  | | 5 |
| (b) | Statement of financial position | | |
|  | Property, plant and equipment | 2½ | |
|  | Trade receivables | 1 | |
|  | Other current assets | ½ | |
|  | Equity shares | ½ | |
|  | Equity option | 1 | |
|  | Revaluation surplus | 1 | |
|  | Retained earnings | 1½ | |
|  | Deferred tax | 1 | |
|  | Loan note | 1½ | |
|  | Current liabilities | ½ | |
|  | Current tax payable | 1 | |
|  |  | | 12 |
| Diluted EPS | | | 3 |
|  | Total for question | 20 | 20 |

31    (a)    Triage Co – Schedule of adjustments to profit for the year ended 31 March 20X6

|  | $'000 |
|---|---|
| Draft profit before interest and tax per trial balance | 30,000 |
| Adjustments re: | |
| *Note (i)* | |
| Convertible loan note finance costs (w(i)) | (3,023) |
| *Note (ii)* | |
| Amortisation of leased property (1,500 + 1,700 (w(ii))) | (3,200) |
| Depreciation of plant and equipment (w(ii)) | (6,600) |
| *Note (iii)* | |
| Current year loss on fraud (700 – 450 see below) | (250) |
| *Note (iv)* | |
| Income tax expense (2,700 + 700 – 800 (w(iii))) | (2,600) |
| Profit for the year | 14,327 |

The $450,000 fraud loss in the previous year is a prior period adjustment (reported in the statement of changes in equity).

The possible insurance claim is a contingent asset and should be ignored.

(b)    Triage Co – Statement of financial position as at 31 March 20X6

|  | $'000 | $'000 |
|---|---|---|
| *Assets* | | |
| Non-current assets | | |
| Property, plant and equipment (64,600 + 37,400 (w(ii))) | | 102,000 |
| Current assets | | |
| Trade receivables (28,000 – 700 fraud) | 27,300 | |
| Other current assets per trial balance | 9,300 | 36,600 |
| Total assets | | 138,600 |
| | | |
| *Equity and liabilities* | | |
| Equity | | |
| Equity shares of $1 each | | 50,000 |
| Other component of equity (w(i)) | 2,208 | |
| Revaluation surplus (7,800 – 1,560 (w(ii))) | 6,240 | |
| Retained earnings (w(iv)) | 17,377 | 25,825 |
| | | 75,825 |
| | | |
| *Non-current liabilities* | | |
| Deferred tax (w(iii)) | 3,960 | |
| 6% convertible loan notes (w(i)) | 38,415 | 42,375 |
| Current liabilities | | |
| Per trial balance | 17,700 | |
| Current tax payable | 2,700 | 20,400 |
| Total equity and liabilities | | 138,600 |

(c)    Diluted earnings per share (w(v))                          29 cents

*Workings* (monetary figures in brackets in $'000)

(i)    *6% convertible loan notes*

The convertible loan notes are a compound financial instrument having a debt and an equity component which must both be quantified and accounted for separately:

| Year ended 31 March | Outflow | 8% | Present value |
|---|---|---|---|
|  | $'000 |  | $'000 |
| 20X6 | 2,400 | 0.93 | 2,232 |
| 20X7 | 2,400 | 0.6 | 2,064 |
| 20X8 | 42,400 | 0.79 | 33,496 |
| Debt component |  |  | 37,792 |
| Equity component (= balance) |  |  | 2,208 |
| Proceeds of issue |  |  | 40,000 |

The finance cost will be $3,023,000 (37,792 × 8%) and the carrying amount of the loan notes at 31 March 20X6 will be $38,415,000 (37,792 + (3,023 – 2,400)).

(ii)   *Non-current assets*

Leased property
The gain on revaluation and carrying amount of the leased property is:

|  | $'000 |
|---|---|
| Carrying amount at 1 April 20X5 (75,000 – 15,000) | 60,000 |
| Amortisation to date of revaluation (1 October 20X5) (75,000/25 × 6/12) | (1,500) |
| Carrying amount at revaluation | 58,500 |
| Gain on revaluation = balance | 7,800 |
| Revaluation at 1 October 20X5 | 66,300 |
| Amortisation to year ended 31 March 20X6 (66,300/19.5 years × 6/12) | (1,700) |
| Carrying amount at 31 March 20X6 | 64,600 |

Annual amortisation is $3m (75,000/25 years); therefore the accumulated amortisation at 1 April 20X5 of $15m represents five years' amortisation. At the date of revaluation (1 October 20X5), there will be a remaining life of 19.5 years.

Of the revaluation gain, $6.24m (80%) is credited to the revaluation surplus and $1.56m (20%) is credited to deferred tax.

Plant and equipment

|  | $'000 |
|---|---|
| Carrying amount at 1 April 20X5 (72,100 – 28,100) | 44,000 |
| Depreciation for year ended 31 March 20X6 (15% reducing balance) | (6,600) |
| Carrying amount at 31 March 20X6 | 37,400 |

(iii)  *Deferred tax*

| Provision required at 31 March 20X6: |  |
|---|---|
| Revalued property and other assets (7,800 + 12,000) × 20% | 3,960 |
| Provision at 1 April 20X5 | (3,200) |
| Increase in provision | 760 |
| Revaluation of land and buildings (7,800 × 20%) | (1,560) |
| Balance credited to profit or loss | (800) |

(iv)   *Retained earnings*

|  |  |
|---|---|
| Balance at 1 April 20X5 | 3,500 |
| Prior period adjustment (fraud) | (450) |
| Adjusted profit for year (from (a)) | 14,327 |
| Balance at 31 March 20X6 | 17,377 |

(v)    The maximum additional shares on conversion is 8 million (40,000 × 20/100), giving total shares of 58 million.

The loan interest 'saved' is $2.418m (3,023 (from (w(i)) above × 80% (ie after tax))), giving adjusted earnings of $16.745m (14,327 + 2,418)).

Therefore diluted EPS is $\dfrac{\$16,745,000 \times 100}{58 \text{ million shares}}$ = 29 cents

32

---

**Text references.** Chapter 19.

**Top tips.** It's not all about the ratios. You have to look at the financial statements combined with the information in the question and work out what is going on with the company. In this case it's important to consider the group aspects.

**Easy marks.** The ratios were easy marks and if they were considered in the light of the rest of the information it should have been possible to get good marks for the comments.

**Examining Team's comments.** This question combined interpretation with an element of consolidation and candidates found it challenging. In part (a) most candidates launched into irrelevant detail regarding ratio movements without stopping to consider the reason for the difference between the two years' financial statements. The ratio calculations in part (b) were generally well done. The comments on comparative performance were generally inadequate – to say that a ratio has gone up or down and that this is good or bad is not enough.

---

**Marking scheme**

|  |  |  | Marks |
|---|---|---|---|
| (a) | 2 marks for each reply to the CEO's observations | 8 | |
|  |  |  | 8 |
| (b) | 1 mark for each pair of ratios | 4 | |
|  | 1 mark per relevant comment up to | 8 | |
|  |  |  | 12 |
|  | Total for question |  | 20 |

---

(a)    **Note.** References to 20X6 and 20X5 are to the years ending 31 March 20X6 and 20X5 respectively.

Comment (1): I see the profit for the year has increased by $1m which is up 20% on last year, but I thought it would be more as Tamsin Co was supposed to be a very profitable company.

There are two issues with this statement. First, last year's profit is not comparable with the current year's profit because in 20X5 Gregory Co was a single entity and in 20X6 it is now a group with a subsidiary. A second issue is that the consolidated statement of profit or loss for the year ended 31 March 20X6 only includes six months of the results of Tamsin Co, and, assuming Tamsin Co is profitable, future results will include a full year's profit. This latter point may, at least in part, mitigate the CEO's disappointment.

Comment (2): I have calculated the EPS for 20X6 at 13 cents (6,000/46,000 × 100 shares) and at 12.5 cents for 20X5 (5,000/40,000 × 100) and, although the profit has increased 20%, our EPS has barely changed.

The stated EPS calculation for 20X6 is incorrect for two reasons. First, it is the profit attributable to only the equity shareholders of the parent which should be used and, second, the 6 million new shares were only in issue for six months and should be weighted by 6/12. Thus, the correct EPS for 20X6 is 13.3 cents (5,700/43,000 × 100). This gives an increase of 6% (13.3 – 12.5)/12.5) on 20X5 EPS which is still less than the increase in profit. The reason why the EPS may not have increased in line with reported profit is that the acquisition was financed by a share exchange which increased the number of shares in issue. Thus, the EPS takes account of the additional consideration used to generate profit, whereas the trend of absolute profit does not take additional consideration into account. This is why the EPS is often said to be a more accurate reflection of company performance than the trend of profits.

Comment (3): I am worried that the low price at which we are selling goods to Tamsin Co is undermining our group's overall profitability.

Assuming the consolidated financial statements have been correctly prepared, all intragroup trading has been eliminated, thus the pricing policy will have had no effect on these financial statements. The comment is incorrect and reflects a misunderstanding of the consolidation process.

Comment (4): I note that our share price is now $2.30, how does this compare with our share price immediately before we bought Tamsin Co?

The increase in share capital is 6 million shares, the increase in the share premium is $6m, thus the total proceeds for the 6 million shares was $12m giving a share price of $2.00 at the date of acquisition of Tamsin Co. The current price of $2.30 presumably reflects the market's favourable view of Gregory Co's current and future performance.

(b)

|  | 20X6 | 20X5 |
|---|---|---|
| Return on capital employed (ROCE) (7,500/74,300 × 100) | 10.1% | 11.3% |
| Net asset turnover (46,500/74,300) | 0.63 times | 0.53 times |
| Gross profit margin (9,300/46,500 × 100) | 20.0% | 25.7% |
| Operating profit margin (7,500/46,500 × 100) | 16.1% | 21.4% |

Looking at the above ratios, it appears that the overall performance of Gregory Co has declined marginally; the ROCE has fallen from 11.3% to 10.1%. This has been caused by a substantial fall in the gross profit margin (down from 25.7% in 20X5 to 20% in 20X6); this is over a 22% (5.7%/25.7%) decrease. The group/company have relatively low operating expenses (at around 4% of revenue), so the poor gross profit margin feeds through to the operating profit margin. The overall decline in the ROCE, due to the weaker profit margins, has been mitigated by an improvement in net asset turnover, increasing from 0.53 times to 0.63 times. Despite the improvement in net asset turnover, it is still very low with only 63 cents of sales generated from every $1 invested in the business, although this will depend on the type of business Gregory Co and Tamsin Co are engaged in.

On this analysis, the effect of the acquisition of Tamsin Co seems to have had a detrimental effect on overall performance, but this may not necessarily be the case; there could be some distorting factors in the analysis. As mentioned above, the 20X6 results include only six months of Tamsin Co's results, but the statement of financial position includes the full amount of the consideration for Tamsin Co. (The consideration has been calculated [see comment (4) above] as $12m for the parent's 75% share plus $3.3m [3,600 – 300 share of post-acquisition profit] for the non-controlling interest's 25%, giving total consideration of $15.3m.) The above factors disproportionately increase the denominator of ROCE which has the effect of worsening the calculated ROCE. This distortion should be corrected in 20X7 when a full year's results for Tamsin Co will be included in group profit. Another factor is that it could take time to fully integrate the activities of the two companies and more savings and other synergies may be forthcoming such as bulk buying discounts.

The non-controlling interest share in the profit for the year in 20X6 of $300,000 allows a rough calculation of the full year's profit of Tamsin Co at $2.4m (300,000/25% × 12/6, i.e. the $300,000 represents 25% of 6/12 of the annual profit). This figure is subject to some uncertainty such as the effect of probable increased post-acquisition depreciation charges. However, a profit of $2.4m on the investment of $15.3m represents a return of 16% (and would be higher if the profit was adjusted to a pre-tax figure) which is much higher than the current year ROCE (at 10.1%) of the group. This implies that the performance of Tamsin Co is much better than that of Gregory Co (as a separate entity) and that Gregory Co's performance in 20X6 must have deteriorated considerably from that in 20X5 and this is the real cause of the deteriorating performance of the group.

Another issue potentially affecting the ROCE is that, as a result of the consolidation process, Tamsin Co's net assets, including goodwill, are included in the statement of financial position at fair value, whereas Gregory Co's net assets appear to be based on historical cost (as there is no revaluation surplus). As the values of property, plant and equipment have been rising, this in effect favourably flatters the 20X5 ratios. This is because the statement of financial position of 20X5 only contains Gregory Co's assets which, at historical cost, may considerably understate their fair value and, on a comparative basis, overstate 20X5 ROCE.

In summary, although on first impression the acquisition of Tamsin Co appears to have caused a marginal worsening of the group's performance, the distorting factors and imputation of the non-controlling interest's profit in 20X6 indicate the underlying performance may be better than the ratios portray and the contribution from Tamsin Co is a very significant positive. Future performance may be even better.

Without information on the separate financial statements of Tamsin Co, it is difficult to form a more definite view.

# ACCA

# Financial Reporting (FR)

# Mock Examination 3

# December 2016 exam

Time allowed: 3 hours 15 minutes

This mock exam is divided into three sections:

Section A – ALL 15 questions are compulsory and MUST be attempted

Section B – ALL 15 questions are compulsory and MUST be attempted

Section C – BOTH questions are compulsory and MUST be attempted

Do NOT open this question paper until instructed by the supervisor.

Do NOT record any of your answers on the question paper.

This question paper must not be removed from the examination hall.

# Section A – ALL 15 questions are compulsory and MUST be attempted

1   Which of the following is a possible advantage of a rules-based system of financial reporting?

   A   It encourages the exercise of professional judgement
   B   It prevents a fire-fighting approach to the formulation of standards
   C   It offers accountants more protection in the event of litigation
   D   It ensures that no standards conflict with each other

2   IFRS 10 *Consolidated Financial Statements* states that 'A parent shall prepare consolidated financial statements using uniform accounting policies for like transactions and other events in similar circumstances'.

   Which of the following situations requires an adjustment because of this constraint?

   A   A subsidiary has been acquired and its land is to be included in the consolidated financial statements at fair value

   B   A subsidiary carries its assets at historical cost but the parent's assets are carried at revalued amounts

   C   There have been intragroup transactions during the year which have resulted in unrealised profit in inventory at the year end

   D   There has been intragroup trading which has resulted in intragroup balances for receivables and payables at the year end

3   The following trial balance extract relates to Topsy Co as at 30 April 20X6:

|  | $'000 | $'000 |
|---|---|---|
| Land at cost | 800 | |
| Building: | | |
|     Valuation at 1 May 20X2 | 1,500 | |
|     Accumulated depreciation at 30 April 20X5 | | 90 |
| Revaluation surplus at 30 April 20X5 | | 705 |

   On 1 May 20X2, when the carrying amount of the building was $750,000, it was revalued for the first time to $1.5m and its remaining useful life at that date was estimated to be 50 years. Topsy Co has correctly accounted for this revaluation in the above trial balance. However, Topsy Co has not yet charged depreciation for the year ended 30 April 20X6 or transferred the excess depreciation from the revaluation surplus to retained earnings at 30 April 20X6.

   In February 20X6, the land, but not the building, was independently valued at $950,000. This adjustment has yet to be made for the year ended 30 April 20X6.

   What is the balance on the revaluation surplus of Topsy Co as at 30 April 20X6 after the required adjustments have been made?

   $ ☐

4   Plow Co purchased 3,500 of the 10,000 $1 equity shares of Styre Co on 1 August 20X4 for $6.50 per share.

Styre Co's profit after tax for the year ended 31 July 20X5 was $7,500. Styre Co paid a dividend of $0.50 per share on 31 December 20X4.

What is the carrying amount of the investment in Styre Co in the consolidated statement of financial position of Plow Co as at 31 July 20X5?

A   $25,375
B   $22,750
C   $27,125
D   $23,625

---

5   Identify, by selecting the relevant box in the table below, which of the following statements are correct when calculating the impairment loss of an asset?

| | | |
|---|---|---|
| Assets should be carried at the lower of their carrying amount and recoverable amount | True | False |
| Assets should be carried at the higher of their carrying amount and recoverable amount | True | False |
| The recoverable amount of an asset is the higher of value in use and fair value less costs of disposal | True | False |
| The recoverable amount of an asset is the lower of value in use and fair value less costs of disposal | True | False |

---

6   Which of the following statements is NOT true?

A   In some countries, accounting standards can be a detailed set of rules which companies must follow.
B   Local accounting standards can be influenced by the tax regime within a country.
C   Accounting standards on their own provide a complete system of regulation.
D   Accounting standards are particularly important where a company's shares are publicly traded.

---

7   Merlot Co had issued share capital on 1 January 20X9 of 2,000,000 equity $1 shares. On 1 October 20X9, a rights issue was made on a one for four basis which was fully taken up.

On 30 September 20X9, each share had a market value of $3.25, giving a theoretical ex-rights value of $2.84 per share.

Using the drop down box to select your answer what is the weighted average number of shares in issue for the year ended 31 December 20X9, in accordance with IAS 33 *Earnings per Share*?

Picklist

2,341,549 shares
1,935,769 shares
2,125,000 shares
2,431,778 shares

---

8   Which of the following would result in a credit to the deferred tax account?

(1)   Interest receivable, which will be taxed when the interest is received
(2)   A loan, the repayment of which will have no tax consequences
(3)   Interest payable, which will be allowable for tax when paid
(4)   Prepaid expenses, which have been deducted to calculate the taxable profits of the previous year

A   1 and 2
B   3 and 4
C   1 and 4
D   2 and 3

9    IFRS 15 *Revenue from Contracts with Customers* states that, where performance obligations are satisfied over time, entities should apply an appropriate method of measuring progress.

Which **TWO** of the following are appropriate **OUTPUT** methods of measuring progress?

☐  Total costs to date of the contract as a percentage of total contract revenue
☐  Physical milestones reached as a percentage of physical completion
☐  Surveys of performance completed to date as a percentage of total contract revenue
☐  Labour hours expended as a percentage of total expected labour hours

---

10   Fifer Co has a current ratio of 1.2:1 which is below the industry average. Fifer Co wants to increase its current ratio by the year end.

Which of the following actions, taken before the year end, would lead to an increase in the current ratio?

A    Return some inventory which had been purchased for cash and obtain a full refund on the cost
B    Make a bulk purchase of inventory for cash to obtain a large discount
C    Make an early payment to suppliers, even though the amount is not due
D    Offer early payment discounts in order to collect receivables more quickly

---

11   On 1 October 20X8, Picture Co acquired 60% shares in Frame Co. At 1 April 20X8, the credit balances on the revaluation surpluses relating to Picture Co and Frame Co's equity financial asset investments stood at $6,400 and $4,400 respectively.

The following extract was taken from the financial statements for the year ended 31 March 20X9:

|  | Picture Co $ | Frame Co $ |
|---|---|---|
| Other comprehensive income: loss on fair value of equity financial asset investments | (1,400) | (800) |

Assume the losses accrued evenly throughout the year.

What is the amount of the revaluation surplus in the consolidated statement of financial position of Picture Co as at 31 March 20X9?

A    $4,520
B    $4,760
C    $5,240
D    $9,160

---

12   A local authority department is responsible for waste collections. They have an annual budget to provide a regular collection service from households in the local area. The budget was increased to enable the department to increase the percentage of waste disposed of in an environmentally friendly manner.

Which of the following is the best measurement to justify the increase in the budget?

A    An increase in the number of collections made during the period
B    The percentage of waste recycled rather than being placed in landfill sites
C    The fair value of the machinery used in making the collections
D    A breakdown of expenditure between the cost of making collections and the cost of processing waste

13    Panther Co owns 80% of Tiger Co. An extract from the companies' individual statements of financial position as at 30 June 20X8 shows the following:

|  | Panther Co | Tiger Co |
|---|---|---|
|  | $'000 | $,000 |
| Property, plant and equipment (carrying amount) | 370 | 285 |

On 1 July 20X7, Panther Co sold a piece of equipment which had a carrying amount of $70,000 to Tiger Co for $150,000. The equipment had an estimated remaining life of five years when sold.

Using the drop down box, select the carrying amount of property, plant and equipment in the consolidated statement of financial position of Panther Co as at 30 June 20X8?

**Picklist**

$591,000
$575,000
$671,000
$534,000

---

14    On 1 July 20X7, Lime Co acquired 90% of Soda Co's equity share capital. On this date, Soda Co had an internally generated customer list which was valued at $35m by an independent team of experts. At 1 July 20X7, Soda Co was also in negotiations with a potential new major customer. If the negotiations are successful, the new customer will sign the contract on 15 July 20X7 and the value of the total customer base would then be worth $45m.

What amount would be recognised for the customer list in the consolidated statement of financial position of Lime Co as at 1 July 20X7?

A    $0
B    $10m
C    $35m
D    $45m

---

15    Which of the following statements relating to goodwill is correct?

A    Goodwill is amortised over its useful life with the charge expensed to profit or loss.

B    On the investment in an associate, any related goodwill should be separately identified in the consolidated financial statements.

C    The testing of goodwill for impairment is only required when circumstances exist which indicate potential impairment.

D    If the fair value of a subsidiary's contingent liabilities can be reliably measured at the date of acquisition, they should be included in consolidated net assets and will increase goodwill.

**(30 marks)**

# Section B – ALL 15 questions are compulsory and MUST be attempted

Please use the grid provided on page two of the Candidate Answer Booklet to record your answers to each multiple choice question. Do not write out the answers to the MCQs on the lined pages of the answer booklet.

Each question is worth 2 marks.

The following scenario relates to questions 16–20.

Artem Co prepares financial statements to 30 June each year.

During the year to 30 June 20X5, the company spent $550,000 on new plant as follows:

|  | $'000 |
|---|---|
| Plant cost | 525 |
| Delivery to site | 3 |
| Building alterations to accommodate the plant | 12 |
| Costs of initial testing of the new plant | 2 |
| Plant operator training costs | 8 |

Artem Co's fixtures and fittings were purchased on 1 July 20X2 at a cost of $50,000. The directors have depreciated them on a straight-line basis over an estimated useful life of eight years assuming a $5,000 residual value. At 1 July 20X4, the directors realise that the remaining useful life of the fixtures is five years. There is no change to the estimated residual value.

Artem Co began a research project in October 20X3 with the aim of developing a new type of machine. If successful, Artem Co will manufacture the machines and sell them to customers as well as using them in their own production processes. During the year ended 30 June 20X4, costs of $25,000 were incurred on conducting feasibility studies and some market research. During the year ended 30 June 20X5, a further $80,000 was incurred on constructing and testing a prototype of the machine.

16    In accordance with IAS 16 *Property, Plant and Equipment*, what is the value of additions to plant for Artem Co for the year ended 30 June 20X5?

$

17    Which of the following is **TRUE** in relation to the change in the remaining useful life of the fixtures and fittings?

A    It is a change of accounting policy which should be retrospectively applied.
B    It is a change of accounting policy which should be disclosed in the notes to the financial statements.
C    It is a change of accounting estimate which should be retrospectively applied.
D    It is a change of accounting estimate which should be prospectively applied.

18    Using the drop down box, select what is the depreciation charge for the fixtures and fittings for Artem Co for the year ended 30 June 20X5 in accordance with IAS 16?

**Picklist**

$7,500
$9,000
$7,750
$6,750

19 In accordance with IAS 38 *Intangible assets*, what is the correct treatment of the $25,000 costs incurred on the research project by Artem Co during the year ended 30 June 20X4?

A They should be recognised as an intangible non-current asset as future economic benefits are expected from the use and sale of the machinery.

B They should be written off to profit or loss as an expense as they are research costs at this date.

C They should be included in tangible non-current assets as machinery which will be put into use once completed.

D They should be set against a provision made for the estimated total cost of the project which was set up at the start of the research.

20 In accordance with IAS 38, which of the following is true when Artem Co moves to the production and testing stage of the prototype during the year ended 30 June 20X5?

A The project has moved to the development stage. If the IAS 38 development expenditure criteria are met, Artem Co can choose whether or not to recognise the $80,000 costs as an intangible non-current asset.

B The project is still in its research stage and the $80,000 costs incurred by Artem Co cannot be recognised as an intangible non-current asset until a product is ready for sale.

C The project has moved to the development stage. If the IAS 38 development expenditure criteria are met, Artem Co must recognise the $80,000 costs as an intangible non-current asset.

D The project is still in its research stage and so Artem Co must expense the $80,000 costs to profit or loss.

The following scenario relates to questions 21–25.

Maykorn Co prepares its financial statements to 30 September each year. Maykorn Co's draft financial statements were finalised on 20 October 20X3. They were authorised for issue on 15 December 20X3 and the annual general meeting of shareholders took place on 23 December 20X3.

On 30 September 20X3, Maykorn Co moved out of one of its properties and put it up for sale. The property met the criteria as held for sale on 30 September 20X3. On 1 October 20X2, the property had a carrying amount of $2.6m and a remaining life of 20 years. The property is held under the revaluation model. The property was expected to sell for a gross amount of $2.5m with selling costs estimated at $50,000.

Maykorn Co decided to sell an item of plant during the year ended 30 September 20X3. On 1 October 20X2, the plant had a carrying amount of $490,000 and a remaining useful life of seven years. The plant met the held for sale criteria on 1 April 20X3. At 1 April 20X3, the plant had a fair value less costs to sell of $470,000, which had fallen to $465,000 at 30 September 20X3.

21 Identify, by selecting the relevant box in the table below, whether the following statements are true and in accordance with IAS 10 *Events After the Reporting Period*, for Maykorn Co?

| | | |
|---|---|---|
| All events which occur between 30 September 20X3 and 15 December 20X3 should be considered as events occurring after the reporting period | True | False |
| An event which occurs between 30 September 20X3 and 15 December 20X3 and which provides evidence of a condition which existed at 30 September 20X3 should be considered as an adjusting event | True | False |

22    In accordance with IAS 10, which of the following events would be classed as a non-adjusting event in Maykorn Co's financial statements for the year ended 30 September 20X3?

A    During October 20X3, there was evidence of a permanent diminution in the carrying amount of a property held at 30 September 20X3.

B    On 1 December 20X3 the acquisition of a subsidiary was completed, following lengthy negotiations which began in September 20X3.

C    The sale of inventory during October 20X3 at a value less than its cost. This inventory was included in the financial statements at cost on 30 September 20X3.

D    The insolvency of a major customer during October 20X3, whose balance was included within receivables at 30 September 20X3.

23    What is the total amount charged to Maykorn Co's profit or loss in respect of the property for the year ended 30 September 20X3?

A    $130,000
B    $180,000
C    $150,000
D    $100,000

24    In accordance with IFRS 5 *Non-current Assets Held for Sale and Discontinued Operations*, what is the carrying amount of the plant in Maykorn Co's statement of financial position as at 30 September 20X3?

Select your answer using the drop down box provided.

**Picklist**

$420,000
$470,000
$455,000
$465,000

25    Which of the following items should be classed as an asset held for sale under IFRS 5?

A    Maykorn Co's head office building is to be demolished, at which point the land will be put up for sale. A number of prospective bidders have declared an interest and the land is expected to sell within a few months of the demolition.

B    An item of plant was put up for sale at the start of the year for $500,000. Six parties have made a bid to Maykorn Co for the plant but none of these bids have been above $200,000.

C    A chain of retail outlets are currently advertised for sale. Maykorn Co has provisionally accepted a bid, subject to surveys being completed. The surveys are not expected to highlight any problems. The outlets are currently empty.

D    A brand name which Maykorn Co purchased in 20X2 is associated with the sale of potentially harmful products. Maykorn Co has decided to stop producing products under this brand, which is currently held within intangible assets.

The following scenario relates to questions 26–30.

Vitrion Co issued $2m 6% convertible loan notes on 1 April 20X2. The convertible loan notes are redeemable on 31 March 20X5 at par for cash or can be exchanged for equity shares in Vitrion Co on that date. Similar loan notes without the conversion option carry an interest rate of 9%.

The following table provides information about discount rates:

|        | 6%    | 9%    |
|--------|-------|-------|
| Year 1 | 0.943 | 0.917 |
| Year 2 | 0.890 | 0.842 |
| Year 3 | 0.840 | 0.772 |

On 1 April 20X3, Vitrion Co purchased 50,000 $1 equity shares in Gowhizzo Co at $4 per share, incurring transaction costs of $4,000. The intention is to hold the shares for trading. By 31 March 20X4 the shares are trading at $7 per share. In addition to the gain on investment, Vitrion Co also received a dividend from Gowhizzo Co during the year to 31 March 20X4.

26  In accordance with IAS 32 *Financial Instruments: Presentation*, which of the following describes an equity instrument?

   A   A contractual obligation to deliver cash or another financial asset to another entity

   B   A contract which is evidence of a residual interest in the assets of an entity after deducting all of its liabilities

   C   A contractual right to exchange financial instruments with another entity under potentially favourable conditions

   D   A contract which gives rise to both a financial asset of one entity and a financial liability of another

27  In accordance with IAS 32, how should the issue of the convertible loan notes be recognised in Vitrion Co's financial statements?

   A   As debt. Interest should be charged at 6% because it cannot be assumed that loan note holders will choose the equity option.

   B   As equity because the loan notes are convertible to equity shares.

   C   As debt and equity because the convertible loan notes contain elements of both.

   D   As debt. Interest should be charged at 9% to allow for the conversion of the loan notes.

28  What amount in respect of the loan notes will be shown under non-current liabilities in Vitrion Co's statement of financial position as at 1 April 20X2 (to the nearest $'000)?

   A   $2,000,000
   B   $1,848,000
   C   $1,544,000
   D   $2,701,000

29  In accordance with IFRS 9 *Financial Instruments*, at what amount will the Gowhizzo Co shares be shown under investments in equity instruments in Vitrion Co's statement of financial position as at 31 March 20X4?

   $ [        ]

30  Where should the gain on the investment in Gowhizzo Co and its dividend be recognised in Vitrion Co's financial statements for the year ended 31 March 20X4?

   A   Both in profit or loss
   B   Gain on investment in other comprehensive income and the dividend in profit or loss
   C   Gain on investment in profit or loss and the dividend in other comprehensive income
   D   Both in other comprehensive income

(30 marks)

# Section C – BOTH questions are compulsory and MUST be attempted

Please write your answers to all parts of these questions on the lined pages within the Candidate Answer Booklet.

31   On 1 January 20X6, Laurel Co acquired 60% of the equity share capital of Rakewood Co in a share exchange in which Laurel Co issued three new shares for every five shares it acquired in Rakewood Co. The share issue has not yet been recorded by Laurel Co. Additionally, on 31 December 20X6, Laurel Co will pay to the shareholders of Rakewood Co $1.62 per share acquired. Laurel Co's cost of capital is 8% per annum.

At the date of acquisition, shares in Laurel Co and Rakewood Co had a market value of $7.00 and $2.00 each respectively.

STATEMENTS OF PROFIT OR LOSS FOR THE YEAR ENDED 30 SEPTEMBER 20X6

|  | Laurel Co | Rakewood Co |
|---|---|---|
|  | $'000 | $'000 |
| Revenue | 84,500 | 52,000 |
| Cost of sales | (58,200) | (34,000) |
| Gross profit | 26,300 | 18,000 |
| Distribution costs | (2,000) | (1,600) |
| Administrative expenses | (4,100) | (2,800) |
| Investment income (note (iv)) | 500 | 400 |
| Finance costs | (300) | nil |
| Profit before tax | 20,400 | 14,000 |
| Income tax expense | (4,800) | (3,600) |
| Profit for the year | 15,600 | 10,400 |

Equity as at 1 October 20X5

|  | $'000 | $'000 |
|---|---|---|
| Equity shares of $1 each | 20,000 | 15,000 |
| Retained earnings | 72,000 | 25,000 |

The following information is relevant:

(i)   At the date of acquisition, Laurel Co conducted a fair value exercise on Rakewood Co's net assets which were equal to their carrying amounts with the following exceptions:

   –   An item of plant had a fair value of $4m above its carrying amount. At the date of acquisition it had a remaining life of two years.

   –   Inventory of $800,000 had a fair value of $1m. All of this inventory had been sold by 30 September 20X6.

(ii)   Laurel Co's policy is to value the non-controlling interest at fair value at the date of acquisition. For this purpose Rakewood Co's share price at 1 January 20X6 can be deemed to be representative of the fair value of the shares held by the non-controlling interest.

(iii)   Laurel Co had traded with Rakewood Co for many years before the acquisition. Sales from Rakewood Co to Laurel Co throughout the year ended 30 September 20X6 were consistently $1.2m per month. Rakewood Co made a mark-up on cost of 20% on these sales. Laurel Co had $1.8m of these goods in inventory as at 30 September 20X6.

(iv)    Laurel Co's investment income consists of:

–    Its share of a dividend of $500,000 paid by Rakewood Co in August 20X6.

–    A dividend of $200,000 received from Artic Co, a 25% owned associate which it has held for several years. The profit after tax of Artic Co for the year ended 30 September 20X6 was $2.4m.

(v)    Assume, except where indicated otherwise, that all items of income and expense accrue evenly throughout the year.

(vi)   There were no impairment losses within the group during the year ended 30 September 20X6.

*Required:*

(a)    Calculate the consolidated goodwill at the date of acquisition of Rakewood Co.        **(7 marks)**

(b)    Prepare the consolidated statement of profit or loss for Laurel Co for the year ended 30 September 20X6.        **(13 marks)**

**(Total = 20 marks)**

32    Landing Co is considering the acquisition of Archway Co, a retail company. The summarised financial statements of Archway Co for the year ended 30 September 20X6 are:

STATEMENT OF PROFIT OR LOSS

|  | $'000 |
|---|---|
| Revenue | 94,000 |
| Cost of sales | (73,000) |
| Gross profit | 21,000 |
| Distribution costs | (4,000) |
| Administrative expenses | (6,000) |
| Finance costs | (400) |
| Profit before tax | 10,600 |
| Income tax expense (at 20%) | (2,120) |
| Profit for the year | 8,480 |

STATEMENT OF FINANCIAL POSITION

|  | $'000 | $'000 |
|---|---|---|
| ASSETS | | |
| *Non-current assets* | | |
| Property, plant and equipment | | 29,400 |
| | | |
| *Current assets* | | |
| Inventory | 10,500 | |
| Bank | 100 | 10,600 |
| Total assets | | 40,000 |
| | | |
| EQUITY AND LIABILITIES | | |
| *Equity* | | |
| Equity shares of $1 each | | 10,000 |
| Retained earnings | | 8,800 |
| | | 18,800 |
| *Current liabilities* | | |
| 4% loan notes (redeemable 1 November 20X6) | 10,000 | |
| Trade payables | 9,200 | |
| Current tax payable | 2,000 | 21,200 |
| | | |
| Total equity and liabilities | | 40,000 |

From enquiries made, Landing Co has obtained the following information:

(i) Archway Co pays an annual licence fee of $1m to Cardol Co (included in cost of sales) for the right to package and sell some goods under a well-known brand name owned by Cardol Co. If Archway Co is acquired, this arrangement would be discontinued. Landing Co estimates that this would not affect Archway Co's volume of sales, but without the use of the brand name packaging, overall sales revenue would be 5% lower than currently.

(ii) Archway Co buys 50% of its purchases for resale from Cardol Co, one of Landing Co's rivals, and receives a bulk buying discount of 10% off normal prices (this discount does not apply to the annual licence fee referred to in note (i) above). This discount would not be available if Archway Co is acquired by Landing Co.

(iii) The 4% loan notes have been classified as a current liability due to their imminent redemption. As such, they should not be treated as long-term funding. However, they will be replaced immediately after redemption by 8% loan notes with the same nominal value, repayable in ten years time.

(iv) Landing Co has obtained some of Archway Co's retail sector average ratios for the year ended 30 September 20X6. It has then calculated the equivalent ratios for Archway Co as shown below:

|  | Sector average | Archway Co |
|---|---|---|
| Annual sales per square metre of floor space | $8,000 | $7,833 |
| Return on capital employed (ROCE) | 18.0% | 58.5% |
| Net asset (total assets less current liabilities) turnover | 2.7 times | 5.0 times |
| Gross profit margin | 22.0% | 22.3% |
| Operating profit (profit before interest and tax) margin | 6.7% | 11.7% |
| Gearing (debt/equity) | 30.0% | Nil |

A note accompanying the sector average ratios explains that it is the practice of the sector to carry retail property at market value. The market value of Archway Co's retail property is $3m more than its carrying amount (ignore the effect of any consequent additional depreciation) and gives 12,000 square metres of floor space.

*Required*

(a) After making adjustments to the financial statements of Archway Co which you think may be appropriate for comparability purposes, restate:

    (i) Revenue;

    (ii) Cost of sales;

    (iii) Finance costs;

    (iv) Equity (assume that your adjustments to profit or loss result in retained earnings of $2.3 million at 30 September 20X6); and

    (v) Non-current liabilities. **(5 marks)**

(b) Recalculate comparable sector average ratios for Archway Co based on your restated figures in (a) above. **(6 marks)**

(c) Comment on the performance and gearing of Archway Co compared to the retail sector average as a basis for advising Landing Co regarding the possible acquisition of Archway Co. **(9 marks)**

**(Total = 20 marks)**

# Answers

DO NOT TURN THIS PAGE UNTIL YOU HAVE
COMPLETED THE MOCK EXAM

# A plan of attack

If this were the real Financial Reporting exam and you had been told to turn over and begin, what would be going through your mind?

Perhaps you're having a panic. You've spent most of your study time on groups and interpretation of accounts (because that's what your tutor/BPP Study Text told you to do), plus a selection of other topics, and you're really not sure that you know enough. So calm down. Spend the first few moments or so **looking at the paper,** and develop a **plan of attack.**

Looking through the paper:

The first section is 15 2-mark questions. These will cover all sections of the syllabus. Some you may find easy and some more difficult. Don't spend a lot of time on anything you really don't know. You are not penalised for wrong answers, so you should answer all of them. If all else fails – guess!

Section B has 15 2-mark questions in total arranged around three scenarios.

*   Scenario 1 is on non-current assets.
*   Scenario 2 is on IAS 10 and IFRS 5.
*   Scenario 3 deals with financial instruments.

Section C has two 20-mark questions

Question 31 is a consolidated financial statements preparation question.

Question 32 deals with accounting adjustments and interpretation of financial statements.

**All of these questions are compulsory.**

This means that you do not have to waste time wondering which questions to answer.

## Allocating your time

BPP's advice is always allocate your time **according to the marks for the question** in total and for the parts of the question. But **use common sense**. If you're confronted by a Section A question on a topic of which you know nothing, pick an answer and move on. Use the time to pick up marks elsewhere.

After the exam…forget about it!

And don't worry if you found the paper difficult. More than likely other candidates will too. If this were the real thing you would need to **forget** the exam the minute you left the exam hall and **think about the next one**. Or, if it's the last one, **celebrate**!

| 1 | C | The other options are advantages of a principles-based system. |
|---|---|---|

2  B  A subsidiary carries its assets at historical cost but the parent's assets are carried at revalued amounts

This situation involves different accounting policies

3  $840,000

|  | $ | $ |
|---|---|---|
| At 30 April 20X5 |  | 705,000 |
| Increase in value of land in the year ($900,000 – $750,000) |  | 150,000 |
|  |  | 855,000 |
| Annual transfer to retained earnings |  |  |
| Depreciation based on revalued amount ($1,500,000/50 years) | 30,000 |  |
| Depreciation based on historic cost ($750,000/50 years) | (15,000) | (15,000) |
| At 30 April 20X6 |  | 840,000 |

4  D  $23,625

| Cost of investment | 3,500 × 6.50 | 22,750 |
|---|---|---|
| Share of post-acq profit | 35% × 7,000 | 2,625 |
| Less dividend received | 3,500 × $0.50 | (1,750) |
|  |  | 23,625 |

5

| | | |
|---|---|---|
| Assets should be carried at the lower of their carrying amount and recoverable amount | True | False |
| Assets should be carried at the higher of their carrying amount and recoverable amount | True | False |
| The recoverable amount of an asset is the higher of value in use and fair value less costs of disposal | True | False |
| The recoverable amount of an asset is the lower of value in use and fair value less costs of disposal | True | False |

6  C  A system of regulation will also include tax rules and company legislation.

7  $2,341,549

| 1 January X9–30 September X9 | 2,000,000 × 3.25/2.84 × 9/12 | 1,716,549 |
|---|---|---|
| 1 October X9–31 December X9 | 2,500,000 × 3/12 | 625,000 |
|  |  | 2,341,549 |

8  C  Interest receivable, which will be taxed when the interest is received

Prepaid expenses, which have been deducted to calculate the taxable profits of the previous year

9  D  Physical milestones reached as a percentage of physical completion

Surveys of performance completed to date as a percentage of total contract revenue

The other options are input methods of measurement.

10  C  This will reduce assets and liabilities by the same amount and so increase the ratio.

11  B  (6,400 – 1,400 loss – (800 loss × 60% × 6/12)) = 4,760

12  B  This measurement relates to the environmental impact.

13    $591,000

Carrying amount 370,000 + 285,000 – 64,000 (see below) = 591,000

The unrealised profit on the sale is 80,000 (150,000 – 70,000) of which 64,000 (80,000 × 4 years/5 years) is still unrealised at 30 June 20X8.

14    C    $35m

This is the valuation at acquisition.

15    D    If the fair value of a subsidiary's contingent liabilities can be reliably measured at the date of acquisition, they should be included in consolidated net assets and will increase goodwill.

Goodwill is not amortised under IFRS and goodwill is not recognised on acquisition of an associate. Goodwill is tested for impairment annually.

# Section B

**16**    $542,000

|  | $'000 |
|---|---:|
| Plant cost | 525 |
| Delivery to site | 3 |
| Building alterations to accommodate the plant | 12 |
| Costs of initial testing of the new plant | 2 |
|  | 542 |

Training costs are not included within the capitalised amount of new plant.

**17**    D    It is a change of accounting estimate and so is applied prospectively.

**18**    $6,750

Carrying amount at date of revised remaining life is (50,000 – (50,000 – 5,000)/8 years × 2 years) = 38,750

Depreciation year ended 30 June 20X5 is therefore 38,750 – 5,000/5 years = 6,750 pa

**19**    B    They should be written off to profit or loss as an expense as they are research costs at this date.

**20**    C    The project has moved to the development stage. If the IAS 38 development expenditure criteria are met, Artem Co must recognise the $80,000 costs as an intangible non-current asset.

IAS 38 does not allow a choice regarding whether or not to capitalise development costs.

**21**

| | | |
|---|---|---|
| All events which occur between 30 September 20X3 and 15 December 20X3 should be considered as events occurring after the reporting period | True | False |
| An event which occurs between 30 September 20X3 and 15 December 20X3 and which provides evidence of a condition which existed at 30 September 20X3 should be considered as an adjusting event | True | False |

**22**    B    On 1 December 20X3 the acquisition of a subsidiary was completed, following lengthy negotiations which began in September 20X3.

This does not provide evidence of a condition existing at the year end.

**23**    B    Property is depreciated by $130,000 ($2,600,000/20) giving a carrying amount of $2,470,000. When classed as held for sale, property is revalued to its fair value of $2,500,000 (as it is carried under the revaluation model, $30,000 would go to revaluation surplus). Held for sale assets are measured at the lower of carrying amount (now $2,500,000) and fair value less costs to sell ($2,500,000 – $50,000 = $2,450,000), giving an impairment of $50,000. Total charge to profit or loss is $130,000 + $50,000 = $180,000.

**24**    $455,000

Carrying amount at 1 April is $455,000 (490 – (490/7 × 6/12)).

**25**    C    A chain of retail outlets are currently advertised for sale. Maykorn Co has provisionally accepted a bid, subject to surveys being completed. The surveys are not expected to highlight any problems. The outlets are currently empty.

This is the only option where there is evidence of a 'highly probable' sale.

**26**    B    A contract which is evidence of a residual interest in the assets of an entity after deducting all of its liabilities

**27**    C    As debt and equity because the convertible loan notes contain elements of both

| 28 | B | $1,848,000 | | |
|----|---|-----------|---|---|
| | | 120,000 × 0.917 | 110,040 | |
| | | 120,000 × 0.842 | 101,040 | |
| | | 2,120,000 × 0.772 | 1,636,640 | |
| | | | 1,847,720 | rounded to 1,848,000 |

29      $350,000

50,000 shares at $7 each

30    A    Both in profit or loss

The Gowhizzo shares are held for trading rather than long term investment purposes.

# Section C answers

**Text reference.** Chapter 9.

**Top tips.** This question requires calculation of goodwill on acquisition and the preparation of a consolidated statement of profit or loss. Take care in calculating retained earnings at acquisition, which must include the first three months of the current year. Whenever you see note (v) realise that you are dealing with a mid-year acquisition. This means that the income and expenses of the subsidiary must be multiplied by 9/12 throughout. Note that all of Laurel's investment income (per note (iv)) will be disregarded.

**Easy marks.** The goodwill calculation is straightforward as long as you take care in calculating the retained earnings.

## Marking scheme

|  |  |  |  | Marks |
|---|---|---|---|---|
| (a) | Goodwill |  |  |  |
|  | Share exchange |  | 1 |  |
|  | Deferred consideration |  | 1 |  |
|  | NCI |  | 1 |  |
|  | Net assets: | Equity shares | ½ |  |
|  |  | Retained earnings | 1½ |  |
|  |  | Fair value adjustments | 2 |  |
|  |  |  |  | 7 |
| (b) | Statement of profit or loss |  |  |  |
|  | Revenue |  | 1½ |  |
|  | Cost of sales |  | 4 ½ |  |
|  | Distribution costs |  | ½ |  |
|  | Administrative expenses |  | ½ |  |
|  | Investment income |  | 1½ |  |
|  | Finance costs |  | 1 ½ |  |
|  | Income tax |  | 1 |  |
|  | NCI |  | 2 |  |
|  |  |  |  | 13 |
|  |  |  |  | 20 |

(a) Laurel Co: Consolidated goodwill on acquisition of Rakewood Co

Investment at cost

|  | $'000 | $'000 |
|---|---|---|
| Shares (15,000 × 60% × 3/5 × $7.00) |  | 37,800 |
| Deferred consideration (9,000 × $1.62/1.08) |  | 13,500 |
| Non-controlling interest (15,000 × 40% × $2.00) |  | 12,000 |
|  |  | 63,300 |
| Net assets (based on equity) of Rakewood Co as at 1 January 20X6 |  |  |
| Equity shares | 15,000 |  |
| Retained earnings at 1 October 20X5 | 25,000 |  |
| Earnings 1 October 20X5 to acquisition (10,400 × 3/12) | 2,600 |  |
| Fair value adjustments: |  |  |
|    plant | 4,000 |  |
|    inventory | 200 |  |
| Net assets at date of acquisition |  | (46,800) |
|  |  |  |
| Consolidated goodwill |  | 16,500 |

(b) Laurel Co: Consolidated statement of profit or loss for the year ended 30 September 20X6

|  | $'000 |
|---|---:|
| Revenue (84,500 + (52,000 × 9/12) – (1,200 × 9 months) intragroup sales) | 112,700 |
| Cost of sales (working) | (74,900) |
| Gross profit | 37,800 |
| Distribution costs (2,000 + (1,600 × 9/12)) | (3,200) |
| Administrative expenses (4,100 + (2,800 × 9/12)) | (6,200) |
| Investment income (400 × 9/12) | 300 |
| Income from associate (2,400 × 25% based on underlying earnings) | 600 |
| Finance costs (300 + (13,500 × 8% × 9/12 re deferred consideration)) | (1,110) |
| Profit before tax | 28,190 |
| Income tax expense (4,800 + (3,600 × 9/12)) | (7,500) |
| Profit for the year | 20,690 |
| Profit for year attributable to: |  |
| Owners of the parent | 18,370 |
| Non-controlling interest |  |
| ((10,400 × 9/12) – 200 re inventory – (1,500 depreciation – 300 URP) × 40%) | 2,320 |
|  | 20,690 |

*Working in $'000*
Cost of sales

|  | $'000 |
|---|---:|
| Laurel Co | 58,200 |
| Rakewood Co (34,000 × 9/12) | 25,500 |
| Intragroup purchases (1,200 × 9 months) | (10,800) |
| Fair value inventory adjustment | 200 |
| URP in inventory at 30 September 20X6 (1,800 × 20/120) | 300 |
| Additional depreciation (4,000/2 years × 9/12) | 1,500 |
|  | 74,900 |

32

---

**Text reference.** Chapter 19.

**Top tips.** This is an interpretation question taking account of a prospective acquisition. As always with interpretation questions, most of the marks are not for ratios. You must take account of all the information and consider the group aspects. How would Archway's results look following its acquisition by Landing?

**Easy marks.** The ratios based on the amended figures are an easy five marks – but don't spend too long on them.

---

Marking scheme

|  |  |  | **Marks** |
|---|---|---:|---:|
| (a) | Revenue | ½ | |
|  | Cost of sales | 2 | |
|  | Loan interest | ½ | |
|  | Equity | 1½ | |
|  | Non-current liabilities | ½ | |
|  |  |  | 5 |
| (b) | 1 mark per ratio |  | 6 |
| (c) | 1 mark per relevant comment |  | 9 |
|  |  |  | 20 |

32    (a)    Archway Co's restated figures

On the assumption that Landing Co purchases Archway Co, the following adjustments relate to the effects of notes (i) to (iii) in the question and the property revaluation:

|  | $'000 |
|---|---|
| Revenue (94,000 × 95%) | 89,300 |
| Cost of sales (see below) | 76,000 |
| Loan interest (10,000 × 8%) | 800 |
| Equity (10,000 + 2,300 RE + 3,000 revaluation) | 15,300 |
| Non-current liabilities: 8% loan notes | 10,000 |

The cost of sales should be first adjusted for the annual licence fee of $1m, reducing this to $72m. Half of these, $36m, are net of a discount of 10% which equates to $4m (36,000/90% – 36,000). Adjusted cost of sales is $76m (73,000 – 1,000 + 4,000).

(b)    These figures would give the following ratios:

| Annual sales per square metre of floor space | (89,300/12,000) | $7,442 |
|---|---|---|
| ROCE | (13,300 – 10,000)/(15,300 + 10,000) × 100 | 13% |
| Net asset turnover | (89,300/(15,300 + 10,000)) | 3.5 times |
| Gross profit margin | ((89,300 – 76,000)/89,300 × 100) | 15% |
| Operating profit margin | ((13,300 – 10,000)/89,300 × 100) | 3.7% |
| Gearing (debt/equity) | (10,000/15,300) | 65.4% |

(c)    Performance

|  | Archway Co As reported | Archway Co as adjusted | Sector average |
|---|---|---|---|
| Annual sales per square metre of floor space | $7,833 | $7,442 | $8,000 |
| ROCE | 58.5% | 13% | 18.0% |
| Net asset turnover | 5.0 times | 3.5 times | 2.7 times |
| Gross profit margin | 22.3% | 15% | 22.0% |
| Operating profit margin | 11.7% | 3.7% | 6.7% |
| Gearing (debt/equity) | nil | 65.4% | 30.0% |

A comparison of Archway Co's ratios based upon the reported results compares very favourably to the sector average ratios in almost every instance. ROCE is particularly impressive at 58.5% compared to a sector average of 18%; this represents a return of more than three times the sector average. The superior secondary ratios of profit margin and asset utilisation (net asset turnover) appear to confirm Archway Co's above average performance. It is only sales per square metre of floor space which is below the sector average. The unadjusted figure is very close to the sector average, as too is the gross profit margin, implying a comparable sales volume performance. However, the reduction in selling prices caused by the removal of the brand premium causes sales per square metre to fall marginally.

As indicated in the question, should Archway Co be acquired by Landing Co, many figures particularly related to the statement of profit or loss would be unfavourably impacted as shown above in the workings for Archway Co's adjusted ratios. When these effects are taken into account and the ratios are recalculated, a very different picture emerges. All the performance ratios, with the exception of net asset turnover, are significantly reduced due to the assumed cessation of the favourable trading arrangements. The most dramatic effect is on the ROCE, which, having been more than three times the sector average, would be 27.8% (18.0 – 13.0)/18.0 × 100) below the sector average (at 13.0% compared to 18.0%). Analysing the component parts of the ROCE (net asset turnover and profit margins), both aspects are lower when the reported figures are adjusted.

The net asset turnover (although adjusted to a lower multiple) is still considerably higher than the sector average. The fall in this ratio is due to a combination of lower revenues (caused by the loss of the branding) and the increase in capital employed (equal to net assets) due to classifying the loan notes as debt (non-current). Gross margin deteriorates from 22.3% to only 15.0% caused by a combination of lower revenues (referred to above) and the loss of the discount on purchases. The distribution costs and administrative expenses for Archway Co are less than those of its retail sector in terms of the percentage of sales revenue (at 11.3% compared to 15.3%), which mitigates (slightly) the dramatic reduction in the profit before interest and tax. The reduction in sales per square metre of floor space is caused only by the reduced (5%) volume from the removal of the branded sales.

Gearing

The gearing ratio of nil based on the unadjusted figures is not meaningful due to previous debt being classified as a current liability because of its imminent redemption. When this debt is replaced by the 8% loan notes and (more realistically) classified as a non-current liability, Archway Co's gearing is much higher than the sector average. There is no information as to how the increased interest payable at 8% (double the previous 4%) compares to the sector's average finance cost. If such a figure were available, it may give an indication of Archway Co's credit status although the doubling of the rate does imply a greater degree of risk in Archway Co seen by the lender.

Summary and advice

Based upon Archway Co's reported figures, its purchase by Landing Co would appear to be a good investment. However, when Archway Co's performance is assessed based on the results and financial position which might be expected under Landing Co's ownership, the recalculated ratios are generally inferior to Archway Co's retail sector averages. In an investment decision such as this, an important projected ratio would be the return on the investment (ROI) which Landing Co might expect. The expected net profit after tax can be calculated as $2m ((3,300 before interest and tax – 800 interest) × 80% post-tax), however, there is no information in the question as to what the purchase consideration of Archway Co would be. That said, at a (probable) minimum purchase price based on Archway Co's net asset value (with no goodwill premium), the ROI would only be 7.9% (2,000/25,300 × 100) which is very modest and should be compared to Landing Co's existing ROI. A purchase price exceeding $25.3m would obviously result in an even lower expected ROI. It is possible that under Landing Co's management, Archway Co's profit margins could be improved, perhaps coming to a similar arrangement regarding access to branded sales (or franchising) as currently exists with Cardol Co, but with a different company. If so, the purchase of Archway Co may still be a reasonable acquisition.

# Review Form – Financial Reporting (FR) (02/18)

Name: _____    Address: _____

_____

_____

**How have you used this Kit?**
*(Tick one box only)*

☐ On its own (book only)

☐ On a BPP in-centre course_____

☐ On a BPP online course

☐ On a course with another college

☐ Other _____

**Why did you decide to purchase this Kit?**
*(Tick one box only)*

☐ Have used the complementary Study Text

☐ Have used other BPP products in the past

☐ Recommendation by friend/colleague

☐ Recommendation by a lecturer at college

☐ Saw advertising

☐ Other _____

**During the past six months do you recall seeing/receiving any of the following?**
*(Tick as many boxes as are relevant)*

☐ Our advertisement in *Student Accountant*

☐ Our advertisement in *Pass*

☐ Our advertisement in *PQ*

☐ Our brochure with a letter through the post

☐ Our website www.bpp.com

**Which (if any) aspects of our advertising do you find useful?**
*(Tick as many boxes as are relevant)*

☐ Prices and publication dates of new editions

☐ Information on product content

☐ Facility to order books

☐ None of the above

*Which BPP products have you used?*

| *Study Text* | ☐ | *Passcards* | ☐ | *Other* | ☐ |
| *Kit* | ☑ | *i-Pass* | ☐ | | |

*Your ratings, comments and suggestions would be appreciated on the following areas.*

| | *Very useful* | *Useful* | *Not useful* |
|---|---|---|---|
| *Passing FR* | | | |
| *Questions* | | | |
| *Top Tips etc in answers* | | | |
| *Content and structure of answers* | | | |
| *Mock exam answers* | | | |

| *Overall opinion of this Practice & Revision Kit* | *Excellent* ☐ | *Good* ☐ | *Adequate* ☐ | *Poor* ☐ |
|---|---|---|---|---|

**Do you intend to continue using BPP products?**    Yes ☐    No ☐

**The BPP author of this edition can be emailed at: accaqueries@bpp.com**

**Review Form (continued)**

**TELL US WHAT YOU THINK**

Please note any further comments and suggestions/errors below.